To Reggie a great
Publisher of River love.
With kind regard.
Capt Wm O Burwell Sr
05/29/08

Ol' Man RIVER

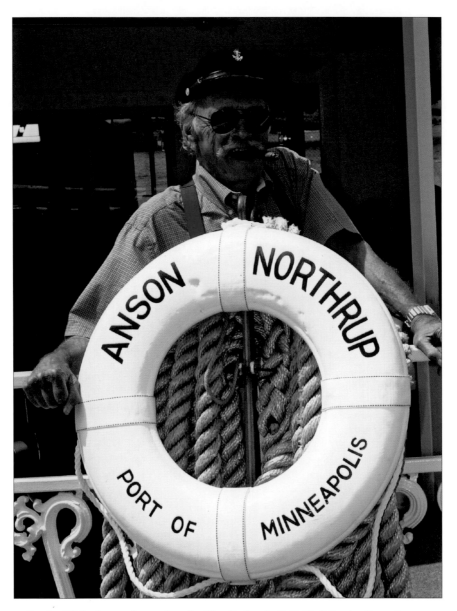

In the 1980s, I opened a series of radio ads for the Padelford Packet Boat Company by announcing, "THIS IS CAPTAIN BOWELL. COME ABOARD!"

Ol' Man RIVER

Memoirs of a Riverboat Captain

Capt. Wm. D. Bowell, Sr.

EDITED BY
BILOINE YOUNG

CARTOONS BY JERRY FEARING

Afton Historical Society Press

Dedicated to all the Padelford Packet Boat Company employees past, present, and future

Photographs for OL' MAN RIVER were provided by William D. Bowell Sr., with additional images from the following sources:

Captain William Bowell River Library, National Mississippi River Museum and Aquarium, Dubuque, Iowa
"Pig's Eye" Parrant and Father Lucien Galtier's chapel (p. 128); the *Virginia* (p. 206); Jackson Street Landing (p. 207); Zebulon Pike, Harriet Bishop, Father Lucien Galtier, and Abigail Snelling (p. 210).

Per Breiehagen Photography, Minneapolis, Minnesota
Bowell with grandfather's portrait (p. 208); Bowell with model boat (back cover).

Jerry Fearing, Scandia, Minnesota
Cartoons on pages 33, 35, 36, 46. 56, 72, 80, 85, 102, 103, 109, 110, 118, 135, 138, 157, 160, 168, 170, 187, 202, 203.

Minnesota Historical Society, St. Paul, Minnesota
Union Stockyard Exchange Building (p. 32); Harriet Island pavilion (p. 43); the *Capitol* (p. 48); E. K. Thomas painting of Fort Snelling (p. 96); the *Avalon* (p. 120).

National D-Day Museum, New Orleans, Louisiana
Lawson Field, Fort Benning (p. 60).

The Padelford Packet Boat Company, St. Paul, Minnesota
Jonathan Padelford (front cover); *Harriet Bishop* (p. 184); *Jonathan Padelford* (p. 192); *Minnesota Centennial Showboat* (p. 195).

St. Paul Pioneer Press, St. Paul, Minnesota
Bowell on flooded Mississippi, 2001, photograph by Craig Borck (p. 188); Bowell delivering new *Centennial Showboat* (p. 198).

Page 2: High school photo of William D. Bowell Sr.
Frontispiece: William D. Bowell Sr. on the foredeck of the **Anson Northrup.**

Copyedited by Michele Hodgson
Designed by Mary Susan Oleson
Production assistance by Beth Williams
Printed by Pettit Network, Inc., Afton, Minnesota

Library of Congress Cataloging-in-Publication Data

Bowell, William D., 1921-
Ol' man river : memoirs of a riverboat captain / by William D. Bowell Sr.; edited by Biloine Young.—1st ed.
    p. cm.
ISBN-13: 978-1-890434-69-4 (hardcover : alk. paper)
ISBN-10: 1-890434-69-8 (hardcover : alk. paper)
1. Bowell, William D., 1921- 2. Ship captains—Mississippi River—Biography.
3. Paddle steamers—Mississippi River—History—20th century.
I. Title: Old man river. II. Young, Biloine W., 1926- III. Title.

VK140.B685A3 2005
386'.3'092—dc22

Printed in China

2005014479

Afton Press receives major support for its publishing program from the Sarah Stevens MacMillan Foundation and the W. Duncan MacMillan family.

W. Duncan MacMillan
President

Patricia Condon Johnston
Publisher

Afton Historical Society Press

P.O. Box 100, Afton, MN 55001
800-436-8443
aftonpress@aftonpress.com
www.aftonpress.com

Contents

FOREWORD

A BIOGRAPHY THAT IS written years, decades, even centuries after the subject has lived has the benefit of hindsight. It analyzes the distant events of that person's life with the certainty of historical research and perspective, and it judges the wisdom of that person's actions with a critical, if not jaundiced, eye. Yet a biography can and often does lose something in the translation. For me, it is the *immediacy* of a person's thoughts and actions, written in his own words and in the framework of his own times, that often makes the study of his life so fascinating.

Written as the first draft of history, an autobiography documents the events of the author's life with nothing more (and nothing less) than his personal perspective. Only he knows for certain what hand he was dealt. Only he knows for sure how he played it and with what consequences. He judges the wisdom of his actions only to the extent that his advancing years will allow. He tells his tale boldly and bravely, perhaps even brashly—an unapologetic, entertaining, and occasionally embellished slice of life.

Ol' Man River is one such autobiography, the no-holds-barred personal account of Captain William Bowell, founder of the Padelford Packet Boat Company in St. Paul, Minnesota. That he survived his dangerous missions as a paratrooper in World War II to return home and get a college education, raise a family, make a small fortune in printing and plastics, and build a successful riverboat excursion company is a riveting tale in itself. That he also beat the odds as a child of the Great Depression doubles the intrigue. Indeed, his story is a model for how he and others of his generation shaped their country in the second half of the twentieth century.

Bill Bowell was born in St. Paul, the fourth oldest of twelve surviving children. He grew up at a time when poverty was real and financial survival was not easy, especially in a family as large as his. He and his brothers spent their boyhood shining shoes, selling magazines, sweeping floors, selling popcorn—doing whatever it took to help put food on the table. The work ethic Bill developed and the survival skills he learned in the 1920s and 1930s would

FOREWORD

certainly serve him well in the Civilian Conservation Corps, the Minnesota National Guard, and the U.S. Army. That work ethic and those skills also have served him well throughout his life.

Bill Bowell is a veteran of World War II, but not just any veteran. As a paratrooper, he jumped into Normandy on D-Day and he fought in the Battle of the Bulge—two of the most decisive campaigns during the war. My uncle, John Verret, was the chaplain assigned to Bill's unit, the 507th Parachute Infantry Regiment. Uncle John coined the motto of the 507th, "Down to Earth." For the paratroopers of the 507th, the motto meant that they would accomplish their dangerous assignments without fear of failure. As it turns out, the motto has come to epitomize all of Bill's personal and professional accomplishments, both before and after the war. He has met every challenge with common sense, practicality, and fearlessness.

Bill has always been a risk-taker, and a creative one at that. To advance in his careers—as a museum curator, copywriter, print salesman, catalog publisher, co-owner of a plastic-mold injection company, and, last, as the owner of the Padelford Packet Boat Company—he was willing to risk success as well as failure.

To say that Bill is hardworking is woefully inadequate. He has an uncanny ability to envision what needs to be done and he gets it done successfully. He has marched to the beat of his own drum and has hated rules and regulations that he deemed meaningless. Paradoxically, he has expected his own rules and regulations to be followed to the letter. A self-professed Captain Bligh, Bill is an enemy of mediocrity who often uses confrontation as the opening gambit in dialogue, raising "cold pricklies" at the drop of a hat. Once you penetrate that feistiness, however, you won't find a more loyal or generous man.

Bill's love for the Mississippi River is renowned, both locally and nationally. He has been vitally instrumental in reshaping St. Paul's downtown riverfront over the past thirty years and in rebuilding the *Minnesota Centennial Showboat* in 2002 for the University of Minnesota's theater department. His Captain William Bowell River Library at the National Mississippi River Museum and Aquarium in Dubuque, Iowa—which since June 2004 has housed his massive collection of river books, paintings, and artifacts—is a remarkable repository for river historians and scholars. *Ol' Man River*, Bill's fascinating autobiography, now takes its rightful place on those library shelves, a record of his life's journey along the river he has loved so long and so well.

Paul A. Verret
PRESIDENT EMERITUS
THE SAINT PAUL FOUNDATION
JANUARY 2005

ACKNOWLEDGMENTS

I WANT, FIRST OF ALL, to thank my daughters, Shelley and Beth, and my wife, Lillian, who encouraged me to write about my life. They put together a list of stories that I had told over the years and I used it as an initial outline for this book.

Many friends also have suggested that I write the story of my life, and I have always wanted to for my own satisfaction. Fortunately, I kept a diary that encompassed my years as an army paratrooper, from 1942 through 1945, and my business life from 1957 to the present. The diaries have been incredibly helpful to me in writing this book.

I acknowledge that certain aspects of my speech are not appropriate in polite society, and so what you read on the following pages is a cleaned-up version of my true vocabulary. Profanity comes very easily to me, which doesn't seem all that unusual for a fellow who spent a year in the CCC, a year in the National Guard, three years in the army, and fifty years as a riverboat man. My swear words punctuate my thoughts. I call it my river language.

Life has been very kind to me. It seems that whenever I want something, it comes to me. About the time I started writing this book I met Freya Schumacher, a bright young woman working on her graduate degree at the University of St. Thomas, who agreed to become my part-time secretary and research assistant. Freya helped me not only on this book but also on other projects, such as a bibliography of all books written about the rivers of America. The list, which I have been working on for many years, includes more than six thousand books. We are also writing an article about the Red River of the North that will cover the era of the first steamboats that ran up there. Freya is wonderful.

For their editorial suggestions and help I am indebted to Billie Young and Michele Hodgson. Billie Young is the author of seven nonfiction books, including *River of Conflict, River of Dreams: Three Hundred Years on the Upper Mississippi,* and she worked closely with me for two years on my manuscript and its photos, making sure every thought and anecdote and image was assimilated into the right spot of every

ACKNOWLEDGMENTS

chapter. She also wrote the book's introduction and the chapter lead-ins that give the book its historical perspective. Michele Hodgson, the former managing editor of *MPLS.ST. PAUL Magazine*, is a remarkably talented editor who meticulously combed through my manuscript, pressing for details, continuity, and accuracy. The cartoons are by legendary St. Paul editorial cartoonist Jerry Fearing. The book was beautifully designed by Mary Sue Oleson.

Ol' Man River probably would not have come about if not for Patricia Johnston, publisher of Afton Historical Society Press. In the early 1980s Patricia wrote one of the best articles ever written about me, which ran in *Twin Cities Magazine*. She and her staff have published a remarkable collection of regional history books over the past ten years, and I am humbled that my book is among them. I want to thank Patricia, as well as Duncan MacMillan, president of Afton Historical Society Press, for their vision in creating this exceptional regional press, and for encouraging me to contribute my autobiography to their endeavors.

I designed the Norska for my retirement and built this model of it in my workshop on the garage level of my apartment building. I designed her so I could drive a car onto the deck and into the living area. A retractable floor would cover the elevator shaft after the car descended into the hold. The Norska may never become a full-scale reality.

Named for one of my ancestors, the J. M. Bowell *was a short-trade packet boat piloted by Captain Jesse Bowell on the Monongahela River. In October 1889, Jesse Bowell got into a shouting match that turned ugly with the captain of a second boat. Captain Bowell was hit with a rock, fell unconscious, and died.*

INTRODUCTION

THE MISSISSIPPI RIVER, that pulsing artery of North America, exerts a spell on those who live near its banks. Mark Twain was not the only person to succumb to its magic. Mississippi River lore is replete with the stories of men, and a few women, who lived lives of such drama and richness that tales of their daring have been recounted for generations.

Minnesota's history includes many such tales. There was Lieutenant Zebulon Pike, who in 1805 poled a keelboat up the Mississippi River from Missouri to the Minnesota Territory, where he negotiated the treaty for land on which Fort Snelling and the Twin Cities of Minneapolis and St. Paul stand. There was Harriet Bishop of Vermont, who in 1847 rode a steamboat to the Sioux Indian village of Kaposia, Minnesota, and across the river to St. Paul in a dugout canoe to become the state's first school-teacher. And there was Abraham Lincoln's cousin, Stephen B. Hanks, who began working at a lumber camp on Minnesota's St. Croix River in the 1840s and fashioned rafts the size of an aircraft carrier flight deck that he then piloted downriver.

Those who made their living as riverboat captains were held in awe. Daniel Smith Harris, a lead miner from Galena, Illinois, built some of the most commanding paddle wheelers ever to cruise on the Upper Mississippi and became the model for every boy who wanted to be a steamboat captain. His *War Eagle* led the parade of boats from Rock Island, Illinois, to St. Paul on the Grand Excursion of 1854, a journey that carried no less a visitor than a former U.S. president to inspect the new lands of the Great Northwest. River men like Captain Philip Suiter, who began skippering boats on the Mississippi in 1856, passed on their skills to new generations. Suiter's three sons, two grandsons, and two great-grandsons all served as pilots or captains, running their boats between St. Paul and the Quad Cities of Iowa and Illinois. They learned about the river by memorizing every detail of every stretch and bend of water—the shadows cast by a bank of trees, the ever-changing shape of the natural channel, the look of the water as it rippled before the wind. River men were cantankerous, obsessed individuals who challenged the gods of weather and chance as they strove to understand the moods of the mysterious Mississippi.

Those who travel on the Mississippi know that the river has two faces. Below St. Louis, the traveler sees nothing on the horizon but miles of levees, earthen walls that contain the broad sheet of water as it flows uninterrupted on its journey to the Gulf of Mexico. Above St. Louis, particularly north of Keokuk, Iowa, the river is lined with bluffs and towering rocks that reminded many an early visitor of ancient ruins of castles. Today, the Mississippi's sometimes turbulent flow is held back by twenty-nine locks and dams, creating alternating cataracts and silent, slow-moving pools.

Government officials, recognizing the two faces of the river, have officially divided it into the Lower Mississippi and the Upper Mississippi. The lower river begins at Pilot Town, Louisiana, Mile Marker 0, ninety-five miles below New Orleans, and extends northward to the mouth of the Ohio River at Cairo, Illinois, Mile 955.8. The Upper Mississippi starts at Cairo, Mile Marker 0, and ends at Camden Avenue in Minneapolis, Mile 857.6. Camden Avenue is at the northern end of the U.S. Army Corps of Engineers' dredged shipping channel in the Mississippi. St. Paul is at Mile 839.6.

The character of the river changes more dramatically in the Twin Cities than any-where else along its entire 2,350-mile length. Between downtown Minneapolis and Fort Snelling, the Mississippi flows through the only true gorge on the river. At its upper end it is wild and shallow. The river then narrows to create the gorge below the Falls of St. Anthony, the only waterfall on the Mississippi. The falls, an icon of Minneapolis, originated in St. Paul, where the Wabasha Street Bridge now crosses the river. Over the twelve thousand years of its life, the falls receded upstream at a rate of about four feet per year. The falls were still backing up the river when European settlers arrived in the 1800s. Wanting to use the falls for water power, they stabilized the cataract.

The human saga of the Upper Mississippi River is that of a love story gone awry. In the beginning, everyone was in love with the river. Insofar as an affair of the heart can be dated, at least for nonnatives, the story began on May 10, 1823. On that date the first boat, the steamboat *Virginia*—stopping every thirty miles to take on wood—plied her way past the treacherous rapids at Rock Island, Illinois, and up the Mississippi to Fort Snelling. The voyage of the *Virginia*, belching steam and threatening to blow up at any moment, brought the mythic Mississippi River into the consciousness of the world.

The river was the highway into the Great Northwest—and, since there were no other roads, it was the only highway. Before the captain of the *Virginia* demonstrated that bold river pilots could bring their boats to the head of navigation, the rich farmlands of Minnesota, Wisconsin, northern Illinois, and Iowa had been effectively barred to settlement by Europeans. For the region's early settlers, the river was the lifeline that connected them to the outside world. Every city and village was established where it was because of the river. A place on the riverbank where boats could dock to unload cargo and passengers was the single most important consideration governing the establishment of a town. The levee was a community's most valuable piece of real estate. Every town had warehouses for goods, hotels, and saloons—all to serve the commerce brought to them by the river. The sound of a steamboat whistle brought residents of river towns rushing to the levee to welcome visitors and get the latest news.

Just as the beginning of the love affair with the river can be given a date, so can the disillusionment, the falling-out-of-love. In 1854, on February 22, an engine pulling five yellow coaches arrived in Rock Island, Illinois. It was the first train to reach the Mississippi River from the East Coast and the entire country celebrated. The technological marvel of the trains quickly eclipsed the romance of the riverboats. Within a few short years, the freight, passengers, and news that once traveled by river now rode the rails. In

1868, a record 1,068 steamboats docked during the season at St. Paul; by 1900 there was hardly a commercial boat left on the river. As railroad tracks snaked along the shores of the river, blocking access to the water, the Mississippi, like a rejected lover, faded from the consciousness of the community.

Instead of remaining a cherished stream, the great river became everyone's dumping ground. Communities put their junkyards and housed their poorest citizens on the banks of the Mississippi. Towns blocked their views of the river with warehouses and freight yards. Lumber mills dumped waste into the river in such quantities that sawdust piled up twenty feet deep on the banks and steamboats became stuck in the muck. The river reeked of pollution as all the sewers of the Twin Cities emptied untreated effluent into it. At the beginning of the twentieth century, the Mississippi was of less significance to the residents of the region above St. Louis than it had ever been since European occupation.

The last great raft of lumber went down the river in 1915, piloted for a short distance by ninety-four-year-old Stephen Hanks. The white pine was depleted, the steamboats were no longer needed, the wheat that once had flowed downriver on the boats now went to markets on the rails. Residents of river towns looked out on an empty stream, devoid of all but fishermen and government dredges.

Migrating birds shared the riverbanks with cattle awaiting slaughter in packing plants. St. Paul railroad baron James J. Hill gave a speech stating that the era of river traffic was over and calling for an end to federal spending on river navigation.

With the steamboats gone and barge traffic dependent on a nine-foot channel that had yet to be dug, only two groups of river enthusiasts were still on the Mississippi at St. Paul. The first, the Minnesota Boat Club, was organized in 1870 and is the state's oldest athletic institution. The second, the St. Paul Yacht Club, was organized around 1915 by a group of motorboat enthusiasts. To avoid the polluted river, however, many members took their boats to the cleaner tributary of the St. Croix, southeast of St. Paul.

Other than the motorboaters, the rowers, and the grain shippers who dreamed of transporting the Midwest's wheat crop to New Orleans, few in the early twentieth century gave much thought to the river. Responding to pleas for help from shipping companies, the U.S. Army Corps of Engineers began dredging the river, creating first a four-and-a-half-foot channel and then a six-foot channel. Even with the greater depth, riverboats and barges could not compete with the railroads in shipping commodities. Shipping on the Mississippi came to a standstill until Congress, in 1930, approved the digging of the present nine-foot channel. Although this would

require building twenty-three dams and modifying three existing dams along the Upper Mississippi, it would also allow the big grain-carrying barges to travel all the way to the head of navigation at St. Paul. The Corps of Engineers completed the building of the dams and dredging of the nine-foot channel in 1938. The locks on the Upper Mississippi River—600 feet long and 110 feet wide—were built as a necessary step to create the shipping channel, and effectively turned what had been a free-flowing river into a series of pools that incrementally step down to St. Louis, Missouri. As a boat passes up or down through the locks, the gates are closed and the water level either raised or lowered.

The success of the nine-foot channel, controversial when it was proposed, astounded even its most ardent supporters. Approximately 2,500 to 3,000 barges pushed by 250 towboats now ply the Upper Mississippi at any one time between March and late November. The barges carry corn, soybeans, and potash from Canada downriver and return upriver with salt, fertilizer, and molasses that is used for animal feed. The barges transport about 151 million tons every year on the Upper Mississippi. Grains comprise 60 million tons of the total. Towboats on the Upper Mississippi are limited to pushing fifteen barges, which pass through the locks in two sections called cuts. The first cut is pulled out of the chamber by winches on the lock walls and tied off; the second cut is pushed through the lock by the towboat. Below St. Louis, where there are no more locks, towboats may push as many as forty-five barges.

The love affair with the river did not begin again for almost one hundred years. Even then, only a few individuals resonated to its power and beauty. Certainly no one in the 1920s could have guessed that a skinny youngster growing up on the streets of St. Paul would be the one to reawaken Twin Citians to an appreciation of the river.

That kid was Bill Bowell, who grasped the romance of the Mississippi a generation sooner than did most of his contemporaries. Greg DenBleyker, commodore of the St. Paul Yacht Club, says of Bowell, "He was the first person to value the river. He came down here, started from nothing, and built it up."

For Bill, the river is a special place. "The Mississippi is secretive, almost unknown to many people who live within a few miles of her," he says. "Down in her valleys it is as primitive and unchanged as it was in the 1800s. When we enter that wooded canyon, closed on both sides by high banks where the river's edge looks wild and private, it's not hard to take yourself back in time. Here we are, in the middle of a metropolitan area of 2.5 million people, and we see deer along the river or eagles flying overhead. There are egrets out here and falcons and beaver—right in the middle of a great city."

Bill has the soul of an archivist. Thanks to his voluminous diaries, collection of clippings and memorabilia, and phenomenal memory, he has put together an engaging account of his long and eventful life. He and I met regularly for more than a year so that he could recount for the tape recorder details of his boyhood on the streets of St. Paul, his service as a paratrooper in some of the most demanding battles of World War II, and his vision for building the Padelford Packet Boat Company on the Mississippi River. Bill's wife, Lillian Bowell, and nephew Stephen Bowell helped fill in dates and details. Son-in-law Jim Kosmo made available for my examination the many notebooks of clippings at the boat company, and Bill's daughter, Shelley Kosmo, tracked down one of the essential pictures for the book: the picture of Bill on the University of Minnesota's *Centennial Showboat* on page 198.

It was a pleasure to work on this book with Bill—this shoeshine boy turned war hero, inventor, tycoon, and legendary riverboat captain who, inspired by great river men of the past, led the Capital City in its historic return to the Mississippi. Bill Bowell is truly St. Paul's "Ol' Man River."

Biloine (Billie) Young
St. Paul, Minnesota
January 2005

17

This formal family photograph, taken in 1923, shows Phyllis on Mother's lap, Mary and Robert on the left, and Betty Jane and me on the right. I was two years old.

1
BEGINNINGS of a RIVER MAN

AFTER THE GREAT WAR ended and Minnesota's veterans returned home, the 1920s roared through St. Paul as boldly as James J. Hill's Great Northern Railroad. Minnesota Congressman Andrew J. Volstead had just succeeded in passing the Volstead Act of 1919, which prohibited the sale of alcohol throughout the country. But in St. Paul, bootleg liquor flowed freely from bars, drugstores, and the wine cellars of the mansions along Summit Avenue, the stately street on which Hill lived and F. Scott Fitzgerald wrote his first novel, *This Side of Paradise*. The book was published in 1921, the same year General Mills of Minneapolis introduced American housewives to the mythic Betty Crocker, the Cathedral School of St. Paul organized the nation's first school patrol—and future riverboat captain Bill Bowell was born.

FAMILY MATTERS

I was born on Valentine's Day in St. Paul, Minnesota, a town nurtured by the rhythms of the Mississippi. St. Paul defines its neighborhoods not by their relation to the points of the compass, but by

their relation to the river. I spent much of my childhood in the communities of West St. Paul and South St. Paul. Never mind that West St. Paul is not west of the downtown; it is south. And South St. Paul is not south; it is east. Forget the cardinal directions. In St. Paul what matters is that the West Side lies on the west side of the *river* and South St. Paul lies on the south.

For residents of the several St. Pauls, the great S-curve of the river flowing through the capital city is a more defining landmark than the compass directions. Like the city, my life has been shaped by the Mississippi. For more than eighty years I have fought it, cussed it, lived on it, and loved it. I catch myself thinking of it as *my* river. The tranquility, the aura that surrounds you when you're on the water—it's almost like you've got a halo protecting you.

My parents lived at 634 Marshall Avenue in St. Paul on February 14, 1921, when I was born at St. Paul Hospital, at 668 Robert Street on the hill next to the State Capitol. That place on Marshall Avenue was the first house they owned, and, at the time, they were pretty well off financially. Leone Padelford Bowell and Ralph Raymond Bowell already had three children—Betty Jane, Mary, and Bob—before I arrived. My mother told me that I was so small when I was born they used a cigar box for my bed. Nine more children would be born to my parents, and twelve of us would survive to adulthood.

My mother, who also was born in St. Paul, had moved a lot as a child, but all of her moves were within the Twin Cities. She lived in eighteen places before she married my dad in 1916. When she was a young woman, my mother, who was Norwegian and English, was very attractive, very stylish, with a slim figure and black hair. She always wore fresh dresses and did not put on weight until she was older. Dad, 100 percent English, was born in Plymouth, Indiana. In his younger days he was short and dapper, with black hair. As a child he had infantile paralysis—polio—so one leg was shorter than the other and he limped. Some people called him "Shorty" and others called him "Limpy." Both of my parents graduated from high school, and Dad took postgraduate courses at Culver Military Academy in Culver, Indiana, before moving to St. Paul. I have no idea what he studied or what his interests were at that time.

Both sides of my family were part of the westward movement, with each generation settling a little farther west. When I was a

My mother, Leone Padelford Bowell, grew up in St. Paul. This photo was taken when she was fourteen.

child, my Grandfather Frank Nelson Padelford told me that an ancestor had made a chart that traced the family history back through several generations to my tenth great-grandfather. One of the first things I did after I began working at the Minnesota Historical Society in 1949 was to ask Miss Fawcett, the librarian, for assistance in searching for that chart. A few days later, to my surprise, she located a Jonathan Padelford genealogical chart in Boston. It had been compiled by S. C. Newman and printed in Providence, Rhode Island, in 1859. When I heard I could buy a copy of the chart for $6.50, I sent away for it.

The chart traced Jonathan Padelford's descendants from 1628, when Jonathan emigrated from England to America, to 1858. Someone had presented the chart to another descendant, Edward Everett, the man who gave the speech before Abraham Lincoln's Gettysburg Address. Everett had been governor of Massachusetts and president of Harvard University. My great-grandfather on my mother's side, Henry James Padelford, drove horses and mules on the Erie Canal before he came to Minnesota in 1856, two years before the

territory became a state. He settled in Northfield, where he had a big livestock farm and ran a hotel. My grandfather Frank Padelford had a drayage company in St. Paul, and most of his sons ended up as truck drivers.

The Bowell side of the family came from Plymouth, Indiana, where my grandfather, John Bazel Bowell, had a hotel called the Ross House, as well as an interest in the Maxinkuckee Inn in Culver. My father and his brother, John Walter (known as

My grandfather Frank Nelson Padelford (third man from left) ran a drayage company in St. Paul. According to family lore, he drove famed Minnesota trotting horse Dan Patch in races and never lost a one.

My father, Ralph Bowell, was an Indiana native and had polio as a child. He is shown here at age fifteen.

Walter), moved to St. Paul as young men because of their friendship with the Reverend Walter Howard, later the pastor of Christ Episcopal Church in downtown St. Paul. When Father Howard moved to Minnesota from Indiana, my father and uncle decided to come here too.

Some years ago, my wife, Lillian, did a lot of work tracing the Bowell family. Together we traveled back east in search of my great-great-great grandfather's grave around Uniontown, Pennsylvania. We found that one, and some time later we began looking for the grave of the missing link in the Bowell family, the man who left Pennsylvania to move west to Indiana. We were poking through a cemetery around Memphis, Indiana, hunting for this guy, Bazel Bowell, when I looked down, scraped at the soil, and there, carved in the stone, saw the name "Bazil Bowel."

"Well, goddamn it," I said, "I finally found you, and you didn't even know how to spell your name." He was my dad's great-grandfather.

One day in 1969 when my boat, the *Jonathan Padelford*, was under construction in Iowa at the Dubuque Boat and Boiler Works, I was talking with Dennis Trone, the hydraulics engineer.

"Are you any relation to the J. M. Bowell who's written up in *Sons and Daughters of Pioneer Rivermen*?" Trone asked me.

"How did he spell his name?" I asked.

"Same way you do," Trone replied.

I was flabbergasted. I found a copy of the publication and learned that J. M. Bowell and I had a common ancestor, and that J. M. had been a steamboat captain on the Monongahela and Allegheny Rivers. His packet boat was named the *J. M. Bowell*.

Besides running a boat line that carried mail, passengers, and freight, Captain Bowell was superintendent of schools in Belle Vernon, Pennsylvania. One day he got into an argument on the street with a Captain Abrams over a four-dollar freight bill. When Bowell turned and walked away, Abrams picked up a rock and threw it at him, hitting Bowell squarely in the back of the head. A couple of days later Bowell died. J. M.'s riverboat friends arranged an eleven-steamboat funeral to take his body from Belle Vernon to his hometown of Brownsville, Pennsylvania, a distance of about twelve miles by river. Abrams was charged with murder, but he eventually got off without serving any time. I went back to Belle Vernon, researched all of the papers, and found a picture of the *J. M. Bowell*. So my affinity for the river has roots in my ancestry.

EARLIEST MEMORIES

The earliest thing I remember is a guy threatening to cut off my ears. It was 1926, and we were living in Minneapolis at 5240 Twenty-seventh Avenue South, where my sister Nancy Jeanne had been born that January. Phyllis, Tommy, and Jimmy had already been added to the family. Somebody in the house across the street, I don't know who, was dying, or we thought he was, and we kids had been sent outside. We were listening at a window to the moans and groans coming from either the dying individual or the mourners. There

was a Chevrolet coupe parked on the street in front of the house. Some of us must have been running around because one of those little things on the side of the car that looked like candles got broken. I have no idea how it happened, but the guy blamed me. He was only kidding me that he was going to cut my ears off, but I believed him and was terrified.

My dad really loved cars and was in the automobile business for many years. His love of cars rubbed off on me, and I have been a car nut most of my life. One of his fancy automobiles was a Wills St. Clair, the first car to put a V-8 engine into production. The car had double cutouts, a device that cuts out the muffler so you can hear the raw sound of the engine. My dad loved the powerful sound that car made. I was riding with him one time when he decided not to stop for a stop sign at Marshall and Snelling in St. Paul. Instead he cut through a filling station on the corner. Every time I go by that intersection I think of it.

In the 1920s my dad was a contractor and owned seven trucks, three of them Pierce-Arrows. Pierce-Arrows were unique because their headlights were formed as part of the fender. Dad's other trucks were Fords and Chevys. He was one of the subcontractors on the building of the Ford Bridge in St. Paul. One day he bid on a job hauling gravel somewhere on the St. Croix River near Taylors Falls, Minnesota. He bid against Joe Shiely and won. He then found out that Shiely had bought the one pit where Dad was planning to get his gravel. Shiely was the owner of the well-known Shiely Sand and Gravel Company in St. Paul. Dad never had a chance, and he led us kids to believe that Shiely had bought the gravel pit on purpose to keep Dad from making good on his bid. I don't know about that, but years later, in 1952, Shiely was my first charter-boat customer on the St. Croix. He liked to throw big parties for his employees. I gave them rides all day with my first boat, the *Toka.*

For a time Dad was general manager of the Burch-Wilson Ford Company in South St. Paul. Then he and a friend, a fellow salesman named Red Leonard, bought out a Ford agency in Hastings, Minnesota. We have a family story that Dad sold twenty-five Model A Fords in one day. I think he probably sold a fleet of cars to some corporation. Nevertheless, he was a great car salesman and must have been pretty successful to be able to buy a Ford dealership. Dad was proud of his large family and he used us as part of his sales pitch. He would brag about us, show off our pictures, and tell potential customers how many mouths he had to feed.

We lived in eight more houses before the family moved to Seventh Avenue in Hastings in about 1931. This was a happy era in our lives. We kids were pretty proud to be the children of a Ford dealer. I can clearly remember a 1931 Ford roadster on

display on the showroom floor with a Santa Claus sitting in it. Right next to it was a Ford Victoria just like the one my mother drove. All the walls were darkened and my dad had hung what looked like snowdrops coming down from the ceiling. They were actually hundreds of cotton balls strung on black thread to look like snow. Dad had also put cotton batting on the fenders of the cars in the showroom to make it look like snow had fallen on them. I thought it was the most beautiful thing I had ever seen.

My other memories of Hastings are a little scattered. I remember we had a barn behind our house and I was enamored with a girl who lived out back of us. I used to go out to the barn and peek through the slats, hoping to see her when she was in her yard. I also remember the day when we kids were walking in the country and found a good automobile tire, still on its rim. We rolled it for miles back to town, and my dad gave us a dollar and a half for it. That was big money at that time.

THE ROAD TRIP

My mother liked to load us kids into her cute little Ford Victoria and drive to Nerstrand, a village near Northfield, Minnesota, where her grandfather had settled. I remember how happy our relatives were to see all of us. As we came and went through Hastings, I was always impressed with the Spiral Bridge. We often drove over the wooden bridge that looped down to Main Street, at about ten miles an hour, and strained to peer out the windows to the river flowing far below.

But the most memorable event of our lives at that time took place in the summer of 1930, when Dad took the twelve of us (ten kids—the last two had not yet been born—plus the two adults) in his Model A Ford two-door sedan on a thirty-six-hundred-mile trip to Detroit. The trunk on the car was a special model, called a Karonteen trunk, which held a lot of luggage but folded down to about half its size when not in use. I think my dad wanted to go to Detroit to see the people who made that trunk and perhaps negotiate for a distributorship.

The four eldest children (thirteen-year-old Betty Jane, twelve-year-old Mary, ten-year-old Robert, and nine-year-old me) rode in the back seat. Dad put a bench in the car between the front and back seats, and the four younger children (Phyllis, eight, Tommy, six, Jimmy, five, and Nancy Jeanne, four) rode there.

The Bowell family took a car trip to Michigan and Indiana during the summer of 1930. This picture was taken at 10:00 a.m. on July 21 in South Bend. The temperature at the time was 100 degrees. From left: Ralph Bowell, 37; Leone Bowell, 33; Jack, 11 weeks; Betty Jane, 13; Mary, 12; Robert, 10; Billy, 9; Phyllis, 8; Tommy, 6; Jimmy, 5; Nancy Jeanne, 4; and Patty, 15 months. Donna and Richard were born in 1934 and 1935, respectively.

Ol' Man RIVER

When they wanted to rest, the younger ones would lean back and put their heads in our laps. My parents rode in front with Patty, who was fifteen months old, and Jack, who had been born only eleven weeks before. So we traveled four, four, and four. I don't remember any fights among us kids during the trip, but my parents got into a big argument one night while driving through Chicago. My dad became lost and stopped the car over some railroad tracks. My mother opened the door and we thought she was going to get out and all of us would be killed by a train. As it turned out, she did not get out of the car and nothing happened, but the whole experience was pretty traumatic as far as we kids were concerned. Then, while we were driving through Chicago, someone bailed out of a high window right in front of us and landed on the sidewalk. Dad yelled, "Don't look!" But we did.

I have no idea what our mother fed us on that trip, but I don't believe we ever went into a restaurant. In South Bend, Indiana, we just happened upon a community picnic and won a big ham with a crust of dough on it for being the largest family there. So we stayed for the picnic. When we got to Detroit, our parents left us in a park someplace where there was a swimming pool. We would go in, get wet and cold, and then come out and lie on the pavement to warm up.

On the way back home my parents ran out of money, so we stayed with Dad's relatives in South Bend. His sister Martha was married to Roy Morgan, who owned a store there. One day I was helping Uncle Roy in the store near some big sacks of flour that were stacked high. Damned if some of those bags of flour didn't fall right down on my back. They knocked the wind out of me, and for a few minutes I thought I was never going to be able to take a breath again. Even though my parents were out of funds, we followed a meandering course through Battle Lake, Minnesota, then Fargo and Grand Forks, North Dakota, and Winnipeg, Manitoba, before we arrived home at last. At the end of our road trip my dad said, "Let's do it again!"

We never did. Not long after the trip, two men from the Ford agency brought our father home. "Your dad's sick," one of them explained to us kids as they helped him into the house. Though I was only ten years old, I knew he was drunk. The Bowell-Leonard Agency had to file for bankruptcy during the Great Depression, propelled in part, we kids were told, because Henry Ford—who was having his own financial troubles at the time—made his dealers buy parts for Ferguson tractors (which Ford sold in addition to automobiles) whether they could sell them or not. The financial strain was too much for my father, who turned to the bottle and became an alcoholic. His drinking made the Depression years an especially hard time for our family.

2
BUDDING ENTREPRENEUR

THE SLIDE INTO the Great Depression began in the early 1920s, when federal spending grew three times faster than tax collections. When the government reduced spending to balance the budget, a severe recession resulted. In the three years preceding 1932, thirteen million Americans lost their jobs. More than 25 percent of America's workforce was unemployed, and 60 percent of all Americans lived below the minimum subsistence level. Across the nation, just two hundred corporations controlled more than half of all American industry; the richest 1 percent owned 40 percent of the nation's wealth. Ten thousand banks, more than 40 percent of banks existing in 1929, failed in three years.

In Minnesota, 491 banks had closed by 1930—a third of the state's roster in 1921. Ninety-three banks closed in 1931 alone. Mining in the Iron Range came to a standstill, while 86 percent of manufacturing firms reported operating losses. Thousands of Minnesotans lost their jobs, and tens of thousands faced destitution. Farmers were hard hit when the value of their land dropped 40 percent and their incomes fell 60 percent. In 1933 sixty of every one thousand Minnesota farmers went bankrupt.

Despite the bleak times, the U.S. Army Corps of Engineers built a series of eleven locks and dams in the 1930s to aid navigation along the Upper Mississippi between St. Paul and Guttenberg, Iowa. The first lock and dam built in the Twin Cities, Lock and Dam 1 in Minneapolis, is the only twin-chamber lock in the St. Paul District of the Corps of Engineers. It was constructed in 1917 and refurbished in 1929, the year the stock market crashed.

HOME LIFE

Our fortunes changed dramatically when my dad's Ford dealership went under. It was the depths of the Depression, and from time to time my parents went on relief. The financial strain affected their marriage and they argued a lot, especially over Dad's binge drinking. He would go three months sober, then drink for two weeks at a time. He didn't come around the house very much when he was drunk, which also meant there was no money coming in to feed us.

Ol' Man RIVER

We left Hastings and moved to 1494 South Concord Street in South St. Paul. There were steps right next to the house leading up the hill to Washington School, which all the Bowell kids attended. We didn't know who owned the house we were living in. The guy never came around for the rent, and eventually we moved because my parents were afraid he might show up someday and claim they owed him all that money. We lived in about sixteen houses while I was growing up. We moved about once a year, just ahead of the rent collector, I suspect. Some of our boxes never got unpacked between the moves.

I was godfather to my sister Donna, whom I am holding. My brother Robert is standing beside me.

My parents continued to have children. Diane, born in 1933, died as an infant. Donna was born in 1934, and Richard came along in 1935. Although they were certainly poor, my parents must have felt they could share what little they had. Because our house was close to a hobo jungle and railroad track, the bums came to our door for peanut butter sandwiches that my mother handed out to them. She always had homemade bread and margarine and peanut butter in the cupboard. I never knew anyone to be turned away hungry at our kitchen door.

One day my mother sent me to the store for some groceries, including a jar of peanut butter that cost twenty-one cents. On the way home I dropped the grocery bag and broke the jar. I was petrified to tell my mother. All that afternoon she sat at the kitchen table, picking splinters of glass out of it. And we ate that peanut butter.

Mother was always baking bread in a big pan that was at least three feet across. You could see the dough rise, lifting the cover off the pan. We would watch as she kneaded the dough before cutting off chunks to make individual loaves. My mother spent most of her time preparing food for all of us. She kept a lock on the door of the icebox and wore the key on a cord around her neck.

Our stove was a big, wood-fired porcelain piece that we moved with us from house to house. It had big drawers for pots and pans and warming ovens built into a frame that rested on top of the cooking surface. Sometimes my parents burned tires in the stove instead of coal. One time they had another couple over and had a hell of a good time feeding pieces of tire into the stove. Every time they opened the stove door to put in another piece of tire, black smoke rolled out. They laughed as if it were funny.

One day I was fiddling around in the kitchen and accidentally pulled the top section of the stove—the part with the drawers full of pans—over on top of me. There was a tremendous crash and everyone came running. My dad had forgotten to bolt the top section of the stove to the cook top. He was not mad at me and told me it was not my fault that the stove had tipped over.

We all ate together at two tables, the big table and a little table with smaller chairs for the younger children. I always ate at the big table, since I was one of the older kids. All of us avoided sitting next to Dad because you never knew what he would do. One time at dinner when I was sitting next to him, I must have made some kind of smart remark. The next thing I knew he hit me, knocking me off my chair and onto the floor, where I lay with my head against the wall. I wasn't hurt, but I began to say, "Tweet, tweet, tweet," as if I had a concussion and was seeing birds circle my head, like in the comic books.

We ate a lot of stews, Cream of Wheat, and oatmeal with milk. One thing we did not like to eat was cornmeal. Worst of all was cornmeal mush and corn bread. My family rarely ate meat because it was so expensive. Occasionally I would have lunch or dinner with my friend Pedro, who was Mexican. His father worked for the railroad, and his family lived in a railroad car they had converted into their home. I was impressed that their meals always included meat.

We also ate margarine instead of butter. We kids preferred the taste of butter, of course, but we ate the margarine because it cost less. When you bought it, the margarine looked like a pound of white lard. Inside its box was a beanlike pod of vegetable dye. You put the lard and the pod into a bowl and mixed the two until they were the color of butter. The coloring did not improve the taste, but since it made the stuff look like butter, it made the concoction palatable. We also preferred that Dad do the mixing. With his strong arms and hands he did a better job than our mother was ever able to do.

One of the things I hated most in my life at that time was coming home and hearing the washing machine running and smelling rutabagas cooking. When that washing machine was going, it meant that Mother was busy and we were not going to get anything good for lunch, usually rutabagas. How I hated them!

Ol' Man RIVER

There was always a massive pile of laundry. Some of the houses we lived in had laundry chutes. Another house had knotholes in the walls and we poked Dad's horsewhips down those holes. I always felt he was fair when he whipped us, but we hid the whips all the same. We kids were not the only ones to hide things. Every so often we would run into caches of Dad's empty bourbon bottles stashed here and there. Sometimes we would find a dozen bottles at a time, hidden in the toilet tank and in the false ceilings.

Despite my father's drinking, we all attended church pretty regularly. When we lived at 395 Eichenwald Street, our house was close to St. Peter's Episcopal Church. Most of my brothers and sisters and I were confirmed there. After we were confirmed, my mother told us that we could do what we wanted about attending church. We

The Bowell family, circa 1939. Front row from left: Jack, Dad, Dick, Mother, Donna, and Patty. Second row, seated: Nancy Jeanne and Phyllis. Third row: Mary, Robert, Billy, Tom (wearing my Humboldt High School letter sweater that I won for being on the varsity tumbling team), Jim, and Betty Jane.

quit going. Years later the church was demolished when the area was cleared for I-35. Christ Episcopal is now located in Woodbury, a St. Paul suburb.

We had an uptown friend named Louie Ferguson, who lived in a big house up in South St. Paul. Louie's father was a handsome man and his wife came from money. When Louie would visit us, we kids were always neatly dressed, but we did not like to have him come up to our bedrooms because they were such a mess. Four of us slept in one room. Invariably I would stand with my foot against the door while he pushed from the other side, saying, "Let me in!"

Louie had some rabbits he wanted to get rid of, so his mother asked my brother Bob, who was about fourteen at the time, to kill them. I witnessed it. That was awful. To think they would let some fourteen-year-old kid do something like that.

EARNING OUR KEEP

South St. Paul was a railroad and stockyards town. In the late 1800s, Charles Wilbur Clark and Alpheus Beede Stickney were largely responsible for the growth of the city's commerce, situating the stockyards next to the Chicago and Great Western Railroad line and along the Mississippi. The business of trading livestock took place in a five-story Romanesque stone palace on Concord Street called the Union Stockyard Exchange Building. The Victorian-style structure was designed by MIT architect Charles Reed, who also designed the Saint Paul Hotel. In 1930 the building housed ninety-eight firms for whom the "commission men" handled the buying and selling of livestock. The commission men were experts in negotiation, communicating their sales with gestures as much as words. Their transactions were personal, based on experience, reputation, trust, and a kind of gentleman's agreement to respect each other's positions in the pens. A single company might handle a million dollars' worth of livestock in a single day.

In 1934 the totals of livestock brought to the yards reached amazing proportions. On August 27, 12,249 calves came into the yards. On September 4, 31,862 head of cattle were received. On October 8, 70,824 head of sheep arrived. In the early 1900s the Union Stockyard in South St. Paul was the largest stocker, feeder, and milch-cow market in the United States. By 1974 it was the largest of its kind in the world.

I can't remember that we kids were worried that much about finances, but it was understood that we had to do what we could to help support the family. We made frequent visits to the South St. Paul "commission house," otherwise known as the Stockyard Exchange Building. The commission offices bought and sold the cattle that the farmers brought to the stockyards for sale and slaughter. By 1935, in the middle of the Depression, South St. Paul ranked with Chicago and Kansas City as one of the top cattle markets in the United States. It was a good place for my brothers and me to sell issues of monthly magazines.

As long as I can remember we kids sold magazines—the *Saturday Evening Post*, *Collier's, Ladies' Home Journal,* and *Woman's Home Companion*. My dad would read each new issue and pick out the stories we were to push to get sales, while my mother kept the books. We ended up winning a national championship for selling the most *Collier's* magazines. We had a sales spiel that went like this: "Hey, hey, *Collier's* magazine. Only a nickel, half a dime. Keeps you reading all the time. If you can't read, there are plenty of pictures to look at."

Each commission house had a front counter. We always helped ourselves to the free pencils on the counter that were stamped with the commission house name. We were particularly friendly with the man who ran the apple stand on the main floor. He knew every one of the Bowell boys by name. His

The castlelike Union Stockyard Exchange Building was one of our preferred places to go to sell magazines. The truck pictured in front of the building is similar to the one that tipped over when I was riding my brother's bike.

stand was well stocked with cigarettes, cigars, fruit, and snacks of all kinds.

The stockyards were one of our favorite hangouts. My brother Bob knew everybody. One good friend was Felix, an artist who painted all the signs on the trucks that brought cattle to the yards. Whenever we saw a truck without a sign on its door, we would tell the owner about Felix. If our referral brought him a job, Felix would give us a commission. In the stockyards we stood on the narrow plank walkways over the pens and watched the men herd the pigs with pig-flappers. Pig-flappers were short-handled sticks with a long, rectangular piece of canvas on the end. It made a lot of noise when the men slapped a pig with it, but it did not hurt the animal or bruise the meat.

All of us kids loved animals. One of our neighbors was a woman we called Old Lady Logan. (Everyone over thirty seemed old to us.) Old Lady Logan liked us kids. Every day during the summer, she walked all the way to the downtown of South St. Paul, pulling a little wagon loaded with vegetables she sold on the streets. She also kept a goat or two on her acreage behind our house above Concord Street. We were shocked when some renegade youths tortured one of her goats by putting hot tar on it.

We had the occasional pet, including, briefly, a pig. President Franklin D.

Roosevelt, with one of his New Deal programs, must have done something to make pigs practically worthless because they were running loose all over the stockyards. We caught a really young one and took it home. We had a screen door with a spring on it, and somehow or other when the little pig was escaping out the door, the screen slammed shut on its head and killed it.

Once we had a dog called Shep that kept getting pregnant. My parents must have wanted to get rid of her because one day the police came and took Shep to the dump across Concord Street from our house and

shot her. I remember her raising her head, trying to figure out what was going on. I don't remember how long we had Shep, just that she was our dog. We kids surely felt bad about the situation. These days you can't imagine how that could happen.

Our house was on the western edge of the dump, which ran about a hundred yards east of where Helen Murr ran her beauty shop. The dump was a halfhearted attempt to fill in a peat bog, and we kids used it as a playground. There was water at the back of the dump, and we built rafts in the summer and floated around on the shallow pool. One day when I was twelve, we were playing in the dump with a Buddy "L" toy steam shovel that had a smokestack on it and a compartment where you could build a fire. We were cutting up bits of rubber and shoving them into the fire when a piece popped out and burned my hand.

Just at that moment a boy ran up and yelled, "Your sister's dead!" Forgetting my injury, I hightailed it home and learned that Betty Jane, the oldest, had released the brake on Dad's car, and when it began to roll she tried to hold it back. As the car rolled down the driveway with Betty Jane holding onto it, the fender ripped her throat. My sister Mary knew enough about first aid to put her hands around the wound to stop the bleeding. They got Betty Jane to the West Side Hospital on Prescott Street and sewed her up, and she survived. For some reason Betty Jane thought Mother's

car was parked too close to Dad's and she tried to move one of them. My parents did not own these cars. Because of my father's connections with the automobile business, he could sometimes use cars that did not belong to him.

We kids were sitting on our porch one day when a Model T pickup drove past. Apparently the passenger in the car was counting money as she and the driver were coming from the market and she was laying it on the seat next to her when it blew out of the window without her noticing. We kids raced into the street to pick up the money. A few minutes later the car and driver came slowly back up the street, looking for the lost cash. An older kid who had not gotten any of the money shouted, "We have your money!" So we had to give it all back. That older kid had an old Pontiac without a muffler on it and you could hear him coming from miles away. I just loved the sound of that car.

THE CATTLE TRUCK TRIP

Cattle trucks constantly zoomed along the roads of South St. Paul, and we kids would hitch rides on the back and hang on from stop sign to stop sign. It was easy to do because we could catch hold of the slotted boards that enclosed the cattle. Sometimes we would ride way out in the country to a stop sign that was close to a truck farm, where we would feast on musk melon, watermelon, tomatoes, radishes,

BUDDING ENTREPRENEUR

and carrots. One day in 1934 my brother Jim and I hooked onto the back of a cattle truck heading west and didn't let go. He was nine and I was thirteen. When night came we found ourselves in Dawson, Minnesota, about 150 miles from St. Paul and not far from the South Dakota border. Some farmer bought us a meal in a restaurant and then took us out to his land to help shock his grain. This was back when farmers still shocked grain by hand, taking bundles of cut wheat and setting them on end to dry in the shape of little teepees.

We spent the night at the farmer's house, and early in the morning, when it was cool, we began shocking grain. We did all right until the sun came up. When it start-

ed beating down on us, we decided this job was for the birds. As soon as the farmer got down to the far end of the field on his tractor to cut the wheat, we took off. Jim and I decided to go to California just for the fun of it. We hitched several rides toward the South Dakota border, and were out on the highway thumbing yet another ride when a car stopped for us. We piled into the backseat, and no sooner were we settled than the driver turned onto another road. "Hey, we're not going that way," I called out. "We're going west."

"Well, you gotta come with me," the driver replied. He reached over and opened his glove compartment. "See this?" he said. We looked over the front seat into the compartment and there sat a big revolver. "Are you the sheriff?" we asked. "Yep," he replied.

He took us a few miles to the courthouse in Madison, and put us in a cell at the jail but left the door open. It was a place for us to sleep. We ended up staying a week or so, mostly because the officials had a problem getting hold of our parents. The police in St. Paul thought we were in Madison, *Wisconsin,* and that caused a big mix-up. The sheriff and his wife took wonderful care of us, practically adopting us. Their son was a veterinarian, and the sheriff took us out to the farms and let us watch the vet work, castrating pigs and stuff like that. We were thrilled. Eventually the St. Paul police located our parents and the sheriff put us on a bus and sent us back to St. Paul. Mother and Dad were smiling when they saw us again. If they were ever worried about us, I never saw it.

I had one other adventure with a cattle truck. My older brother, Bob, had somehow come into the possession of an old bicycle. It was one of those turn-of-the-century bikes with a high bar at the seat level. The only way we could ride it was to put our legs through the bike, under the bar, and pedal by holding the bike out to the side at an angle. We made a kind of a Y going down the street, with the bike leaning one way and our body leaning the other. One day, when I was twelve, I begged Bob to let me ride his bike. He said, "Go ahead," and told me he would wait for me.

I wobbled down the street to where the old Inver Grove streetcar used to turn around on the borderline between Inver Grove and South St. Paul. Barren's Grocery Store was down there. To turn that bike around I had to swing into the filling station and make a wide turn. When I got back onto the street, damned if the bike tire didn't get caught in the streetcar track. As I struggled to get the tire out of the track, I heard this rumbling noise behind me. I looked over my shoulder and, God, there was this truck full of cattle bearing down on me! I went one way and the cattle truck went another. Then I swerved back and the cattle truck changed direction. The two of us rocked back and forth, trying to miss each other. All of a sudden the truck tipped over, tumbling the cattle into the middle of the street. I was right in front of it, scared stiff. I took off,

and when I got home I must have looked like a nervous wreck because Bob asked me, "Did you do something down there?" "No," I replied. "No, I don't think so."

Bob went down the street on his bike to see what was going on, and he got blamed for the accident. When I got my nerve back I went down there too. The driver was still sitting in the cab of his truck, laughing so hard he couldn't get himself out. He said he had never in his life seen a kid go so fast on a bicycle, holding it off to the side with his leg stuck through the opening.

THE WORLD'S FAIR

The 1933 Chicago World's Fair was designed to celebrate the centennial anniversary of the incorporation of Chicago. Four decades earlier the Windy City had produced the enormously popular World's Columbian Exposition, commemorating the four hundredth anniversary of Columbus's discovery of America. The exposition opened May 1, 1893, ran for six months, and attracted 27.5 million visitors—almost half the number of people then living in the United States. The promoters had every reason to believe that the 1933 Chicago World's Fair, celebrating a "Century of Progress," would be equally successful.

The goals of the World's Fair, which ran for six months in 1933 and six months in 1934 and drew 48.7 million visitors, differed markedly from those of the earlier exposi-

tion. The 1893 fair had created a model ancient city that glorified an idealized past. The 1933 fair celebrated the America of the future, with streamlined high-rise constructions dedicated to science, industry, and the arts. Many exhibits showed how things were done rather than merely celebrating the finished object. The General Motors Building, for example, featured an entire Chevrolet production line. For Americans living on little more than hope during the Great Depression, the Chicago World's Fair was a promise of better times to come.

One July day in 1934, my brother Bob, a mature fourteen-year-old, asked me, an immature thirteen-year-old, if I wanted to go to the World's Fair. I said, "Why not?" Without saying anything to our parents, the two of us took off hitchhiking down Highway 12 to Chicago. We had a buck and a half between us. At the end of the first day we had gone only as far as Hudson, Wisconsin, about twenty miles east of St. Paul, where a guy who had given us a ride let us sleep on his front porch. The next day we had a hard time getting rides on Highway 12. Cars kept whizzing by. While we waited I dug in the soft tar on the road with a stick, and damned if I didn't turn around and accidentally sit in it. I jumped back up, but the damage had been done to the khaki shorts I was wearing. For the rest of the trip, whenever other people were present, I hung my hands behind me to hide the stain on the seat of my pants.

Robert and I sent this postcard home as we made our way to the Chicago World's Fair. Verbatim, it reads: "Dear Mother & Dad. We are going to the Worlds fair and we can get in for a nickel Thursday. We are o.k. so don't worry. We are going to try and bring back a souvenir for each of you. Wishing you good luck. Robert & Billy."

BUDDING ENTREPRENEUR

When we reached Eau Claire, Wisconsin, Bob sent a postcard home to our parents to let them know where we were. By the next night, we made it to the Wisconsin Dells, where we slept in a real Indian teepee that was part of a roadside display. It got so cold in the middle of the night that we got up and looked around for a warmer place. A four-door car with mohair seats was parked nearby. Its doors were unlocked, so we crawled in and spent the rest of the night sleeping in the car.

When we got to Chicago and onto the grounds of the World's Fair, we never left. We toured every exhibit, just soaking up everything there was to see. We found one of those big canvas magazine sacks and carried it everyplace we went, filling it with brochures we collected from the exhibits. Our biggest problem was being cold at night. We found places to sleep in a construction area where we could cover ourselves with the big paper sacks that workers had left on the ground. I don't remember ever being hungry because we found work, sweeping up grocery stores for food. We ate a lot of bismarcks and overripe fruit.

We were particularly happy to get into the racetrack where stunt driver Barney Oldfield was putting a 1934 Plymouth through its paces. Oldfield would drive onto a ramp that would tilt the car up on two wheels as he careened around the track. At the end of the circuit he would bring the car back down on its four wheels, get out, and ceremoniously bow to the crowd. The car he drove had the muffler removed so it made a roaring sound, making the car sound powerful. We loved it. Dad had met Oldfield, so we went up to the daredevil and said, "Our dad knows you!" "Oh yeah?" he replied. When we told him we were the sons of Ralph Bowell, Oldfield smiled, patted me on the head, and said, "I know Ralph," and moved on. We were thrilled.

About a week later Bob and I hitchhiked back home to St. Paul. No one in the family expressed any concern over our absence or said anything about missing us. Instead of scolding us, I think they wished they could have gone along. If it occurred to our parents to worry about us, they never said anything about it. They were simply happy to have us back so we could add to the family's income.

When we dumped our bag full of brochures and catalogs on the dining room table, everyone gathered around to look at them and marvel at the wonders we had seen. The gift we brought our mother was a penny we had put into a machine that elongated it and stamped it with a design that showed a world spinning through space with the fair's slogan, "A Century of Progress, Chicago, 1934." I still have that coin and some of the postcards we sent to our parents from the fair. I also have the advertising broadside from the South St. Paul newspaper that probably gave us the

BARNEY OLDFIELD, WORLD'S MOST FAMOUS RACE DRIVER — FIRST MAN TO DRIVE AN AUTOMOBILE A MILE A MINUTE

"I've been driving cars ever since they've been built but I've never driven a car that I like as well as the new Plymouth. How this car performs! More power and speed than I ever require and no vibration, due to Floating Power engine mountings. Plymouth's Individual Front Wheel Springing accounts for the softest, smoothest ride imaginable. And the protection of Safety Steel bodies and Hydraulic Brakes make all speeds safe. That's why I like my Plymouth."

—Barney Oldfield.

My autographed picture postcard of Barney Oldfield.

idea for the trip. When we got back, Bob and I had $1.75, which was a quarter more than we had when we left.

EXPLORING DOWNTOWN

Sometime before the World's Fair trip, my family moved from South St. Paul to 206 Prescott on the West Side. It was here that we kids were exposed to the streets of downtown St. Paul and began exploring opportunities to make money.

We four older boys—Bob, Tom, Jim, and I—were always on the streets, trying to make a buck. For a time I ran errands for the Concord Drug Store. One day a lady offered us fifty cents if we could find an angora cat for her. We found one, and when I leaned down to pick him up, that son of a bitch bit my hand. I still have the scar.

We sold magazines and then started selling newspapers too, especially the *St. Paul Dispatch and Pioneer Press*. As kids selling newspapers in downtown, we thought we were in the big time. To this day I can remember the sound of downtown St. Paul early on a Sunday morning. The streets gave off a hollow sound and our voices would echo back to us. The Sunday papers were a heavy load. We collected lots of dimes and quarters for those papers.

We used to go up on Cathedral Hill to sell because of the many apartment buildings there. In the winter it was a good place to keep warm while you sold magazines. We would knock at every door. One day, in answer to my knock, a woman came to the door and said, "We don't want any." After she closed the door she called out to her husband, "It's that same ugly-looking kid that comes by here all the time." I overheard her remark through the transom. Her comment sickened me as I already had a terrible inferiority complex. I was shy, introverted, and convinced I was homely. I was bucktoothed, small, and thin.

There was a Chinese place on Cedar Street and Ninth that sold good luck charms, beautifully formed images made of plastic. We bought these little figures, four for a nickel, and resold them to guys in the beer joints for twenty-five cents each. The charms had a little ring on them so you could hang them around your neck. My brother Jim was little and cute with curly blond hair. We would rub dirt on his face and then send him into the joints to sell the charms. If the men had had a couple of drinks, they would buy the charms to take home to their girlfriends.

My brother Bob moved up to delivering postal telegrams, and the rest of us—Tom, Jim, and I—joined him by getting jobs at Western Union. We were all good salesmen, and it wasn't long before we started selling Western Union greetings in beer joints, just as we had done with the Chinese good luck charms. It was not too hard to convince guys who had had a few drinks that it was a heck of an idea to send a telegraphed greeting. Norwegian guys here on a visit bought a lot of them. The greetings cost only twenty-five cents to send to any place in the United States and could be used for any of the holidays. That was big money. We did so well that the head guy in Chicago called the St. Paul Western Union office to ask how in

the heck he was beating everyone in the United States selling those greetings. Our boss told him about us.

All of the money we earned we turned over to our mother. I used to say that she stood at the door with a tin cup to collect when we came home. That is not quite true, but nearly so. One day my brother Tom and I saw Bob eating a chocolate éclair. When Tom asked, "Where did you get the money for that?" Bob replied, "I took it out of the magazine money." Shocked, Tom said, "My God! Mom will have a fit." Bob countered with a smile and said, "Mother would not want us to go hungry."

Mother liked her treats too. She was a great reader and read whenever she could. In the evening she would sit in a chair, reading the newspaper, a bowl of jelly beans in her lap. While my younger sister Donna stood behind her and combed her hair, the rest of us sat at Mother's feet, watching every jelly bean go down. It was clearly understood that this was her time and her candy.

THE POPCORN WAGON

Harriet Island, across the Mississippi River from downtown St. Paul, was named for Harriet Bishop, St. Paul's first schoolteacher. Dr. Justus Ohage, St. Paul's public health officer in the early 1900s, bought the island and turned it into a public park. Largely at his own expense, Ohage gave St. Paul residents a recreational area with bathhouses and beach, playgrounds, tennis and handball courts, a cafeteria, bandstand, pavilions, childcare facilities, and picnic grounds. Between 1900 and 1906 attendance at the park exceeded six million visitors.

Recurring flooding and increased pollution of the river forced the baths to close in 1919. In the 1920s an entrance at the south end of the Wabasha Street Bridge was added to Harriet Island to increase accessibility to the public. Park use continued to decline, however, despite its central location in the city. In 1942, in an attempt to revitalize the park, the Works Progress Administration built a stone pavilion on the island. Its architect was Clarence Wigington, St. Paul's chief design architect and the first black city architect in the country. In the early 1950s the water channel separating Harriet Island from the mainland was filled in, creating the Harriet Island Regional Park of today.

My mother liked to talk about the good times she had as a teenage girl on Harriet Island. She frequented the zoo and the public baths, and joined the crowds that swam in the river under the watchful eyes of handsome lifeguards. My father reminisced about the fast boats that raced past the island (one of them at seventy miles an hour) between the Wabasha Street Bridge and the High Bridge, and about the day when aerial stuntman Charles "Speed" Holman flew his biplane under the Wabasha Street Bridge. On that day, Holman—a

Minnesota native who became the first pilot for Northwest Airways (now Northwest Airlines)—had a passenger with him: Julius Perlt, the announcer at the University of Minnesota's football and basketball games and Northwest's first office manager. When Holman got past the bridge he did a barrel roll over the river, turned around, and repeated the whole feat going the other way. (The Robert Street Bridge had not yet been built.) Perlt just held on for dear life. Holman was killed in 1931 during a performance at the dedication of the Omaha, Nebraska, airport. His funeral was the largest in Minnesota history, attracting one hundred thousand mourners along the route to the cemetery.

Dad was a creative person who always looked for ways to make money. In 1934 he bought a used ton-and-a-half Model A Ford truck and designed a popcorn wagon with a castlelike motif to fit on the truck's frame. He was a nut for quality and insisted on placing a beautifully varnished solid oak Hire's root beer barrel as the truck's centerpiece. From the barrel we dispensed either clear or foamy root beer at five cents a frosted glass. Popcorn, ice cream, and hamburgers filled out the menu.

Dad booked the wagon into carnivals and county fairs. When he could not get it into a fair, he would park the wagon at a busy location, such as Harriet Island or Lake Phalen, and disappear for the day while we kids ran the business. From time to time irate public officials would try to kick us out of our spot, but with Dad gone no one could drive the truck. The officials had no choice but to let us stay right where we were.

One night when Dad was driving the popcorn truck home down Concord Street, we came upon a dummy that someone had put in the middle of the street. Dad swerved and dodged the dummy, but the window panel through which we served customers had been left on the floor of the truck and it broke all to pieces. Dad stopped the truck to cuss out whoever put the dummy in the street and to bemoan the fact that repairing the shattered window would use up all of the profit we had made that day.

We were proud of the Model A popcorn wagon, but we did not have it for long.

None of us remembers exactly what happened to the truck and popcorn structure, but it was probably repossessed by a finance company. We were left with one piece of the original equipment: the popcorn popper. As soon as the weather warmed up, we older children ran a makeshift portable popcorn concession on weekends at Harriet Island. Our move from South St. Paul to Prescott Street on the West Side put us within walking distance of the island, which really *was* an island in those days. We had to cross a narrow, rickety old bridge to get to it. At the west end of the island was a Victorian-style pavilion that was the center of activity, with dances and booyas every weekend. The pavilion was on pilings to keep the dance floor high above the floods that inundated the island every few years. We

This circa 1910 photo shows the Harriet Island pavilion, where we had our popcorn stand on the lower level.

set up our stand under the pavilion. This location kept us out of the rain, allowed the smell of popcorn to waft up to the dancers, and gave us access to the crowds that came to Harriet Island for the day's activities.

Dad was proud to be the owner of a new type of popcorn popper, called—we believed—the Peerless Popper. It looked like a cylinder with a round bottom and two floppy hinged covers on the top. There was a handle geared to a center shaft that ran at right angles to the bottom of the kettle and stirred the kernels inside with a four-pronged mixer. The popper sat in a stand heated with a propane gas flame. The flame had to be set just right, about 450 degrees. We put the oil and corn in the kettle, and when we heard the last pops we took it off the flame and dumped it into a two-by-three-foot galvanized tin container, about twelve inches deep, that Dad had made. It had a screen bottom to allow the old maids to drop out. We added the salt later. If we put the salt in with the oil and kernels before popping, it made the popcorn rubbery and tough.

We bought our popcorn and Mazola oil from Midwest Feed on Seventh Street. Dad had a fetish about how important it was to use Mazola oil to get the right flavor. He thought that particular oil created the luscious fragrance that enticed customers to buy our popcorn. Supposedly this was the first popper to use cooking oil inside the popper to pop the corn. As each kernel

popped, of course, it turned inside out with the oil and flavor neatly contained inside.

"French-fried popcorn!" we shouted to everyone who came near our popper. Dad coined the slogan, "It sharpens your teeth and combs your hair and makes you feel like a millionaire. It's only a nickel, half a dime, and keeps you eating all the time."

Over the years I kept my eye out for one of the old Peerless Poppers of my childhood to have as a memento. Then one day, leafing through an East Coast catalog, I spotted a popper that looked like our old Peerless, made by the Felknor Company in Monon, Indiana. I called the company and talked with the president, Bill Felknor. When I described our old popper to him, Bill said, "Wait a minute while I go look in our storage area." When he came back on the line, he told me he had the exact popper I had described to him, except the brass nameplate on the cover said "Feerless" instead of "Peerless." It was the same popper; we had just remembered the name wrong all those years.

Bill Felknor later graciously sold the old popper to me. Much as I loved it, I never put it on one of my boats because I didn't want the mess on the carpet. Around 1992 I re-created the identical stand that my dad operated and occasionally set it up for special events on Harriet Island. We would sell popcorn for ten cents a box or five cents a bag, which is the price we charged in the middle-1930s. In recent years we have put fancy modern popcorn machines on all of our boats. We don't use the Feerless for special events anymore, so I'm still trying to figure out what to do with that old popper.

SHOESHINE BOY

In 1934, while I was a student at Roosevelt Junior High, I learned tumbling and how to play the snare drum. (My dad had also been a drummer as a young man.) I also got a job as a shoeshine boy at Dell's Barber Shop on Concord Street on the West Side of St. Paul. It was like I had found my element. I learned how to snap the rag as I shined shoes—and how to comb my hair back and slick it with that pomade we used to use. My stand was solid oak with a drawer where I kept my supplies. I had to buy my shoe polish, but I did not have to pay any commission to Dell Mallinger, the shop owner. However, between shoeshines I was expected to ring up the sale, usually $1.25, and sweep up the hair around the three barber chairs after each customer left. I also wound the barber pole that hung outside the building and cranked the awning up and down. Every day I drew a sign on the sidewalk with colored chalk reading "Shoe-Shines 10 Cents."

One day I had a rabbi in the chair who wore paper-thin kangaroo leather shoes. As I was enthusiastically brushing his shoes I missed and clobbered his foot with the heavy wood backing on the brush.

"Ouch, boy, you hurt my foot!" he cried out. Everyone in the shop turned and looked at me. I was thoroughly embarrassed and the barbers kidded me for days.

One of my best customers was Herman Marthaller, one of the wealthy commission house salesmen from South St. Paul. He owned a mansion up on the hill on Prescott Street. I was shining his shoes one day while he was getting a shave when Dell mentioned that I was struggling to earn enough money to buy a dilapidated bike that was leaning against the outside wall of the barber shop.

"How much is the bike?" Marthaller asked.

"A dollar fifty," the barber replied.

After he had his shave, Marthaller came up to me and said, "I'll give you the dollar and a

half for the bike and take it out in shoe-shines." I was thrilled. I bought the bike, but Marthaller never collected on my debt. He always insisted on paying for his shoeshines.

I worked at the barbershop Monday through Friday from three o'clock, when I got out of school, until six o'clock. Saturdays were big days and I worked from eight until after six.

Once, Dell became angry with his brother Claire (also a barber) because Claire had purchased a fancy car, an Oakland. It had these candelabras on the sides and an elegant mohair interior. It was a big day when Claire gave me a ride in his car. Claire and Dell also thrilled me to death one Christmas when they took me to a dry-goods store on the corner called Henley's and bought me a pair of corduroy trousers. Every Saturday night after they closed up, the brothers would take me to a corner restaurant and buy me a hamburger steak. Man, that was good food. I loved that job and remained lifetime friends with Dell and Claire.

One of my jobs at the shop was to deliver the rent check to the landlord, Bud Moeller. Once a month I went to Bud's house with the check and over time I became friends with Bud and his wife, Lucille. Years later, in the 1970s, I ran into Bud at the Cherokee Sirloin Room in West St. Paul and we resumed our friendship. Bud told Lucille that, at his death, she was to give his sixteen-foot Dingle rowboat to me.

Dingle boats are legendary. Joseph Dingle began his boat works in St. Paul in 1880 and became famous for the quality and workmanship of his boats. The largest boat he built was the 120-foot river cruiser *North Star* for the Mayo family of Rochester, Minnesota. Bud had been a friend of Fred Dingle, one of Joseph's sons, who later took over his father's boatyard. Along with the boat, Lucille gave me Fred's tobacco can, which was leather-covered with the initials "F. D." on it. When I opened the can, I found his last pipe tobacco, his last Harvester cigar, a full bag of Bull Durham tobacco, a Dingle Boat metal nameplate, and a Golden Wheel lighter Bud had given to Fred. The lighter is engraved "MFD" on one side and "From Bud. Xmas, 1927" on the other. The nameplate was not usually put on Dingle boats, according to Todd Warner, a boat restorer and founder of Mahogany Bay Vintage Boats Company. Todd has restored a beautiful runabout that Dingle built for $25,000 in the late 1920s, and he would have liked the nameplate I inherited, but I later gave the Dingle boat to the Minnesota Historical Society. The Society displayed it with the tobacco can and its contents, including the nameplate.

When we kids weren't working, we hung out at the Neighborhood House, a nearby settlement house on Robertson and Indiana Streets, close to where Highway 52 crosses the intersection today. It was founded in the late 1800s to help Eastern European Jewish immigrants resettle; it is now called the Paul and Sheila Wellstone Center for Community Building. We played football and basketball, we wrestled—we did everything down there at the Neighborhood House. Some of our pals lived on the other side of the Mississippi and we thought nothing of swimming across to hang out with them. We swam back and forth in the river just above Harriet Island. One day I watched a little Mexican kid fishing condoms out of the river and blowing them up like balloons. I was about twelve years old at the time and I was petrified when I saw it.

One of my good friends was Harold Lipshultz, who lived on State Street near Concord. Every Friday night for several years, I went to his house around six to turn off all the lights and light candles for his family as they got ready to observe the Jewish Sabbath. The Jewish people have a name for it: I was a *shabbas goy*. Two other friends were Art and John Nasseff. We became friends at Roosevelt Junior High. Art was about my age and John was a year or so younger. I never missed an opportunity to go to their house to eat because their mother served such good food.

Other well-known fellows on the West Side, all of whom were friends of mine, were Joey Specter, Bernie Kessel, "Poncho" Rodriquez, "Dutch" Weber, John Slater, Jim Henley, Bill Kuehn, Melvin Spiegler, George Kuehn, Harry Lieberman and his partner Marvin Hunsaker (both druggists at State and Concord Streets),

Benny Sugarman, Harry Gaston, "Mac" McArdle (he owned the candy store), "Beans" Kane, Art Rockwater, Sidney Applebaum, and Stuart Applebaum.

As far as school was concerned, I was not very interested in it and so was not a good student. One of my favorite teachers was Gretchen Moos, the sister of Malcolm Moos, a future president of the University of Minnesota. Miss Moos taught me the Palmer Method of handwriting. Thanks to her efforts, I have received compliments throughout my life on my penmanship. Two other teachers I appreciated were Mr. Gustafson, who taught woodworking, and Mr. Munch, who taught electrical wiring.

THE CAPITOL

The only excursion boat left on the river during my youth was the *Capitol*, which took hundreds of passengers on cruises down to Hastings and back. She was built in Cincinnati, Ohio, in 1879 and given her original name of the *Pittsburgh*. For two decades the *Pittsburgh* operated in the regularly scheduled packet trade on the Upper Mississippi. In 1897, while docked at the St. Louis riverfront, the boat's entire upper works were stripped off by a cyclone that struck Missouri. The old Diamond Jo Reynolds Line bought the wrecked steamboat and had it rebuilt at Dubuque, Iowa. For more than twenty years it ran on the Upper Mississippi as the *Dubuque*. The boat sank in 1901, but was refloated and purchased by Streckfus Steamers of St. Louis, which turned it into an excursion boat by adding a deck and a dance cabin. The remodeling began in 1920 at Keokuk, Iowa, and was completed at Davenport, where the boat was renamed the *Capitol*.

On June 13, 1920, the *Dubuque Telegraph-Herald* described the *Capitol*: "More than 2,000 electric lamps alone are used to illuminate the dancing deck . . . and the effects are vari-colored, giving the semblance of a beautiful ballroom. The steamer carries an excellent jazz band . . . a novel cafeteria. . . . Decorated with silken Japanese lanterns, terra cotta flower boxes, vari-colored lights, and enclosed mahogany stairways, the 'Capitol' will create a very favorable impression."

For twenty-five years the *Capitol* operated on the Mississippi River between St. Paul and New Orleans, and by 1945 she was broken up at the steamboat graveyard in St. Louis. As kids, however, my brothers and I boarded her several times to sell newspapers. I also spent a lot of time at the Jackson Street Landing just looking at her. In those days, a river excursion boat was the epitome of luxury, and to me the *Capitol* was the biggest thing in town. The thought of taking a cruise on that huge, glamorous riverboat seemed an unattainable dream. Looking back now, I think the *Capitol* probably set the hook in my soul for the river. But I had to leave home and grow up before I could feel the tug of that connection pulling me back to the Mississippi.

This photograph of the Capitol *excursion steamer was taken by John Runk at the Stillwater levee in June 1931.*

3
THE CCC and NATIONAL GUARD

ON MARCH 9, 1933, five days after Franklin D. Roosevelt became president, he asked the Secretaries of Interior, War, and Agriculture to devise a plan that would employ 500,000 youth in America's national parks and forests. He wanted the plan on his desk by the end of that day. By nine o'clock that evening Colonel Kyle Rucken, the army's judge advocate general, brought Roosevelt an outline for the Civilian Conservation Corps. The CCC program was designed to employ jobless young men and to put much-needed cash in the hands of their families.

Congress approved the program, and President Roosevelt signed the CCC bill into law on March 31. The young men would help with flood control, the prevention of forest fires and soil erosion, removal of undesirable plants, insect control, and construction and maintenance of trails and fire lanes on public lands. In return they would receive uniforms, food, housing, medical attention, and a monthly salary of thirty dollars, of which up to twenty-five dollars was to be sent home to the worker's family.

By early July, 250,000 youth between the ages of eighteen and twenty-five were employed in forest and park camps throughout the nation—representing the greatest mobilization of men in peacetime and marking the beginning of a nationwide state parks system. Before the CCC program ended in 1942, two million workers in 895 camps planted trees, built dams, fought forest fires, constructed log buildings and stone bridges, and completed hundreds more conservation and restoration projects. In the CCC's nine years of existence, 711 state parks also were established. In Minnesota, eighty thousand men worked in more than one hundred CCC camps.

FIRST TASTE of SERVICE

I was a terrible student at Humboldt High School. In the ninth grade I got a C in English and D's in history and biology. In the tenth grade even my English had dropped to a D. My brother Bob had joined the CCC and, since nothing else was working out for me, I joined too. I was a five-foot-six, 110-pound seventeen-year-old who, on July 13, 1938, signed up for a one-year term in the CCC. Although the program was designed for eighteen-year-olds, they were willing to take me.

When I reported for duty, a guy in an army uniform gave me two dress uniforms, two work uniforms, and two pairs of army shoes, and warned me that if I lost them my family would have to pay for the replacements. Then they loaded us up in trucks for the ride up Highway 1, the Ely-Finland Trail, to Camp 704, about nine miles south of Ely, Minnesota. Every day began at six-thirty when the night watchman walked through our barracks blowing his whistle. We had to get up and make our bunks with just six inches of white

sheet showing beneath the pillow. If we were quick, we could manage to get in a fast dip in the lake before breakfast.

The chow bell rang at seven o'clock and at eight we lined up in front of our barracks for roll call before piling in trucks to ride to our work site. Our main job was to plant trees and to keep the new trees from being overcome by weeds. On my first day they gave me a sixteen-pound bar to jam in the ground and shove back and forth to open the soil and make a hole. Then I was to plant a tree seedling in the hole and pack in the dirt. I was not accustomed to working hard, to doing physical labor, and this was difficult for me. Besides, I suspect that I was basically lazy. For the first six

Every morning at eight, after having a big breakfast, we reported to our CCC crew leader and boarded the trucks that took us to our job site. In the winter we usually cut aspen to thin the forest; in summer we planted trees.

months I was pretty miserable. On August 23, 1938, I wrote to my mother: "I went to a fire the other day and got my fill of smoke and heat. Although it was a small fire, the forester said it was hot and unusually smoky. . . . I hope you don't think there's any education in grub-hoeing. . . . I am hoping you could spare a little dough. I just spent 95 cents in the canteen for various necessary items. . . . Please write soon and send some money." She did.

After watching me struggle with the iron bar for six months, my boss must have decided I was not a very effective tree planter because he made me a coffee cook for a logging crew. I really liked this job and soon developed a reputation as the best coffee cook in camp. I made the coffee in cleaned-out five-gallon lard cans with a contrived wire handle. To make the coffee I got eggs from the commissary and mixed the whites in with the coffee grounds to make a perfectly clear brew.

For breakfast we had what we called CCC rolls. These were big, four-inch frosted rolls stuffed with cinnamon and raisins. One was usually enough to fill you up, what with the eggs and potatoes and everything else they served for breakfast, so there were always a whole bunch of rolls left on the tables. After breakfast I went around with a sack and picked up all the leftover rolls. Then, when we had our coffee breaks at ten o'clock out in the lumber camps, I'd break out the rolls and pass

them around. The guys just loved them. Then I whittled V-shaped toasting sticks so that when the guys came in from the woods for lunch and picked up their peanut butter and jelly sandwiches, they could toast them on the fire I made. Toasted peanut butter and jelly made a very tasty sandwich out there in the middle of the woods.

Work for the day ended at three o'clock. They trucked us back to the camp, where we cleaned up and changed into our regulation uniforms. We were then free to do what we wanted until dinner at five. There was a recreation room with five pool tables and two Ping-Pong tables. We could also take courses for high school credit. I took three courses, including one in radio and another in touch-typing. I graduated with high marks in practically all the army radio schools I later went to. My Morse code speed was up around twenty words a minute, which was very good.

My most exciting times in the CCC were spent fighting fires. Our crews were generally stationed about ten miles from our camp. Each truck had a telephone in its cab, and after unloading the crew the truck driver would connect the wires from the phone to the nearest telephone line. Then, if the foresters in the lookout towers spotted a fire, they could call the nearest CCC camp crew to go fight it.

Once, we got a call on a fire a considerable distance from camp. We started out late at night and traveled the roads by truck, crossed the lakes by a series of barges powered by outboard motors, and ended up hiking the last nine miles. A third of the men made camp while the others went on to fight the fire, which covered about one and a half square miles of forest. Even that far from our base camp the CCC fed us well. For the noon meal that first day we had baked ham and fresh apple pie made in the camp's makeshift cook stove. For the two weeks we spent fighting the fire, an airplane flew back and forth to bring in food. To have fresh apple pie and baked ham twenty miles from civilization really impressed me.

The abundance of food in the camps must have made a big impression on my brother Bob too, because he mailed the CCC Thanksgiving menu to our parents. On the cover is the word "THANKSGIVING" in capital letters, followed by "Company No. 701, Civilian Conservation Corps, Camp F-2, Isabella, Minn., November 26, 1936." The menu included consommé, celery, pickles and olives, roast turkey with cranberry sauce, two kinds of potatoes, dressing, peas, Waldorf salad, and hot mince pie. The meal concluded with coffee, candy, nuts, and cigarettes. My Thanksgiving dinner at Company 704, Camp F-1, Ely, Minnesota, in 1938 must have been similar. In a country where a shocking percentage of the population was begging for food, such abundance was news worth writing home about.

On September 6, 1938, I wrote to my mother: "I would like to come back to school but I would rather stay here for my term. For this week, by doing extra work I am going to make $3.25. I work from 7 [p.m.] to 7 [a.m.] as a night watchman. During the night I got a quart of milk, nine eggs, a dozen jelly rolls, pound of butter, coffee, bread and three oranges. That was just for snacks for me between rounds—all that and $3.25 as a night watchman. Not bad!"

I learned how to press clothes with three pleats in the back of our uniform shirts and two pleats in the front, like they did in the army. I made pretty good money pressing clothes on the side, and my financial situation continued to improve. In May 1939, I sent my mother some quills from a porcupine I had killed and wrote, "Well, I think I can make the $22 by the end of the month. I haven't taken out any canteen books yet so I'll have $7.80 coming pay day." I enclosed two dollars for the family.

One day we had an unusually bad blizzard. It was a camp rule that if the temperature hit twenty below zero we didn't go out. A group of us were looking out the window over Birch Lake, which was about a mile across, when one of the men wagered a dollar that no one could get across the lake and back in the storm. A dollar was a lot of money to us at that time. I took the bet, dressed as warmly as I could, took a bearing with a compass, and went out into the blizzard. About the time

I got across the lake to a tree trunk, where I placed a note (the agreed-upon evidence that I had gotten there), the storm let up and the guys over in the barracks could see that I had made it. When I got back to the barracks, the guy tried to welsh on his bet, but the other fellows made him give me the buck.

I was honorably discharged from the CCC on July 13, 1939. I weighed 137 pounds, had close to two hundred dollars in the bank, and had three certificates for courses that I had taken. Moreover, I was a changed youth. I had matured. The year in the Ely CCC camp was the best year of my life in an organization. The first thing I did when I got back to St. Paul after serving in the CCC was to enroll in Harding High School, where my grades immediately jumped from almost failing to A's and B's.

QUITTING SCHOOL

I don't know why I did it or what I was thinking of, but with only half a semester left to get my diploma, I quit high school in 1939 to attend St. Paul Vocational School to become an electrician. Soon I was working as an apprentice with a journeyman electrician, replacing the 110-volt knob and tube electrical systems with 220 volts so people could install the new electric cook stoves and clothes washers in their homes. My employer, Mr. Nelson, had a 1930 two-door Model A Ford sedan. It was jam-packed with fuses, wires of

every gauge, tools to bend pipe, and all the other necessities of our trade. The car was functional, but it looked like a mess.

One time we were working in a huge building with printing presses in it and my screwdriver got grounded. There was a loud cracking noise and I watched the screwdriver melt in my hand. We were working with 440 volts. My boss sent me out to his car in a hurry to find a 60-amp fuse to replace the one I had blown. The whole floor of presses was out of commission until I could bring back that new fuse, but my boss never chewed me out for what I had done.

For a brief time I held a clerical position with Glendenning, a St. Paul trucking firm at Raymond and University. My job was to log the tachometers on the trucks that ran to Chicago and back to St. Paul. I knew every stop between here and Chicago and can still recite the towns where the drivers made stops. I earned enough money to buy my first watch. A wristwatch was a serious purchase in those days. The two guys I worked with discussed the purchase at some length with me, and I ended up negotiating with a jeweler for a Bulova.

ARRESTED for CAR THEFT

My brothers and I were still scrounging to make some money. One of the things we did was make buttons to sell at University of Minnesota football games. We took the wires out of the buttons, put ribbons in, replaced the wires, and fixed up the buttons so they looked really good. The whole thing was Bob's idea and it made tons of money. Bob, Tom, and I went to one of the Gopher games in the fall of 1939 to sell buttons and somehow the two of them got into the stadium and I didn't.

There I was, outside the stadium, and it was a long walk back to our house on the West Side at 504 Orleans Street. As I trudged home, I saw this car parked on the street with its key in the ignition. When I thought about how far I was from home, I just said, "What the hell," and got in the car. I think it was a 1927 or 1928 Nash. It did not have a ignition starter. I looked around the inside and saw this bailing wire sticking up out of the floor. When I pulled on the wire, it activated the starter and the engine fired up. I found it fairly simple to steer it over the High Bridge and to our neighborhood, where I parked the car a couple of blocks from our house.

I left the car where I had parked it for about a day and a half. Then, figuring the car was probably out of gas, I siphoned some from another parked car into a can and carried it back to "my" car and poured it in. Then I got in, yanked on the wire, and had gotten about three blocks down the street when a police car pulled up beside me. An officer pointed what looked like a handheld 20-millimeter cannon right at me. I raised my hands and in my excitement let

the car jump over the curb. I think the officer felt sorry for me.

The police took me to my house, and I asked them to please park in the back so the neighbors would not see what was going on. The officers did. After talking with my mightily upset mother and sister, they hauled me off to jail. I spent about a week there, scared to death, before going before a judge and being put on probation. The charge was reduced to taking a vehicle without the owner's permission. I had turned eighteen just a few months before, which was a problem because now I was no longer a juvenile but an adult. The court let me out of jail and assigned a probation officer named Willard Esau to me. Mr. Esau was an absolute prince. I went to see him once a week and took very seriously everything he said to me. At the end of my probation, Mr. Esau got me a "pardon extraordinaire" from Governor Edward John Thye, which wiped the offense from my record. I don't think I had ever stolen anything before the car episode, and I certainly have never taken anything that did not belong to me since. I have often thought that I would like to establish an honorarium at the Hennepin County Probation Office for Mr. Esau. One of these days I am going to do that.

WRESTLING in the NATIONAL GUARD

The idea of a militia, or body of citizen soldiers as distinct from career soldiers, was borrowed from England and, in North America, dates from 1636, when three militia regiments were organized to defend the Massachusetts Bay Colony. Minnesota formed its first National Guard unit, called the Territorial Enrolled Militia, in 1850, but the unit did not actually get started until April 1856, when the first uniformed volunteer company of Pioneer Guards was formed in St. Paul. When the Civil War broke out in April 1861, Minnesota's militia organizations formed the nucleus of the First Minnesota Volunteer Infantry Regiment. The First Minnesota is officially recognized as the senior regiment in the Union Army because Alexander Ramsey of Minnesota was the first governor to offer state troops to President Abraham Lincoln. The regiment is legendary for its gallant and casualty-heavy charge at Gettysburg on July 2, 1863.

Members of the Minnesota Guard fought in the Philippines from 1898 to 1899 and served on the Mexican border and in France during World War I. In June 1931, a field training site was opened north of Little Falls, Minnesota, called Camp Ripley, named for a long-abandoned nineteenth-century army post.

I joined the Minnesota National Guard in 1940 to get the shoes. As kids growing up in the Depression we never went hungry, but we did experience all the privation and problems that came with a lack of money. Because I had learned Morse code while

in the CCC camp, the Guard put me into a radio section at Camp Ripley. I was on KP duty one day, peeling potatoes, when the cooks began talking about the big wrestling and boxing match that was coming off that night in the camp.

"Gee," I said, "I used to do some wrestling."

"You're a wrestler?" they asked, casting a skeptical glance at my skinny frame.

"Yeah."

I *had* learned to wrestle, at the YMCA in St. Paul, under a wonderful coach by the name of Chuck Mulalley. His father was a judge and Chuck later joined the police force. Thanks to him, our YMCA team was one of the winningest teams in the region. Convinced that I knew nothing of wrestling and was showing off, the cooks maneuvered a match for me on that night's wrestling program. I showed up for the match wearing World War I britches that laced up the legs. I did not want to get mat burns. When I climbed into the ring there was a smattering of polite applause. Suddenly there was a roar. It was for my opponent, a hairy guy who looked like a mountain. I weighed about 130 and he looked to be 145 pounds at least. Everyone figured I was going to get my ass whipped.

The bell rang. We walked to the center of the ring and touched our arms. Then I did

My brother Jim and I wrestled on the St. Paul YMCA championship team in 1937. Kneeling from left: Jordan Noyes, George Leaman, Don Kennedy, George Schulte, Gordon Rooke, James Bowell, and Homer Ford. Second row: Rocco Soggiorno, William Behr, William Bowell, Walter Kennedy, Dan Holgren, and Art Nielson. Third row: Louis Tallen, Chuck Mulalley, Harold Simon, Frank Turie, and Lew Dahlen.

an immediate leg drop, which took him down to the mat. I tied one of his arms to his body, rolled him over, lay on top of him, and pinned him. I won the match so fast, in less than a minute, that he never knew what happened to him. When I glanced over at the two cooks, who thought they had arranged for my demise, they were in shock. They couldn't get over it. From then on I was their hero and I got a ribbon for it.

None of us knew what real heroism was, of course. That changed after Pearl Harbor.

4
PARATROOPER

BEFORE DECEMBER 1941, few people in the United States had heard of Pearl Harbor. That changed on December 7, when Americans turned on their radios for some Sunday afternoon entertainment and instead learned that the Japanese had bombed the U.S. naval base at Pearl Harbor on the island of Oahu, Hawaii. The night before, Japanese Vice Admiral Chuichi Nagumo had led a thirty-three-ship fleet to a position about 230 miles north of Oahu. From there, 350 airplanes led by Commander Mitsuo Fuchida took off from aircraft carriers to attack the U.S. fleet early that Sunday morning. The surprise attack killed 2,388 people and wounded about 2,000. Twenty-one American ships and more than three hundred airplanes were destroyed. Among the surviving ships was the USS *Ward*, whose crew—including eighty-two reservists from St. Paul—is credited with firing the first shots of World War II.

The attack took place just before 8:00 a.m. on Oahu, which was early afternoon in Washington, D.C. President Roosevelt was having lunch when Secretary of War Henry Stimson informed him what had happened. Roosevelt called for a joint session of Congress the next day, and that evening penned his speech that opened with the memorable statement, "Yesterday, December 7, 1941—a date which will live in infamy—the United States was suddenly and deliberately attacked by naval and air forces of the Empire of Japan." The United States immediately mobilized for war.

JOINING the ARMY

On the day the Japanese attacked Pearl Harbor I was out squirrel hunting with a bolt-action .22-caliber rifle. I liked the sight on it and its accuracy. I was really a good shot. A squirrel had jumped from one tree to the other, and I hit it with the .22 in midair and killed it. It was an improbable shot. On the way back home from hunting I stopped in a little grocery store to get a Paramount Pie for a nickel and heard the radio announcement about Pearl Harbor. I wondered where the hell Pearl Harbor was and why everyone was making such a fuss. I was twenty years old and did not realize how involved I would soon become in World War II.

I volunteered for the army. Three of my brothers also enlisted—Bob in the air force and Tom and Jim in the navy. Bob, who was something of a mechanical genius, took the military's mechanical aptitude test and scored 159 out of a possible 160. He spent the war years in Texas inspecting airplanes. Jim ended up on a minesweeper in the Pacific. During a kamikaze attack, Jim asked permission to go overboard as there were sailors in the water calling for help. He dove into the sea and saved six men. He received the Navy and Marine Corps Medal for his heroism. Tom served his whole time in the Bahamas. If I had stayed in the Minnesota National Guard, I would have spent all of World War II in Riverside, California, in an antiaircraft regiment and would have missed all the action. Instead, I became a paratrooper.

PARATROOPER TRAINING

Because I had learned Morse code and how to operate a radio in the CCC, the army put me in communications school at Camp Roberts, California. On the April day we arrived in 1942, it was 110 degrees on the parade grounds. Toward the end of my thirteen weeks of basic training, officers came around looking for volunteers to join a new and specialized combat unit called the paratroopers. (Everyone who became a paratrooper in World War II volunteered for it.) I submitted my name, and when I had my interview with the colonel he asked me why I wanted to join the paratroopers. My answer reflected the immaturity of a twenty-one-year-old kid: I told him I wanted to come home with medals or not come back. That is how I got into the paratroopers, and I have never regretted it.

Before they let you join, the officers tried to scare the hell out of you. The only training films they had at that time were made by the British paratroopers, who jumped through a square hole in the floor of the plane. Those guys just walked over to the hole and, *whoops*, dropped out of sight. We

Egad—I'm in the army!

did it differently; we jumped out the side door of the airplane.

They sent me to Fort Benning, Georgia, for training in one of the early paratrooper classes, Class 32. I was assigned to the 507th Parachute Infantry Regiment, one of the initial regiments activated in World War II. For a few weeks I wondered if I would make it, the training was so rigorous. In a letter to my mother I wrote: "I never dreamed that anything could be this tough. From 7:30 in the morning until 5 at night if we so much as wiggle an ear we get punished. We do push-ups, sometimes a hundred at a time. If we get caught at any part of the day with our shoulder

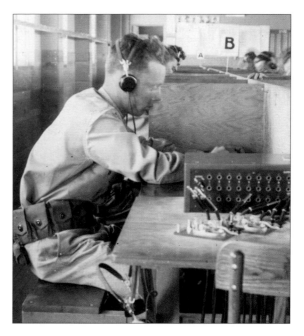

I spent hours on code practice in basic training.

My favorite weapon was a World War I Springfield, which I preferred over the newer Garand M-1 for its accuracy.

Ol' Man RIVER

This prewar postcard shows Lawson Field's hangar number seven at Fort Benning. The 507th Parachute Infantry Regiment still uses this hangar today.

blades not touching and our chests not way out we get push-ups. We may be marching along and if we aren't standing right an instructor will pull us out of line and say, 'Fifty!' and we get down in front of him and do fifty push-ups. You do exercises until your lungs cry for air but the instructors keep hounding you. Kids start sobbing through gritted teeth. . . . We have to have a special menu. Our noon meal is light so that we can make it through the afternoon without throwing up.

"We can leave camp any time we want to. The only reason we keep it up is we think of the wings we'll get and our boots. The paratrooper is the best and toughest soldier of the Army, Navy or Marines. I won't know if I've made it for four weeks yet but I'm giving it every bit of guts I ever had. I could never give this up no matter how tough it gets."

My experience as a tumbler in junior high and as a wrestler helped me as we had to be able to tumble properly when we landed so we wouldn't break a leg. For part of our training we were dropped from a 150-foot tower, high enough to scare the devil out of you. Most of us did not get scared jumping from the free tower; it was the shock harness that shook us up the most. To do it we put on a regular parachute harness without the chute, strapped ourselves in a vertical position, and were hauled by cable up 150 feet, where we hung in midair. When the instructor on the ground counted to three we were supposed to pull the ripcord, which dropped us fifteen feet before jerking us upright. We had to switch the pull cord handle to the other hand as we dropped the fifteen feet. Then it lowered us to the ground. Some of the kids got up there and couldn't pull the ripcord and the instructors wouldn't let them down. I didn't blame the kids too much. At 150 feet up, people below look like ants.

On the day our first parachute jump was scheduled, we all went down to the field, but when we got there it was sprinkling and they decided the cloud ceiling was too low, so they sent us back to the barracks to wait. After a couple of hours they brought us back to the field, found the conditions still unfavorable, and returned us to the barracks a second time. I had never been up in an airplane before, and by this time was beginning to feel shaky.

Finally, in the afternoon, we went down to the field, drew our chutes, climbed into the plane, and up we went. We flew around for half an hour in a kind of daze. Suddenly the jumpmaster said, "Stand up and hook up. Stand at the door." I was the second man in line and I got all set to get the hell out the door when the jumpmaster excitedly said, "Hold it, sit down!" A big wind had come up with sheets of rain. I

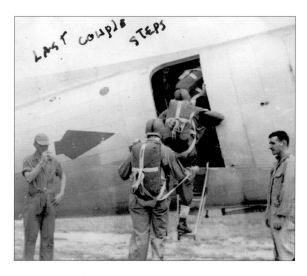

Entering the plane for my first jump.

"What in the hell am I doing up here? Did I hook up? Did I tie my break cord? Maybe it won't open! I should have gone to church last Sunday!"

had a sudden urge to push him aside and jump out the door anyway. I guess common sense held me back. I was disgusted and figured I would never get to make my first jump. We snapped on our safety belts and the plane landed.

Then, before we could get off the plane, the order came through to make the jump after all. The wind had died down and it had stopped raining. The plane took off for the second time and every man had a hell of a scared look on his face. It was silent in the plane except for the roar of the engines. Then the jumpmaster started us singing "You Are My Sunshine." We all joined in and that made us feel a heck of a lot better. Again he said, "Stand up and hook up. Stand at the door." Then he hollered, "Is everybody happy?" We all shouted, "Yes!"

Our regimental patch.

"You are all a bunch of bullshitters!" the jumpmaster yelled back. Then he slapped the first man on the leg and hollered, "Go!" Quick as a flash I got in the door. *"Go!"* Out I went and before I even thought of counting, my chute opened and I felt my head jerk back with a snap. The elation I felt when my chute opened—I don't think there are words to express it. I looked

around and saw the rest of the boys who jumped with me. We all were together in a bunch coming down. Most of us lit like feathers. We were the happiest kids I ever saw, and we all wanted to go back up and jump again.

Despite our jubilation, the day was shadowed. Another group had jumped just a few minutes before us. They were Canadians, led by a major who jumped with his men. They all had bailed out together, and as they were floating down, a press plane that had been photographing them got too close and tore the canopy off the major's chute. He fell about a thousand feet to his death. They covered the spot where he landed, but it made all of us nervous.

On my second jump I was more scared than I had been on my first. I kept thinking about the major who had been killed. However, I knew more about what I was doing this time. I still got a hell of a shock when my chute opened, but it felt good. My third jump was the best of the three. I wasn't nervous or scared and felt cool as a cucumber. I went out the door right on the back of the guy ahead of me and my chute had a good opening. I felt only a slight jar. After that jump I loved what I was doing and wouldn't have traded it for anything.

Before long I had made five jumps and got my sterling silver paratrooper wings. Before I went home on furlough I ordered a tailor-made uniform for myself. A paratrooper at that time was like somebody from outer space. When you walked down the street with your silver wings pinned to your chest, your boots polished to a high gleam, and your pants blossomed into the top of your boots, you were something. (It was against regulations, but we used rubber bands to keep the pants blossomed out perfectly on our legs.)

While at Fort Benning I was assigned to the headquarters company of the 507th Regiment of the 82nd Airborne Division, an elite group of intelligent men. I was impressed by the sophistication of those guys. We were always in some sort of philosophical discussion, and it was then that I began to read the Romantic poets, like Byron and Shelley, as well as Shakespeare. I kept track of what I read in my three-volume wartime diary.

I began growing up in the army, though I was still immature in other ways. While I was a skilled radio operator, ranked at the top of every class I took, I was a poor

The residents of Alliance, Nebraska, loved having the 507th as neighbors. We paraded as a way to thank them.

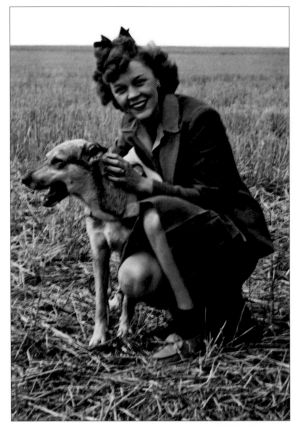

Alliance girlfriend Gladys Nielsen with the 507's mascot, Geronimo, who had his own parachute and sometimes jumped with us.

Sunday dinner with the Nielsen family.

soldier. I did not take it seriously. When I left Fort Benning for Alliance, Nebraska, for further training, for instance, I used to slip off to visit a girlfriend I had in town. Once, when I was hospitalized with bronchitis, I changed out of my gown and into my civilian clothes, which I had hidden in the false ceiling of the hospital porch, before sneaking out. After sneaking back in, a friend saw me and said, "They've been looking all over hell for you." I quickly changed out of my clothes, put on my hospital gown, went down to another ward, and climbed into an empty bed. I lay there for an hour, my hands pressed against my face to make it look like I had slept, and then walked into my ward. "Gee," I said, "I must have fallen asleep in the wrong ward." Officers would say to me, "I really want to raise you in rank, but you keep doing these things."

I got called in one day for some infraction and was standing in front of the officer we called Captain "Big Steve" while this first sergeant stood next to me. His name was Brown, and I never did like the son of a bitch. I was talking to the captain about something and this Sergeant Brown said, "You can't talk to the captain like that," and he hauled off and slapped me in the face. Without batting an eye I said, "Sir, I want to prefer charges against the sergeant for doing that." It was all Big Steve could do to keep from laughing. He told me, "Why don't you go over to the barracks and you'll be restricted there for a while."

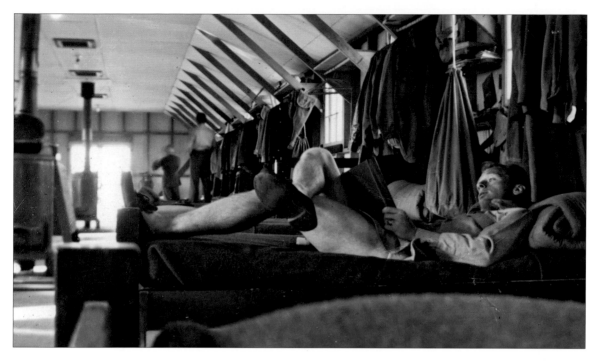

Whenever I had a free moment, I would read in my bunk. I especially enjoyed reading nineteenth-century poetry.

Alliance was nothing but sand hills. At six one morning they told us we would fall out at seven to make a jump. They didn't tell us that the jump was forty miles away and we would have to walk back. We finished the jump at around nine o'clock and started to walk back. We could see Alliance, so help me, thirty miles away. The hike was arduous. For every step we took up the sand hills we'd slide back a step. We had to walk much of the forty miles in the heat of the day. My buddy Bob "Van" Vannatter and I had been out all night the night before and had hangovers. We walked the rest of that day and all night, finally getting back to the base around noon the next day. I wouldn't give up until I got to the gates of the camp. I passed out at the entrance but at least I made it. They had to carry me the rest of the way in. That hike was something else, but it was very, very good training.

SHIPPING OVERSEAS

While I was in Alliance, I found a supplier for sterling silver paratrooper wings. Once you got your original sterling silver set, the only copy a paratrooper could get was a die-cast set, which nobody really wanted. My supplier sold not only the genuine wings, but also miniature silver wings. So I put a deal together where I bought the miniature wings and had somebody put loops on for earrings and put a pair of them in each box.

Ol' Man RIVER

I figured I would make twenty thousand bucks that Christmas selling paratrooper wing earrings. I was all set when somebody walked up and said, "We're leaving for Europe." That killed the whole deal, or so I thought. We shipped out on December 4, 1943, on a British vessel called the *Strathnaver*. The ship was a mess and we were really packed in. It served horrible food. When we arrived at Liverpool, we switched ships and went to Belfast, Ireland. From Belfast they sent us to Port Rush in Northern Ireland, where we were quartered in apartments that had fireplaces.

When I got overseas I discovered that a soldier could send for one package a month from the States. All the guys were sending home for cookies and candy while I was sending off for sterling silver parachute wings from some company in Utica, New York. I'd get a couple hundred of them at a time. The minute they arrived I'd step out in the street in front of our tent and announce, "I got wings!" The guys queued up to buy them. They really sold. I was buying the wings at eight-five cents and selling them for $4.20, which was the exchange rate for a British pound at the time.

I don't know how many I sold, but I made very close to my twenty thousand bucks. Every cent I made I sent to my bank account at home. One time somebody stole four hundred of my wings and I found out who it was. The son of a bitch was a cham-pion fighter, so I decided it might be wiser to just let the damned wings go.

While we were stationed near Port Rush for part of our training I made friends with the Carlisle family, where I spent most of my spare time. Mr. Carlisle had a lot of books on radio, and I read them and played with his powerful receiver, which could pick up American broadcasts and German propaganda messages. I was in Ireland for my twenty-third birthday in February 1944, and the Carlisles gave me half a dozen beautiful Irish linen handkerchiefs. It was nice of them to do that, especially since it took some of their scarce ration coupons. One day Uncle Sam got generous with us and gave each soldier a one-pound box of Fanny Farmer chocolates. It was such a treasure that I hated to eat it. Instead I gave it to the Carlisles.

With materials Mr. Carlisle supplied me I built a Morse code practicing table. It held six partitioned stations, a net control at the head of the table, and an oscillator that duplicated the sounds as if they were coming from real radios. The arrangement allowed seven radio operators to practice field communications in one room as if they were miles apart, just as they would be in an actual combat situation.

When Lieutenant Kay Todd, who was from St. Paul, saw what I had built, he sat me down for a talk. Todd was a Yale graduate and a tremendously nice guy who, unfortunately, was killed on D-Day. Todd read the riot act to me. He had just made someone else a corporal and he told me the position should have gone to me. But he couldn't promote me, despite the talent I had, because he couldn't depend on what I would do next, which was usually to go into town without a pass to visit girls, stuff like that. I just was not a good peacetime soldier.

On the battlefield, however, I was all business. Fortunately, I didn't have much fear in combat. When I saw a job to be done, I just did it. I became a corporal, then a sergeant, and finally a staff sergeant when I was the message center chief. The latter was a battlefield promotion that never got on the record because the guy I replaced returned and got his job back.

Life in the small Irish villages was something to see. Electric lights were few, and for heat there was the ever-present fireplace that burned peat, the major fuel. Housewives did all of their cooking over the fireplace. Usually a long chain hung from the top and different types of kettles and skillets, depending on what she was making, hung from the chain. The older fireplaces had soot from past generations clinging to their sides. For some reason they did not clean the soot from the face of the fireplace, yet the rest of the house would be spick-and-span. The people went in for brass decorations a lot and they were always shimmering like polished gold. Most

houses were a century or more old, and many of them had thatched straw roofs.

As part of a training exercise, my friend Van and I and a few others were put on an enemy detail and sent into the countryside to guard a certain point against an attack from a rifle platoon. The point turned out to be a remote country schoolhouse. We had a lot of fun with the kids and showed them how to play American games. We even had them doing close-order drill. From a local farmer we bought eggs, bread, and jam, and with that and the coffee and C-rations we got from our mess sergeant, we had a feast. As a general rule, no one could get eggs. The civilians received one every two weeks. As it turned out, we paid three shillings a dozen for the eggs, which was about sixty cents in American money.

A few weeks before D-Day I was in the hospital for a minor operation. One day the doctor came through and asked everybody to put their hands out so he could look at their fingers. I had no idea why. He looked at mine and saw that the tips of my the fingers were purple. "I want to put you through some tests," he said. The tests included submerging my hands in cold water, and they determined I had Raynaud's disease—a condition that causes the small arteries in the fingers and toes to suddenly go into spasm on exposure to cold or stress, shutting down the blood circulation. When the doctor saw this he

My sisters Mary and Phyllis, circa 1942.

"Z.I.'d" me. Z.I. stood for "Zone of the Interior." It meant they were going to send me back to the States.

The prospect of being shipped home before the invasion of Europe took place brought me up short. I thought, "My God, I've spent all this time in training for the big day and now I'm going to miss it." We all knew the D-Day invasion was about to take place. We could feel it in the air. We had mixed feelings about the invasion. On the one hand we wanted it to begin and to get it over with. On the other hand, we knew what it would lead to. In the hospital with me were men with broken legs, broken backs. One guy's leg was amputated. They all had been injured in training. We had trained for so long, hiked so many miles, dug so many foxholes, made so many hazardous jumps that now we longed for the real thing. The waiting was making us mentally fatigued. My own nerves were bothering me more and more. Underneath it all, I believe, was a strong dislike for army life. I liked the work I did with radio and found that to be a lot of fun. What was getting to me was the army's heavy schedule of lectures and the discipline.

After thinking about it for a day, I asked my captain to get me out of the hospital so I could go back to my unit and go into combat with my fellow paratroopers. It was an emotional decision because I had a free ticket home, and here I was turning it down. I wrote to my sister Mary on May 28, 1944: "I'm getting out of the hospital today and going back to duty. For a while there they had me scheduled for a trip back to the States. Somehow I managed to scrape out of that deal and now I am anticipating the future. There will be long periods when I'll be unable to write but you can be well assured I'll be taking good care of myself."

NORMANDY and D-DAY

The D-Day invasion of June 6, 1944, began with an attack by American paratroopers. The night before, 822 aircraft carried parachutists or towed gliders to the landing zones. Dropped behind enemy lines to secure needed targets, the paratroopers knew that if the accompanying assault by sea failed, they could not be rescued. Departing from the English coast, the 101st and 82nd U.S. Airborne Divisions were dropped on the Cherbourg peninsula. The 101st was to secure the western end behind Utah Beach and head off an eastern German advance. The 82nd, landing farther inland, was to seize the bridges and halt an advance from the west. Bill Bowell's unit, the 507th Parachute Infantry Regiment, was to be dropped west of the Merderet River, about one-half mile north of the town of Amfreville, in a drop zone that placed them squarely in front of the elite 91st Division. Heavy fog and German gunfire prevented the pilots from landing the paratroopers precisely as planned.

I could have shipped out for home, but instead I went back to southern England, near Nottingham, back to the staging area with all the sand tables showing the area in Normandy where we planned to jump. By now I was a communications sergeant, a battalion radio operator assigned to a crack demolition crew that was ordered to blow up a bridge. Besides jumping with all the usual gear carried by a paratrooper, I was going to have a Number 300 radio set strapped on.

Father John Verret, chaplain of the 507th Parachute Infantry Regiment, said mass to

This is the identifying flag that I wore on my sleeve when I parachuted into Normandy on June 6, 1944. All of the paratroopers were issued similar flags.

London photographers did good business taking pictures of soldiers who were not sure they would survive to return home. This photo of me with my sergeant's stripes was taken on October 7, 1944.

the largest group of communicants of his military career, Catholics and non-Catholics alike. With final letters written home and last-minute adjustments made to equipment, there was no relief from the mounting tensions. We pondered our fate.

Less than a week later, on June 5, 1944, at one hour before midnight, I was waiting with a group of paratroopers on a blacked-out airfield, getting ready to board our plane. The moonlit sky enabled me to distinguish row upon row of army transport planes. Men sat everywhere around me, their faces darkened with burned cork. Each of us had grenades and ammunition attached or in bandoliers around our waists. The pockets of our jumpsuits bulged with K rations, cigarettes, and other small items that would be of use to us when we jumped behind enemy lines. Wearing all of our heavy equipment and the tightly strapped parachute made it difficult to move or walk. Many of us weighed in at ninety to 120 pounds over our body weight.

A note from General Dwight D. Eisenhower, the D-Day mastermind, was handed to each trooper. It read, "The eyes of the world are upon you. The hopes and prayers of liberty-loving people everywhere march with you." We sat calmly but uncomfortably in small circles. Everyone either spoke in low tones or was quiet. Tension hung over us all. Every once in a while a group of men would half-heartedly laugh at a joke a buddy had told, breaking the silence. To my left the lights were still burning in the hangar where the sand table with all of its small reproductions and details of the mission had been carefully laid out. An officer darted by, a roll of maps under his arm.

Our battalion commander suddenly appeared, walked briskly to the center of the clusters of men, and gave the order to secure equipment. We formed a circle around him. He gave us last-minute orders and stated the password again to make sure everyone knew it. Chaplain Verret said a prayer and we moved off to our assigned planes. As I trudged up to my plane, the engines gave a sudden chug, kicked over, and then roared, vibrating with power. Dynamite and TNT were loaded underneath the belly of the aircraft. Climbing into the airplane was a chore because of all the gear we were carrying. I could not get into the plane on my own and they had to lift me in. Within a few minutes our group, our "stick" of men, was on board, strapped in and waiting.

The C-47s left the runway and became airborne, and we were on our way to make history. Our stick was silent in our plane. It was a moonlit sky with a few clouds here and there. Through the windows we could see the dark shapes of the other C-47s as they hovered over the field, maneuvering into tight formations. Finally, with all of the paratroop-laden ships in the air, we crossed the English Channel. D-Day was about to dawn.

The silence in our plane was broken by the German-manned ack-ack guns. The flak was heavy, bursting all around us, and small burning pieces soon pierced the fuselage. Underneath the plane, hanging from bomb racks, were six bundles of explosives. A hit there would blow us into a million pieces. We flew around Cherbourg peninsula, through clouds, to come in from the west side, where the Channel Islands are. As we flew over the peninsula we got intense flak from German antiaircraft guns. All of a sudden the plane seemed to do a back flip. Then it was steady, though we seemed to be losing altitude. "Stand up and hook up!" we were ordered. Every man rose mechanically. This was the moment we had trained for for nearly two years. I had a sick feeling in the pit of my stomach and many of us murmured prayers: "May God be with us."

At that moment we flew into another flak area. We took a bad hit, and the plane lurched again and began to vibrate. Shrapnel flew around the interior of the plane. We sensed it was going down and we were already low to the ground. "Go!" shouted the jumpmaster. I was the eleventh man on the stick. The men were going head first out the door of the plane when the number seven guy slipped and fell. We had wrapped blankets around us to keep warm during the two-hour flight and when

we stood up the blankets fell on the polished aluminum floor, which was slippery as glass. When the guy fell he caused a big pile-up at the door. Every trooper was loaded with at least a hundred pounds of gear, and when one fell it was hard for him to get back up. Number eight fell, then every one of us, down to the last man, fell to his knees. The need to untangle the mess became increasingly urgent because the plane was obviously going to crash. Some of us ended up crawling out.

I managed to push myself out the door and no sooner did my chute open than I hit the ground. I had probably counted to no more than one thousand, two thousand, three thousand, four thousand, and *bam*— I must have jumped at two hundred feet carrying all my equipment, a rifle, and the goddamned Number 300 radio set between my legs. When I hit the ground I sprained my ankle. It was the first time I had been injured in a jump.

For a moment I lay on the ground, writhing in agony in the dead of night. I knew I had to get myself out of my chute before some German bayoneted me. I reached for my knife to cut myself free and in my excitement I dropped it. I had spent weeks sharpening that knife, and when I picked it up I grabbed it by the blade and spent a few panicky minutes trying to cut myself free with the handle. By the time I discovered what I was doing, blood was oozing down my fingers. But I

Ol' Man RIVER

PARATROOPER

managed to cut the harness holding me to the chute and free my rifle. It was two o'clock on the morning of D-Day. I had landed on the wrong side of the Douve River, about ten miles from my drop zone.

At that moment, however, I didn't know where the hell I was. I lay flat on my belly, watching planes and gliders going down around me, when I heard this noise and saw this shadow walking in a crouch toward me. My rifle was next to me. I picked it up quietly so I wouldn't give my position away. Slowly I raised my rifle to fire and whispered the password, "Flash." There was no answer. We had been given metal crickets for signaling, but everybody, I think, had decided they weren't going to use the damn crickets. We were sure the Germans would quickly figure out that everybody had a cricket and the things would give us away.

I gave the password again, only louder. Still no reply. I took up the slack on the trigger and, for the last time, hollered, "Flash!" The guy replied with the right answer—"Thunder!"—and I relaxed. He was one of the men from our stick. Two more figures came forward and immediately gave the password. I hurriedly cut out a panel of fabric from my parachute for a souvenir and the four of us moved out slowly, creeping and crawling through the dark. I was able to hobble along on my sprained ankle. A steady stream of tracers came over our heads, followed by telltale trails of smoke. The sky was periodically lit with flak as more planes came over. One burst into flame and went down in a slow glide, exploding when it hit the ground.

We discovered we were in an orchard and saw the shapes of cows around us. We figured that, because of our premature jump, we were nowhere near our planned jump area. We tried to orient ourselves and find our position on the map. Near us was a highway and running parallel to it was a high-voltage power line. That high line was not on our map, so we decided to wait until daybreak to find some landmark that would help us identify our exact position. Cautiously, the four of us crossed the road and, walking in a crouch, headed for the far end of a nearby field. I didn't know any of the three guys I had hooked up with. One was a lieutenant from some other company and seemed spooky to me. He wore a pair of knitted baby booties hanging around his neck. I firmly believed in not being superstitious, and I did not want to be near that guy for fear he would get blown up and take me with him.

At dawn that morning, we saw a farmhouse and decided to approach it and ask for directions. With my companions spotted around the farmyard to cover me, I knocked at the door. I could hear shuffling inside, but no one came to the door. Suddenly a window opened above me and, looking up, I gazed into the scared eyes of an old woman. I pointed to the American flag patch on my sleeve and said, *"Americano, Americano, ami."* She shut the window and soon an old man in a nightcap, whom I took for her husband, opened the door. Using hand signs and my French translation sheet, I was able to tell him we were lost. Looking at my map, the old man showed me our position. We were ten miles from Amfreville, where we were supposed to have landed, south of the Douve River and deep in German territory, somewhere near the village of Videgrainnerie.

We had to get back to our lines. Though my ankle was bothering me quite a bit, we headed off in a northerly direction. We decided to get rid of our heavy equipment. All of us threw away our musette bags (knapsacks), gas masks, and bayonets. We followed the high line all that day and slept in the bushes that night. Two men stood guard while two slept. During the afternoon, one of the men ventured out on a scouting patrol and found another man who had lost his rifle when the shock of his chute opening had torn it from him. His only protection was a few grenades.

When night fell we continued moving slowly north through orchards and a maze of hedgerows. Near dawn we reached the Douve River. There was only one bridge, and it was heavily guarded by the Germans. Since there was no place where we could cross the river, we hid for the night in a cold ditch. When morning came we saw we were near another farmhouse. With the hope of finding some food, I told the group that I was going to go up to the farmhouse.

"I don't want you to go," said the lieutenant, the guy with the baby booties.

"That's too bad," I replied. "I'm going up there."

"If you do and we get back, I will have you court-martialed," he threatened.

I told him to go to hell. He was the type of guy that was scared of his own shadow. I slipped through the field up to the house. It was a well-built, prosperous-looking farmstead with solid stone buildings. As I was creeping around I heard a sound behind me. I whirled, my M-1 at the ready, and found myself face to face with an old lady who was probably returning from a visit to the outhouse. My first words were, *"Ami, ami,"* French for friend, and I told her I was an American and hungry.

"Aiii!" screamed the woman, and she threw her arms up in the air. She quickly opened the door of the farmhouse and ushered me in, still shouting something in French. Suddenly people seemed to come out of the walls, including an attractive sixteen-year-old girl and men still in their nightclothes. They were all very excited and friendly. The young men looked admiringly at my M-1 Garand rifle. It was obvious they were happy the Americans

had landed. They said they were part of the French underground and they showed me a printed leaflet with a picture of an American paratrooper.

I told them I was hungry and that I had three friends outside. The lady took a big, beautiful loaf of bread, cut it in half, scooped out the center, and filled the loaf with butter. Then she put it back together and handed it to me. One of the men asked me if I wanted some calvados, a potent alcoholic drink. I was a dumb kid from Minnesota and didn't know what calvados was, but I held out my canteen cup and they poured some in. When I kept holding out my cup, they said, *"Oh, ay, ay, ay!"* From their reaction I figured this stuff was not meant to be drunk like coffee. I realized I had committed a faux pas and asked them to pour some of it back in the bottle.

I took the food back to my friends—the French family had given me two loaves of bread and some cider—and everyone decided to go up to the farmhouse. Even the lieutenant, who was scared as hell, decided to come along. The farmer brought blankets for us, put us in the barn adjacent to the house, and told us to get under the haystack in case anyone came around. I went to sleep for about four hours and woke up to the sound of voices. An English-speaking Frenchman was talking to a couple of our boys. The French had made arrangements for us to cross the Douve River in a small boat to try to meet up with the rest of our division. While we spent the rest of the day drinking and feasting, one of the Frenchmen scouted the area where the boat was kept to make sure there were no German troops in the neighborhood. At midnight we drank one last cognac toast to our French friends.

Guided by one of the younger sons, we skirted the Nazi emplacements and came to the river. Much to our surprise we found forty-one more paratroopers there, also waiting to be taken across the river. They too had missed their drop zone. A lieutenant colonel from the 101st was in charge and our group joined them. The boat they used to take us across the river could carry only four men at a time, plus the young man who rowed, and each round trip took thirty minutes. By daylight about half the men had been ferried across and we had to wait for cover of darkness to bring the rest. I crossed the river on the first night. In the direction of our lines we could hear heavy small-arms fire, broken now and then by the booms of field artillery. While we waited, some of the men went on patrols and knocked out a lone tank, some cars, and motorcycles. I slipped away to find food. Bread was hard to get, but if we asked for a canteen of water the French would fill it with cider.

On one of my patrols we found four supply parachutes that had landed in German territory. Two were caught in trees while the other two were laying on the ground.

Ol' Man RIVER

One of the men climbed the trees to cut the bundles down. We hoped they contained food but instead they held two much-needed .30-caliber machine guns. The other two chutes held ammunition. While we worked to get the bundles down without being detected, the sounds of battle raged around us. A large complement of German soldiers was only a few hundred yards away. With only four of us on this patrol, it was impossible to carry both machine guns and the ammunition back to where the rest of the men were hiding. We chose to take one of the guns and sufficient ammunition. We dismantled the other gun and hid a few of the parts so that if the Germans found it they would not be able to use it. On the way back we encountered a German tank and a lone motorcyclist. We were tempted to throw a couple of grenades at the tank, but thought better of it as our objective was to get the machine gun back to the other men.

That night the remaining paratroopers crossed the Douve. We stayed in our position until five in the afternoon, when we decided to make our break through enemy lines. We had no other choice as our rations were growing short. I had been living on D rations (chocolate bars) for two days. We struck off toward the sounds of rifle fire. We expected to go at least three miles or more before meeting heavy resistance. If we succeeded in fighting our way through enemy lines, we still might be subjected to fire from our own troops. We

doubted if the rest of our division even knew we existed and figured many officers were still unaware of how spread out our paratroop drop had been. For four hours, with scouts out front, we moved in single file along the hedgerows across the difficult French terrain.

Suddenly we made contact, and the Germans let loose with a rapid burst of machine-gun fire. I was toward the rear of the column and every man in front of me hit the ground. With bullets whistling overhead, we crawled slowly forward. Hedgerows and steep embankments surrounded most of the tiny French fields. I could hear the unmistakable sound of our .30-caliber machine guns mingled with sporadic fire from our M-1 rifles. The rear of the column moved up into position to face the enemy fire. Our forty-five men formed a square about twenty-five yards across inside a large field, with the majority of the men and firepower facing the front. For two hours we inched forward on our bellies, keeping up a continuous volley to return the fire of the German weapons. It began to rain. The fine dust of the field that had collected on our rifles turned to slimy mud, but those good M-1s continued to fire.

One of the things we blew up was a German pay wagon. Money flew all over the place. One guy had this musette bag with him and he picked up the money and stuffed it in his bag. "That money's not going to be any good," I told him. But later in England he cashed it in for about four thousand dollars. It was all French francs.

When night came, we heard only occasional bursts from the Germans' machine guns. A signal came that we were moving forward. One of the men had knocked out a horse-drawn German artillery cart with a grenade. Unaware of our presence, the men on the cart had come boldly down the road between us and the enemy. We moved forward along a narrow trail and across the dirt road where the artillery cart and its dead horses lay sprawled in a bloody heap. The trail continued on the other side of the road and our men moved up on it. On either side the high banks were covered with heavy foliage, concealing and protecting us. The colonel gave the order to set fire to the artillery wagon.

As we moved up the protecting folds of the narrow, twisting cart trail, we were halted by the sputter of a machine gun. We were blocked at one end of the trail by the machine gun and at the rear by the ammunition that we had set on fire and was going off with terrific explosions. We had no way out. The colonel sent a patrol to try to knock out the Germans blocking our advance. The patrol was unsuccessful and returned minus a couple of men. We lay for hours in the overgrown ditch, hugging the ground as best we could while big mortar shells went off from the burning remains of the artillery wagon. Shrapnel hissed through the trees all around us.

Our position seemed hopeless. The night was cold and we were still drenched from the rain of the day before. At intervals the rattle of the German machine gun one hundred yards to our front broke into the far-off sounds of battle. Patrols of five men went out. Only one or two men would return. The lieutenant with the baby booties, the one who was going to court-martial me when we returned because I had gone up to the French farmhouse, went out on one of the patrols. He did not come back. When a couple of guys went out to look for him, they heard a noise and called out in the darkness, "Is that you, Lieutenant?" "Yah," he said instead of "Yes." Thinking by his answer that he was a German, they threw a grenade that hit him in the head and killed him.

At daybreak our position was still the same. All of us had a sinking feeling that the Germans were waiting for the light of day to move in and mop us up. Except for occasional rifle fire and the distant battle sounds, all was quiet. Then one of our men came running up the cart trail with news that he had met an advance scout of a battalion of our ground infantry. They were only a few hundred yards away. Then somebody hollered, "My God, the troops are breaking through!" The 90th Infantry Division had arrived.

Dirty, unshaven, and shaking from the cold and wet of the day before, the twelve of us who remained from the forty-five that crossed the Douve River climbed out of our ditches and over the high banks. Stepping over German and American dead, we met the troops who had saved our lives. The first thing most of us got hold of was K rations. We were exhausted but thankful to be alive as we slowly trudged toward the rear. Some of us were from one regiment and some from others. We divided into small groups, inquired where our command post was, and headed in that direction. Gas masks, broken rifles, machine guns, ammunition, rations—all were strewn along the ditches on either side of the road. German equipment predominated. Helmets with pieces of skull and bloody mats of hair still clinging to them were everywhere.

I vividly remember looking at this face that was still attached to a body but was missing the entire inside of the head. One of the troopers marching back with the group I was in gave a startled gasp as he recognized the ivory-white face of a buddy. Carefully, and with a prayer, he draped a field jacket over the upper part of the body. All of that affected us very little. We had developed a survival instinct that told us if we paid attention to what we saw, we would be in trouble. So we walked by it without seeing.

All I wanted to do was find my unit. I was walking back on the road when I found a German motorcycle. I was careful picking it up, fearing a booby trap, but then I got on and rode back to my unit in style.

When they saw me on the motorcycle, everyone began laughing. The friends I had last seen at the airport in England I met as if seeing ghosts; many of the others were not coming back. The reunion was emotional. We spent a day regrouping and integrating the new guys who came in to replace the men who had been killed. Two days later we headed back to the hedgerows to fight the Germans.

We walked single-file, including our cook, who was serving as an infantryman because we were going into battle. Damned if the guy behind him was carrying his rifle without the safety on and he accidentally shot the cook in the back. A short time later I was talking with a four-man machine-gun crew during a pause in our forward march when I heard the unmistakable sound of a mortar shell coming in. I started running for the ditch and I knew those guys on the machine gun were wondering what the hell I was doing. From the sound of the shell, I knew I was not going to make it to the ditch, so I threw myself on the ground just as the shell hit. It killed all four of the men I had been talking to.

As the Germans were forced back, they zeroed in on every crossroad and farmhouse so that the 88-millimeter artillery hit us with uncanny accuracy. The sound of the incoming shells with their high shriek was almost as bad as the hits themselves. Our unit proceeded to a crossroads where there was a farmhouse. Shells were raining

PARATROOPER

on us and I was flat on my stomach on the road when I looked up into the face of First Sergeant Stankowitz, the guy who had been my nemesis all during training. Both of us were on the ground, staring into each other's eyes, and I said, "It sure as hell is not like basic training, is it?" I laughed weakly, but he did not. As a radio operator I was one of the best, but I had hated stateside army discipline and had given "Stanky" a lot of trouble, going AWOL and never doing anything right.

Suddenly someone hollered, "We're being flanked!" I ran to the back of the farmhouse, lay on my stomach next to a hedgerow, and poked my rifle through the bushes. We had moved ahead too fast and put a dent in the German lines. Through the thick, shrublike growth I could see the line of enemy soldiers along the hedgerow, hitting us from the right flank. All I could think about was the scene in the World War I movie *Sergeant York*, where York is out hunting and he picks off a row of turkeys beginning at one end of the row so the turkeys at the other end would not know about it. So I started at the rear of the line, picking guys off. I got to number six before they spotted me. All of a sudden a rifle shot went right across the top of my head. I put up my hand to see if the bullet had creased my helmet. No damage.

The Germans let loose with mortars that began detonating in the branches of the small fruit trees above me. I ran for the protection of the farmhouse, first to the front and then to the side facing the Germans. I wanted to get a better angle on the guys who were shooting at me. Suddenly I collided with a German soldier, face to face at the corner of the farmhouse. I reared back with my rifle, my finger on the trigger. The German ran and I shot him in the back, almost by reflex. I don't know if I killed him. I ran again to the other side of the farmhouse, where I found one of my buddies who had caught a piece of mortar shell in the throat. He begged me to save him. "Bowell!" he cried out. "I've been hit, I've been hit!"

I wonder to this day where everybody else was, including Sergeant Stankowitz. The only other guy around was my buddy who had been hit. I put my hand on his throat to slow the bleeding, then walked him a couple of hundred yards back to a crossroads and put him in a Red Cross Jeep. I told a lieutenant there that my friend was probably going to fall off the Jeep, and he said to climb on and hold him. So we took off for the aid station, four hundred yards or so back from the action. They took care of my friend, and as I turned to go, a medical sergeant said to me, "We'd better take a look at you."

"Why?" I asked.

"Well, you've been hit."

"Where?"

"Look at your arm."

I looked at my left arm and shoulder, which were covered with blood. "Sir," the sergeant said to a captain, "this guy's been hit with shrapnel. What shall I do with him?"

"Send him back," said the captain.

At that I started to walk back toward the action, but the captain said, "No, the other way."

Suddenly I felt as if I were in heaven, four hundred yards to the rear of the fighting. I still wonder whether I should have left the battlefield. But it was the fifteenth of June, and I had just come out of ten days of holy hell and was not inclined to go back to the sound of those incoming 88s. As it was, Stankowitz told me after the war

that he thought he had recommended me for a Silver Star for my actions that day.

For the next two days I was handed off from one aid station to the next. Every time I stopped someplace, somebody put a shot in my arm. I just followed the medics' instructions. I was trucked to Utah Beach, and they took us in a small boat out to this huge transport, where some doctor looked at my arm and said, "Hell, we can't take people back with little wounds like this. Has the boat gone yet?" The goddamned boat *was* gone, so I was shipped back to England. I was lucky. Our regiment sent twenty-two hundred men to Normandy on D-Day. We suffered more than 60 percent casualties.

In 1985 the U.S. Army honored World War II's 507th Parachute Infantry Regiment by reactivating the regiment as a training battalion. All of today's paratroopers go through training at Fort Benning with the insignia of the 507th. In 2004, Marty Morgan—an associate of author-historian Stephen Ambrose, who founded the National D-Day Museum in New Orleans—published *Down to Earth: The 507th Parachute Infantry Regiment in Normandy.* The title is the motto of the 507th, and the foreword is written by Lieutenant Colonel Aidis L. Zunde, who until recently was the commanding officer of the 507th Parachute Training Battalion at Fort Benning. Zunde wrote the following about the 507th:

PARATROOPER

IN THE HOT AUGUST days of 1940, the United States paratrooper tradition was born with the first jumps of the Parachute Test Platoon. The troopers of that unit, under the leadership of Lieutenant Ryder, lit the torch of the U.S. airborne forcible entry capability on the fields of Fort Benning.

Soon after, the U.S. Army quickly built up its airborne force, forming a series of parachute and glider regiments. The 507th Parachute Infantry Regiment was one of those initial formations, activated in Fort Benning, Georgia, on 20 July 1942.

U.S. paratroopers distinguished themselves during World War II with a series of awe-inspiring airborne operations, the most legendary of which was the jump onto the fields of Normandy in the early morning hours of 6 June 1944 as the prelude to the D-Day landings. During thirty-five days of combat the regiment accomplished all assigned missions, though it suffered 1,320 casualties in so doing.

For its accomplishments in Normandy alone, the 507th PIR earned the Presidential Unit Citation (streamer embroidered Cotentin), the French Croix de Guerre with Palm (streamer embroidered Ste. Mere-Eglise), and the fourragere to the French Croix de Guerre, as well as the Normandy campaign streamer with arrow head device.

The Normandy campaign, however, was only the beginning for this regiment. Reassigned to the 17th Airborne Division, the 507th PIR went on to fight in the Allied counter attack during the Battle of the Bulge. Later, on 24 March 1945, the regiment was the first unit to parachute into Germany as two airborne divisions (17th U.S. Airborne Division and the 6th British Airborne Division) were dropped across the Rhine River near Wesel in Operation Varsity.

BATTLE of the BULGE

On December 16, 1944, the Germans started their last major offensive of the war. Chancellor Adolf Hitler knew the end was near for Germany unless something could be done to slow the Allied advance. He ordered eight German armored divisions and thirteen infantry divisions to attack five divisions of the U.S. 1st Army at the Ardennes—the same location where Hitler had earlier initiated his surprise attack on France. The 106th Infantry Division was stretched thin, defending a salient—the Bulge—that jutted into Germany. The German forces attacked at this point.

Bastogne was a strategic position within the area that the Germans and Americans both wanted. The American 101st Airborne got there first and occupied the city, but the Germans soon surrounded it. On December 22, German officers, under a flag of truce, delivered a message from General der Panzertruppe van Luttwitz, commander of the Panzerhops, demanding the surrender of Bastogne. When he received the message, Brigadier General Anthony McAuliffe exclaimed, "Aw, nuts," which was his official reply to the request for surrender.

The Battle of the Bulge was the largest land battle fought by the United States in World War II. More than a million men participated, including 600,000 Germans, 500,000 Americans (more than fought at Gettysburg), and 55,000 British. Nineteen thousand American were killed and 100,000 Germans were killed, wounded, or captured.

On June 26 I wrote to my mother from England: "I have returned to my original company area after having been discharged from the hospital. The injury I received in France did little damage. It was only a piece of shrapnel and it hit in the upper part of my arm. As for the nervous condition I left the hospital with those few days before the invasion, it hasn't bothered me a bit. In fact I'm in better condition now than when I left. Over there (in France) we couldn't afford to have nerves. I got rid of mine." The nervous condition I wrote her about was a kind of temporary anxiety neurosis that may have been aggravated by my Raynaud's disease.

The whole regiment came back to England in July for rest and more training. Our original commanding officer, Colonel George V. Millet, had been captured in Normandy and we had a new one, a West Pointer named Colonel Edson D. Raff. Raff started out being hated by all the guys in the regiment. My opinion at the time was no different from the rest. We called him "Boy Scout Colonel" and "Sonofabitch." In a letter to one of my brothers I wrote, "The new commander is hell to live with. The spirit of the 507 is dead. We are no longer anything like we used to be. As much hell and blood as we saw in France, some of us wish we were back there."

Where our former commander had been an athlete and worked on our physical fitness—the hell with anything else, all Millet was really interested in was basketball—Colonel Raff was different. He did care—about military discipline and survival on the battlefield. As any military person knows, that characteristic becomes exposed in wartime. Raff had us standing for inspections and doing training exercises and maneuvers out in the field. He cancelled our passes. Raff was tough, one of the top colonels in the army, and his strictness paid off for us in the Battle of the Bulge. The guy had integrity too. He had been General Matthew Ridgway's chief of staff, and when they put Ridgway up for a Distinguished Service Cross, Raff would not sign the petition. When Ridgway heard about it, he put Raff back on the line and he ended up head of our regiment. He never made general but he should have. Eventually I realized that Colonel Raff was one of the best things that ever happened to the 507th. His West Point training really made the 507th. Very few of my buddies felt the same way.

Come December they wanted us back in France to spearhead General George S. Patton's tanks on their way to free the 101st Parachute Battalion that was trapped in Bastogne. We had been reassigned to the 17th Airborne Division! The weather was so bad they could not parachute us in, but then the fog lifted just enough so that they could fly us to Chartres. It was Christmas Eve and freezing cold when they loaded us into big semitrucks typically used to haul cattle and drove us to our battle position. I was at the bottom of this cattle truck where I figured it would be nice and warm with all the bodies around when we heard *boom, boom, BOOM!*

Someone shouted that a damn "midnight Charlie" was coming in. The German plane was lobbing these 20-millimeter shells right down the middle of the road. The trucks stopped and everybody bailed out and ran for the fields and ditches alongside the road. Since I was at the bottom, I didn't have time to go anywhere. As soon as I got up over the rail and down the side of the truck, the pilot was already coming back and was right on top of the truck with 20-millimeter cannons in the nose of his plane.

I figured the best thing I could do was to get under the engine. I wondered where in the hell was the guy who was driving the truck. He should have been manning the machine gun mounted on the cab. Turns out he was in the field with the other guys. The rest of the seventy-two-hour trip I rode on the sides of the truck where I could get away fast if I had to.

When we got to the front, we went through intense 88-millimeter fire. The Germans were in retreat, but they had everything laid out; they knew where we were going to be next and sent their 88s in on us. On one occasion I heard the *whoosh* of a shell coming in and I ran for a foxhole the Germans had abandoned. Next to it was a five-gallon can of gasoline. As I dove for the foxhole, I saw a flash out of the corner of my eye. When things settled down I looked out and there was the gas can, absolutely shattered. Not one piece of the shrapnel hit me.

The company moved forward and I was left behind to guard our equipment. I waited for twenty-four hours and nobody came back. "To hell with the equipment," I thought, and I left to look for my unit. I got to the 507th just when they were engaged in one of the worst battles of the war. We fought for a week in front of Patton's tanks, and were the company that broke through to Bastogne to free the 101st Parachute Battalion. It was snowing and we did not have the right clothes or

Our beloved chaplain, John Verret, was killed in the Battle of the Bulge while rescuing a wounded soldier.

body else thought was dead. A little while later he was loading the wounded soldier into an ambulance when an 88-millimeter shell came in and killed him. Chaplain Verret was dedicated to all of the troopers in the 507th Parachute Infantry Regiment. It made no difference if you were Catholic, Jewish, or Protestant. He was concerned with our problems and expected that we would unload them onto his broad shoulders. When word passed around the battlefield that Chappie Verret was dead, you could feel the anguish. As the German 88s continued to pound us, I thought that perhaps I was going to join him. The soldier that Chaplain Verret saved recovered in the hospital.

Shortly after we freed Bastogne they moved us to Luxembourg, Belgium, where we were on the line in combat for six weeks living on K and C rations. Everybody in the regiment had diarrhea. My job was to operate the biggest radio set we had, the 284, which was mounted on a Jeep and had a little table you could use to send code. Usually I carried a 300 radio set, which was a backpack with heavy batteries. The one most used by the army was the 536, which was a hand-held walkie-talkie.

equipment. We were fighting in the uniforms we had worn at Normandy. As a result I damn near lost my feet because of the cold. Marshal Karl von Rundstedt's breakthrough caught everyone by surprise. On the way to free the 101st, our regiment survived the Battle of Cake Hill, where we lost quite a few men. Our Catholic chaplain was one of them.

Father John Verret, the chaplain who wrote "Down to Earth," the motto for the 507th, was killed about a hundred yards from where I was dug in. He had crawled out of his foxhole to rescue a soldier every-

We were moved to an area near the Ziegfried line, where we had constant patrols going out, usually at night. I would go on patrol to find spots where I could radio artillery onto the Ziegfried line, which paralleled the Our River at that point. I went into this little town in the middle of the night and set up my radio in an empty room about three or four stories up in a building that might have been a church. I had a perfect view out the window and could even see the Germans moving about. I was sending in our artillery with great accuracy with my radio when I looked out the window and saw a shell from a German mortar come in and splash in the river. A few minutes later there was another explosion, this one on my side of the shore and halfway between me and the river. Then another shell hit just forward of it. I knew damn well where the next shell was going to land: the other side of the eighteen-inch-thick stone wall partition where I was standing. A piece of shrapnel hit my radio, which I had put on the windowsill to improve reception, and blew off the antenna. I was not hurt.

Much of the time I operated the big 284 radio in the Jeep. The people in the town learned about my Raynaud's disease and they brought me hot bricks so that I could sit there in the cold and still operate the radio. Radio operators with numb fingers do not do too well. They use the tips of their fingers to send the dits and dots of Morse code. Holding those hot bricks in my hands helped a lot.

In a letter I sent home to my mother on February 28, 1945, I wrote: "It is still cold here. My feet go through chilblains every morning. We have to have our tents rolled before breakfast. It makes us cold and miserable but impresses the general. We have to scramble for wood every day. It is the only fuel. Fires are allowed from 5:30 p.m. until 8 o'clock the next morning."

The townspeople sometimes invited us to sleep on featherbeds in their houses. They put hot bricks in the beds to warm them for us—something almost unbelievable for guys living the way we were.

The regiment was eventually sent to a rear area near Rheims, France. The cold had aggravated my Raynaud's disease to the point where I could hardly walk. I was hospitalized to save my feet. In the beds next to me were actor Mickey Rooney and

singer Bobby Breen, all fagged out from their appearances in front of the troops. I thought my little brother Jack back home would be really impressed if I got Mickey Rooney's autograph. I was a little embarrassed to ask, but I did and he acted kind of funny.

"Where's your book?" Rooney said. "You're just another autograph hunter."

I happened to have my diary there and I said, "Here, use this. Write on the back page."

He did, and I tore it out and sent it to my brother.

On March 8, I wrote to my mother: "At the moment I am in the local hospital—nothing serious. My feet got a little frost bitten on this last battle. Cold weather and W. B. just don't mix. My hands and feet turn the same bloodless white at the first sign of cold or dampness. I wish, once and for all, they'd find out what it was. Remember, just before Normandy I was in the hospital in England with the same condition except that I hadn't irritated my feet by freezing them. At that time I talked my way out of the hospital to make that big jump. Anyway, I left there without getting anything definite done. I don't know what they'll do here. The hospital is heaven to me. You can imagine how clean sheets, clean wholesome food, rest, a chance to read and just living like a human being

appeals to me after the rough outdoor life we usually live. A sense of security is about the biggest item. Just to lie down at night and know you'll see the light of the morning—believe me, it's a very pleasant feeling."

VICTORY in EUROPE

On March 24, while the rest of my division jumped into Germany during Operation Varsity, I was still hospitalized in England. Eventually I was shipped back to a hospital in Bristol, and after a while my feet were OK. On April 20, I again wrote to my mother from a hospital: "Coming back to England was like coming home. At least the girls over here speak English. I've been here for a week but this is the first letter I've been able to tie myself down to write. At times I get so restless I can't even sit down to read.

"We flew over from France by C-47. It was a real pleasure to go up at least one time with the satisfying feeling that I didn't have to jump out. The plane was loaded with twenty patients, all ambulatory. Some were recently released P.O.W.s—they were human scarecrows. Others were men of the 17th, who had been wounded in the Rhine mission.

"The pilot let me take over the controls. It was quite a thrill to set up there just as if driving a big automobile only the scenery was a good bit different. When we got over the 'Isle' it got pretty rough. It seemed as if the plane was jumping all over the sky. A lot of the poor doughboys got sick. President Roosevelt's death [on April 12] hit as a terrific shock and surprise. Then yesterday Ernie Pyle died or was killed— two very great men in such a short period.

"At the moment I am lying on a blanket out in back of our ward soaking in some vitamin D. This hospital is a mammoth affair. The food isn't too bad. My biggest trouble is getting an appetite to eat. I've lost all the weight I ever owned. I was up to 145 and now I am down to 130. Sooner or later I hope to get it back so I am not worried."

On my last night in England I put on my dress uniform, left the hospital, and went into town, literally going AWOL. There I met a beautiful girl named Lorna. Together we climbed a hill behind the town to a statue of the English explorer John Cabot. While we were sitting there the announcement was made that the war in Europe was over. It was May 8, 1945—Victory in Europe Day. That town absolutely exploded before our eyes. Later we walked down and had dinner. People were hanging out of windows, drinking and hollering, and having a hell of a time. After dinner, Lorna and I went back to the top of that hill. She knew I was leaving the next day and I knew I would never see her again. She was a delightful person. Her father was a major in the English army. When I got back to the hospital the nurses were about

to have a nervous breakdown because of my absence, and I got on the ship home the next day by the skin of my teeth.

My status in the military had been mixed. I had received a battlefield promotion to staff sergeant and then was busted back to private. I didn't receive the Silver Star that Sergeant Stankowitz said he recommended me for, but I was awarded four Battle Stars and an Arrowhead for the European theater of operations campaign (the Arrowhead was for participation in the invasion of Normandy), plus the Presidential Unit Citation, the Combat Infantry Badge, three French Croix de Guerres, the Bronze Star, and the Purple Heart.

Coming home and running down that gangplank in Boston on May 23, 1945, was such an emotional experience that it was almost traumatic. They shipped me by rail first to Camp Miles Standish, Boston, and then to Mayo General Hospital at Galesburg, Illinois, where they continued working on my Raynaud's. One day I went to lunch, came back, and lay down on my bunk for a nap. The next thing I knew a doctor was waking me up. "Did you eat a ham sandwich for lunch?" he asked. "Yeah," I replied. "Well," he said, "you are going to throw up any minute." And right then, *boom*, I, along with everyone else, more than four hundred people, got ptomaine poisoning. I don't know how many more pounds I lost. I was skin and bones when I was discharged on August

15, 1945—Victory in Japan Day, or V-J Day. To keep my Raynaud's under control, advised my doctors, I should stop smoking when I got back to the States and move to the warm South. I did neither.

All three of my brothers in the service—Bob, Jim, and Tom—returned home safely from the war. I was the only one who got wounded. My family did not have much to say on our return. When I arrived in St. Paul, I dropped by the house and someone said, "You're home," and that was it. There was no celebration.

The decision I made in my hospital bed in England—to stay for the D-Day invasion rather than ship home when I had the chance—was probably the defining moral judgment of my life. I discovered that I was a hell of a lot better soldier in combat than I was out of it. Before going into battle, I was constantly getting into trouble, ignoring the rules and the discipline. I was too young then to grasp how that decision to parachute into Normandy on D-Day would affect who I would become. In the end I was just thankful for what I was able to do for my country.

Like so many returning veterans, I had no job waiting for me when I got back home, no concrete plans for my future. So, like thousands of other GIs, I decided to take advantage of the army's offer of a free education. I enrolled in college.

Dad and Mother with me (front) and my brothers Robert (center) and James after the three of us came home to Minnesota after the war.

5
CIVILIAN LIFE

THE FEDERAL government's greatest participation in education was the passage of the GI Bill of Rights, officially known as the Servicemen's Readjustment Act of 1944. The bill provided veterans with tuition, books, and equipment, plus subsistence and counseling services, so they could get advanced educational or vocational training when they returned to civilian life. Education also served as a safety valve that eased the tensions of returning from war to peacetime living. In the next seven years, eight million veterans received $14 billion in educational benefits. About two million enrolled in colleges and universities, while another six million attended other schools or took on-the-job training.

The GI Bill transformed American colleges and universities as young men from a variety of socioeconomic backgrounds shattered the myth that higher education was the privilege of a well-born elite. To deal with the overcrowding, institutions put up temporary classrooms, built crude barracks for student housing, hired more instructors, and added new courses. Percentagewise, the University of Minnesota had one of the largest GI enrollments in the country. In 1945 enrollment at the university was 11,872; a year later, 27,982 students had signed up for courses, 18,929 of whom were World War II veterans. Other public and private colleges in Minnesota experienced a similar jump in enrollment.

COLLEGE DAYS

Although I didn't graduate from high school, I had it in the back of my mind that I wanted to attend Carleton College, which, for some reason, I thought was Episcopalian. (It was Congregational.) I was literally on my way to Northfield, Minnesota, to talk with the folks at Carleton when I stopped at Macalester College in St. Paul. I walked into the admissions office and the person there would not let me leave until I agreed to enroll. I walked around campus and saw all those nubile young women who appeared to be equally interested in seeing a young man and that probably sold me.

Macalester officials gave me a battery of tests and did not seem bothered that I did not have a high school diploma. But because I had attended St. Paul Vocational School to become an apprentice electrician, and because I also had earned a lot of credits from the University of Wisconsin and taken college-level correspondence courses offered by the military, Macalester evidently felt I had the equivalent of a high school education because I was accepted. The only stipulation was that, since I had had very little math and science, I had to take an extra course in algebra. Algebra is one of the worst subjects for me and I don't know why. To this day I'm still horsing around with it, thinking there must be an easier way to figure things out.

I went to Mac under what was called "rehab." It was like the GI Bill, but it was specifically for veterans who had been wounded. The 1940 Selective Training and Service Act ensured job reinstatement for vets, plus training and rehabilitation services for disabled vets. I had been given a 50 percent disability because I still experienced some anxiety neurosis. I can remember lying on the lawn on the campus but never looking up into the sky. As paratroopers we used to fear somebody coming over us with a parachute as we came down in a group. It took me a while to get over that. A couple of years after I graduated, however, I sent a letter to the Veterans Administration telling them I did not feel I should be getting that pension anymore. I felt embarrassed. To me there was a stigma associated with taking money for my wartime disability. The VA wrote

back and told me I should keep 10 percent anyhow. I would not get any money, but I would keep some rights. So I did.

I met my wife, Lillian Flatten, when she was a junior and I was a freshman at Macalester. Lillian was from Sheldon, a small town in southern Minnesota, and a graduate of Houston (Minnesota) High School. Some of my fondest memories are of the trips we made to some of her relatives in the Sheldon area. Lillian was a topnotch honors student majoring in history; I was an economics and business major. We both lived in Kirk Hall, a dormitory building near Snelling and Grand Avenues that housed men and women in separate sections. We were married on February 22, 1946, in the same Episcopal church I attended as a child. We moved into Macville, the college's temporary housing for veterans who were going back to school. Macville was a barracks-type building where we had a two-bedroom apartment. Later that year, our daughter Shelley Ann was the first child born in Macville. We named her for the poet Shelley.

Financially I was doing well. Everything I had earned while in the service I had sent home to the bank. Now I could buy a car, clothes, and books for college, and still have money left. I even lent my dad $650 to buy a 1939 LaSalle that was almost brand new. He paid me back for that about the time he and my mother moved to Artesia, California, a small farming community near Los Angeles, along with my youngest brothers and sisters—Jack, Patty, Donna, and Dick. I don't know why they moved. Mother had some family in California and that may have influenced their decision. Though I don't think he ever saved any money, Dad tapered off his drinking for a time and started selling construction materials for Montgomery Ward. When they got to California they somehow bought two unfinished houses. With his background as a contractor, Dad probably planned to finish them off.

Lillian, Shelley, and I drove out to visit my parents once while I was in college. It was 1948 and I had a brand new car, an Austin A-40 British sedan. I never could trust its hydraulic brakes, which kept going out in the mountains. We hit a chuckhole and lost a hubcap. The hubcaps were hard to get and expensive. I spent an hour looking for it and could not find it. It was getting dark, so we decided we would pull off the road and look for it in the morning. We spent a fitful night on the mountainside, expecting bears, wolves, and robbers to attack us. In the morning I went back up the road to the chuckhole. On my way there I found somebody else's hubcap. When I reached the chuckhole I threw the hubcap I had found down the road in the direction I had lost my hubcap. I watched it as it spun off the road in the distance. I followed it to where it landed and could not believe how many hubcaps were laying there. There must have been fifty, including mine.

The Bowells with daughter Shelley in 1946. Lillian and I were students at Macalester College in St. Paul.

While I was a student at Macalester College, I taught Sunday school for about a year at Christ Episcopal Church. I was considering majoring in theology, a decision I had made on the battlefield that just sort of grew on me. I was pretty sincere in my faith. On the battlefield you are looking for all the protection you can get, and almost everyone in the face of imminent death will commit his thoughts to God. I took sixteen credits in religion at Macalester and, for a thesis, outlined the entire Old Testament. I was pretty proud of the A that I received on that paper.

Lillian and I drove to visit my folks in California in my new 1948 Austin A-40 car.

One of the students in my Sunday school class was a son of St. Paulites John and Betty Musser. One day, Betty stopped by the class and caught me telling the young people a war story. I quickly gave the story a religious cast, but a few days later the superintendent of the Sunday school pulled me aside and said that, much as they appreciated all I was doing for the church, they did not want to encroach on my time as a college student. Perhaps I should just concentrate on my studies, they said. That ended my career as a Sunday school teacher. That was all right, as my ideas about church were changing and I concluded I was not really cut out for the ministry. I tell everybody that the Lord came to me

in the middle of the night and suggested I take up another field of endeavor.

I threw myself into college life. As a veteran who had fought for freedom, I campaigned to abolish compulsory chapel and to establish a grading system for professors. I was president of Macalester's Young Republicans Club; future U.S. vice president Walter Mondale headed the Democratic student organization. Joan Adams, his wife-to-be, was also a classmate and active in the Macalester Christian Association. I also joined the 1948–1949 conference championship wrestling team that was later memorialized in Mac's Athletic Hall of Fame. By the time I was a senior I was photo editor of the yearbook and working as a freelance photographer, taking wedding pictures for studios in Minneapolis.

The popcorn business was still very much on my mind when I attended Macalester. I observed a guy called Popcorn Pete, who, from time to time, brought his little popcorn wagon onto campus. Curious, I asked the college comptroller how much Pete paid Macalester for the privilege of selling popcorn. I was surprised to learn that he did not pay anything. So I offered to pay the college 10 percent of my take if Macalester gave me exclusive rights to all the concessions on campus. The school agreed.

I was in business. Football games were my busiest and most productive times. The biggest event of them all was going to be the 1948 homecoming football game against the College of St. Thomas, about a mile away. I ordered a huge supply of buns for the hotdogs and stored them in big cardboard cartons. I popped corn for two days straight in the gym, stacking the filled boxes in our apartment. Early on game day I sent crews onto the football field to fill large stock tanks with ice and five hundred cases of Coca-Cola in glass bottles. I was still feverishly popping corn an hour before kickoff when a kid wandered into the gym and asked me what I was doing.

"I'm popping corn for the homecoming game," I replied.

"Don't you know they called the game off?"

At first I thought he was kidding, but I could see by the look on his face that he was not. During a freshman team game with St. Thomas the day before, John Eide of Virginia, Minnesota, a Macalester football player, had been injured and later died. The campus was in shock over the incident, but no one dreamed that the varsity game would be called off.

This was a major financial fix I had to solve. Coca-Cola took all of its bottles back without charging me. I sold the hotdogs to the campus cafeteria. For two days I went from grocery store to grocery store selling every

I spent a lot of time in Macalester's darkroom as the yearbook photo editor and as a journalism student. This is one of the Speed Graphic cameras I used.

one of the buns. For the next thirty days I sold popcorn at a reduced rate to the students in the dormitories. When it was all over, I just about broke even.

In 1948 I wrote a twelve-page business plan called "Store and Sales Management" for a popcorn business that would operate citywide in St. Paul. I went so far as to get permission from the city council to operate three popcorn wagons in city parks. The exclusive agreement was to take effect on May 15, 1949. My business plan included drawings of my Jeep-driven popcorn wagons that I named "The Normandy," "The Bulge," and "The Saint Lo." In my plan I wrote, "The names . . . are not meant to indicate that the operation will be run by

a veteran of the last war." I wonder who I thought I was kidding.

Lillian and I graduated on June 6, 1949, the fifth anniversary of D-Day. The *St. Paul Pioneer Press* ran a three-column picture of us in our caps and gowns. Shelley Ann, age two-and-a-half, is between us in the photo, all decked out in a miniature cap and gown Lillian made for her. The newspaper story reported that "they took turns taking Shelley Ann to classes so they wouldn't have to hire anyone to care for her. They staggered their classes and when that couldn't be done, she trotted right along with them."

Although my brothers Jim and Jack also went to Macalester, I was the first and

Macalester's wrestling team won the MIAC conference championship in 1948 and was inducted into the college's Hall of Fame. I'm kneeling at the far left in the front row; my brother Jim is next to me.

Lillian, Shelley, and me on graduation day in 1949.

only one of the Bowell children to graduate from college.

MINNESOTA HISTORICAL SOCIETY

In 1948 the state legislature granted funds to the Minnesota Historical Society to create a new graphic arts department. MHS owned about 384,000 graphic items, from early daguerreotypes to contemporary photography and from prints to paintings. They hired me in 1949 to set up the photographic laboratory, organize it, and plan how to catalog the collection. It was my first job after graduating from Macalester College. I worked with Jim Whitehead, a princely person. He was an assistant to Harold Cater, the director, and to Dan Hill, the head of the library.

During my tenure at the MHS I made an important discovery: the identity of the painter of a historical picture. It all began on January 24, 1951, when Burt Reinfrank called the MHS to report that he had a painting in his St. Paul home that was similar to the Society's Seth Eastman painting that had appeared in a recent story in the *Minneapolis Tribune.* Could it be an undiscovered Eastman?

Seth Eastman was a West Point army officer who was stationed at Fort Snelling in 1830. He was also an artist, and since there wasn't a great deal for army officers to do at the fort, Eastman spent much of his time sketching and painting the Dakota people who lived along the Mississippi River. For a time, he was married to or lived with Stands Sacred, the daughter of the Dakota leader Cloud Man, and they had a daughter, Mary Nancy. Eastman went on to illustrate Henry Rowe Schoolcraft's monumental six-volume *History of the Indian Tribes of the United States* and is considered to be the foremost pictorial historian of Native Americans of the nineteenth century.

I went to Reinfrank's home on Summit Avenue and took both color and black-and-white pictures of his painting. It did look a lot like either a Seth Eastman or a painting by another nineteenth-century artist, James Boal, in the collection at the Minneapolis Institute of Arts. When we compared the three works at the MIA, it was apparent that each had been painted by different artists, but from the same vantage point at Fort Snelling. While we were examining

Ol' Man RIVER

I examine a painting while working in the late 1940s as a curator at the Minnesota Historical Society.

the paintings, we discovered a faint pencil mark on the back of the canvas and frame of the Reinfrank painting. I took it back to the Minnesota Historical Society and photographed the markings with infrared film. When the film was developed and enlarged, we could read the name E. K. Thomas.

There had been a Sergeant Edward K. Thomas stationed at Fort Snelling in 1851 and he had done a number of early paintings. Only one known painting by Thomas had survived, and it was hanging in the Military Affairs Room in the U.S. Capitol in Washington, D.C. Fortunately, there

Fort Snelling, *an oil painting by Sergeant Edward K. Thomas, who was stationed at Fort Snelling in 1851. This is Burt Reinfrank's painting, which had been incorrectly identified as a Seth Eastman.*

was a photograph of the Thomas painting in the Minnesota Historical Society files. When I compared photographs of the two Thomas paintings, it was obvious they had not been created by the same artist. Which one, Reinfrank's signed picture or the one hanging in the nation's Capitol, was by Thomas? The Thomas signature on Reinfrank's painting was under layers of aged varnish, so there was little reason to doubt its authenticity.

While looking closely with a magnifying glass at the lower right-hand corner of the photo of the Thomas painting in D.C., I saw that the shadows formed into words. First there was a capital "S" followed by a period, then an "Ea" followed by two indistinct characters. After this was clearly written "m-a-n." I was electrified when I realized that by inserting an "s-t" in place of the two indistinct characters, it would form the name of one of Minnesota's greatest painters, a man who many experts consider to be the master painter of the North American Indian. The painting hanging in the Capitol had been incorrectly labeled as an E. K. Thomas when it was actually painted by Seth Eastman. Burt Reinfrank now had the only known surviving E. K. Thomas painting.

THE *TOKA*

For as long as I can remember—from the days when I was a twelve-year-old admiring the *Capitol* steamboat—I have been fascinated with boats. As a young man I visited every boatyard for miles around the Twin Cities, looking at boats and dreaming about them. I still remember the first boat I fell in love with. It was the summer of 1950, and the boat was berthed at Clarkson's Marina, located a quarter mile above the Mendota Bridge on the Minnesota River. That sweetheart of a boat was a small cabin cruiser, about twenty-three feet long, that had probably been built about 1930. It caught my eye because it had an inboard-outboard engine. Back then, configurations of this sort were unheard of and did not become popular until twenty years later.

Though I loved that little cruiser at Clarkson's, I knew I could not afford it, so I kept on looking. A short time later, at a marine store on Lake Street in Minneapolis, I found a twenty-six-foot 1946 Steelcraft that had been used on Leech Lake in northern Minnesota as a duck boat. The Steelcraft's cabin was gone, but I thought I could make something of her hull. One of my problems was what to tell my wife. We had a toddler and little money to spare. I knew Lillian would be outraged at my frivolity if I spent twenty-four hundred dollars for a pleasure boat. I would have to find a practical reason for such a purchase. So I didn't tell Lillian that I was buying a boat: I told her I was going into the excursion boat business. At that time no one ran excursion boats on the Mississippi River in the Twin Cities and I thought I saw a business opportunity.

However, it was one thing to buy a boat and quite another to go into business.

I had a welder friend, Red Olson, who did a lot of work for the Muller boatyard in Stillwater. Red told me that if I brought the boat to Stillwater, he would do the necessary welding on the Steelcraft for me. Red and his family lived on an old paddle-wheel boat called the *Doc John*. To board the *Doc John* you had to walk across a ten-inch-wide plank that ran from the riverbank over the water to the deck of the boat. Red's three young children frolicked in the water most of the time. Every time I visited him, I worried that one of the kids would fall into the water as they scampered up the plank to their home on the boat.

No sooner had I bought the Steelcraft than the Mississippi flooded in the spring of 1952. Clarkson's Marina was half under water. For several days, after leaving work at the Minnesota Historical Society, I would stand on the Mendota Bridge, looking down at my boat sitting in its cradle and worrying that the rising water would swamp it before I even had a chance to take possession.

Finally the day came when I could leave the office early and take the boat to Stillwater. I had arranged with Gus Clarkson to launch the boat as soon as I got down to his marina. I climbed aboard and Gus slowly lowered the cradle into

the Minnesota River, near the confluence of the Mississippi. This was the first time I had ever run a boat, so it was a maiden voyage for both of us. The water was flowing fast and I figured I should get out of there in a hurry. As soon as the boat hit the water and I was free of the cradle, I gunned the engine—in reverse.

Somehow I managed to get the boat turned around in the current and headed downstream to the Mississippi. I hoped to make it to the Inver Grove Heights harbor before dark. As I fiddled with the throttle I noticed that the boat began to vibrate if I gave it too many RPMs. When backing off the cradle I had gunned the engine too much and pulled the rudder into the propeller. The rudder was OK, but the prop was damaged and causing the vibration.

Still, my spirits were high. I limped past downtown St. Paul, the airport, and the Pig's Eye railroad bridge. A few drops of rain fell as I passed South St. Paul, and I began to worry about darkness overtaking me as there were no running lights on the boat. At last I could see the Inver Grove Heights railroad swing bridge in the distance. Not knowing how to get into the harbor, I killed the boat's engine so I could be heard as I yelled up to the bridge tender for directions. He told me to turn to the right as soon as I got below the bridge.

I thanked the tender for his help, turned the key in the ignition, and heard a click.

Nothing happened. The generator was not working. The battery on my boat was dead. The rain was coming down harder, it was almost completely dark, and I was drifting helplessly. Growing alarmed, I realized that upbound towboats could not see me in the blackness of the night. As I frantically tried to start the engine, I noticed that my drift was taking me on a course parallel to shore. Ahead, I could dimly see some overhanging branches. Desperately I grabbed one and pulled. Then I caught another and another until I grasped a good-sized tree branch I could tie a line to. The boat was secure.

My boat did not have an exterior cabin, but under the deck in the bow was a tiny cabin with two double bunks, a little kitchen, and a toilet. I crawled into the cabin and fell asleep. It rained all night. I awoke early the next morning to the hum of thousands of mosquitoes—and to a foot of standing water in the cabin. I took off my socks, rolled up my pants legs, and waded onto the deck, figuring that all I had to do was go ashore and walk back to the marina for help.

It was not to be so simple. I was not on the mainland, as I had thought, but on an island. After two hours of waving and shouting I finally attracted the attention of a guy who came over for me in his boat and took me back to the Inver Grove Marina. I ran into Andy Anderson, a chum from Roosevelt Junior High who kept an old paddle-wheel houseboat at the marina. I bought a new battery and Andy took me back to my boat in his.

I was soon under way through the most circuitous part of the Upper Mississippi called the "graveyard." Beyond the graveyard was Lock and Dam 2 at Hastings. I tensed up. What if the engine stalled again before I could get into the lock and my powerless boat drifted over the dam? Fortunately, the battery kept supplying the necessary juice. I made it to Prescott, Wisconsin, and up the St. Croix River to Stillwater without further incident.

I named my boat the *Toka*, after an infamous Dakota chief who used to hang around Fort Snelling, and with Red's help I quickly turned it into a sporty, sixteen-passenger charter boat. I had planned to dock the boat at the Jackson Street Landing in St. Paul and run a ferryboat service across the river to a notorious nightclub on Navy Island called Tug Boat Annie's. To get my license to carry passengers, I went down to Dubuque, Iowa, to the U.S. Coast Guard station, where I met with the commander, a fellow by the name of "Smoker." When I went into his office, Smoker was sitting there with his feet up on a 1910 oak rolltop desk.

"Come on in, son," he said. "I hear you want to get a license to haul passengers."

"That's right."

"Well," he said, "what side is port on?"

"The left side," I replied.

"What side is starboard on?"

"The right side."

"Congratulations, son. You just passed your license test."

Just when I was about to begin my ferry business, the police raided Tug Boat Annie's and put it out of business. We then booked charters wherever we could get them, mainly out of Stillwater on the St. Croix. For two summers we ran excursions on weekends from Lowell Park in Stillwater. I still remember the Sunday afternoon we made eighty dollars—a princely sum in 1952.

My younger brother Tom, who was a great ladies' man, used to steal the *Toka* when I wasn't around. Once he and I took the boat to Hudson, Wisconsin, and, true to Tom's form, we ended up with several girls on the boat. I was barreling out of the harbor when this girl came up and sat next to me in the pilot seat. The next thing I knew I hit the sand beach on the opposite side. I had read someplace that if you run aground you should immediately reverse and the incoming wake will sometimes take the boat back out. I tried it and the *Toka* floated free.

I ran the *Toka* as an excursion boat until I was offered a position with Studebaker Corporation in South Bend, Indiana. I reluctantly sold her and put the river back on hold.

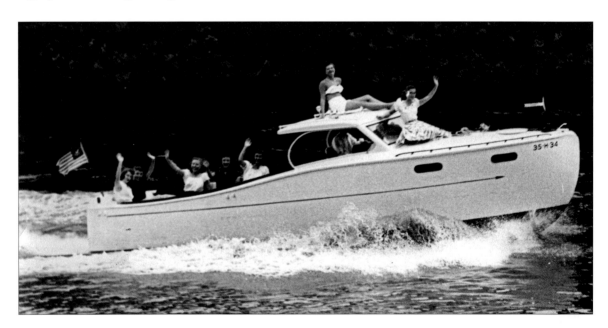

The Toka *on a run down the Mississippi River in 1952 with some of my Macalester classmates.*

6
TYCOON

AFTER AMERICAN soldiers returned home from World War II, the national birth rate and the economy soared. After the deprivations of the Depression and the war, growing young families were hungry for the good life, their appetite for cars and other merchandise fueled by advertisements on a new medium called television. The number of automobiles produced annually quadrupled between 1946 and 1955.

In 1952, the year Bill Bowell joined Studebaker, the company celebrated a century in business. Though he could not know it at the time, the organization was headed on its downward slope. Studebaker had been the only company to make a successful transition from wagon-making to manufacturing automobiles. Begun in 1852 by two brothers who opened a blacksmith shop in Indiana, the company began making luxury automobiles in Detroit in 1920. Production moved to South Bend, Indiana, where Studebaker went into receivership in 1933, a victim of the Depression. New leadership revived the company, and by 1939 it was again the largest independent auto-maker in the country.

When World War II broke out, Studebaker shifted its production from automobiles to trucks for the army. Following the war, the company again manufactured cars and became famous for the bullet-nosed design of its 1950s models. Though Studebaker designed some of the most attractive cars ever conceived, management was on a course that led to the company's eventual demise in 1966.

STUDEBAKER

After two and a half years at the Minnesota Historical Society, I thought I had better get my fanny out of that business because it was never going to make me any money. Lillian and I now had two children (our son, Bill Jr., was born in 1950), and I decided to go back to Macalester College to take a second major in journalism and add writing skills to my photography expertise. I worked closely with two professors, Phil Beedon and Ivan Burg, head of the department. Ivan put me in charge of the photographic laboratory. We students could handle the cumbersome four-by-five-inch Speed Graphic as if it were a

35-millimeter camera. We also competed to see who could get the most pictures published in the local newspapers. I had seventy-five to one hundred printed in the Minneapolis and St. Paul papers. One of the students who worked with me in my last year at Macalester became famous—Tom Abercrombie of *National Geographic*.

One day in 1952 a recruiter from the Studebaker Corporation in South Bend, Indiana, came to Macalester and offered me $379 a month ($2,728 in today's money) to work for the company. At that time I was working the night shift at the Twin Cities Army Ammunitions Plant in

New Brighton, a place so loud I suffered hearing loss. Without finishing my second degree, I moved to South Bend.

Going with Studebaker was a big deal. I was a sales trainee in the publications department with about five guys who did not have the drive that I had. I would do any job anybody asked me to. The big boss, Mr. Robinson, had an office at the end of the department that overlooked fifty yards of desks. One day he said to me, "I can always spot you out there."

"How?" I said.

"Because you're the only one with his coat tails sticking straight out."

I got a $1,400 raise the first year ($9,898 in today's money), which was unheard of. Lillian and I bought our first house. I also had an opportunity to take a higher-level job after I had been at Studebaker for only a couple of years. I have very good mechanical aptitude, and so I became the liaison engineer—the link between the engineering department and the sales department. I wrote the technical stuff for the dealers and the salesmen's training manuals, and put into writing the techniques for selling automobiles.

My photography experience at the Minnesota Historical Society and at Macalester paid off at Studebaker. I ended up directing the slide films that were used

in the dealer shows around the country. One day I was photographing a clay model of the 1953 Studebaker Starliner coupe created by Raymond Loewy, the famed American industrial designer who had also designed Zephyr trains. Loewy's collar was standing out from his suit jacket. I had never seen anything quite like that, so I thought I was doing him a favor when I commented to him, "Mr. Loewy, your collars are sticking out of your suit." He gave me a pitying look and said, "Son, I pay $150 for a shirt that will do that."

When it came time to show the slide films, the easiest thing for the top brass to do was to take me with them to all the big automobile shows and dealer presenta-

tions. I brought a twenty-foot portable rubber screen with me and used it to show slides of the new automobiles. Sometimes we flew in the company's corporate airplane, a Douglas DC-3, but when we went to the West Coast we flew on a commercial aircraft. I would sit in the cocktail lounge, back in the tail of the plane where it felt as if it were wiggling itself through the air. Anyone who has flown in the old three-tailed Constellations knows what I am talking about.

Traveling with the top brass as I was, I found out that Studebaker was in major financial trouble and that most of the executives were going to quit. We were at a big dealer council meeting at the Morrison Inn

I'm at the wheel of a 1954 Studebaker convertible, a one-of-a-kind car that was never put into production. It was designed by the famed Raymond Loewy. I was Studebaker's liaison sales engineer at the time.

on the Notre Dame campus, where we had seen all the new Studebakers parading around the oval track at the stadium. That evening after dinner, the corporate sales manager, "Big Bill" Keller, got up in front of the meeting and said, "Fellows, you all saw the automobiles today. I don't know what the hell you're going to do, but I know what I'm going to do." He slammed his notebook shut and said, "I quit." With that he walked out of the meeting. I lost no time in getting my resume out on the street.

EDWARDS and DEUTSCH

One of the companies that interviewed me in 1955 was Edwards and Deutsch Litho in Chicago. Edwards and Deutsch had just landed the contract to produce the *Oldsmobile Rocket Circle* magazine that went

to all Oldsmobile owners—about one and a half million copies. The Oldsmobile magazine, which was published nine times a year, was similar to *Ford Times*. It had a center-page spread that contained the technical information on the car. The president of Edwards and Deutsch at that time was an older guy, Arthur Meding. His son-in-law, Dean Milburn, was also with the company. Edwards and Deutsch was mainly in the billboard business, inexperienced in publications. They did have Sheldon Widmer, who had come from Brown and Bigelow, a St. Paul printing company, and who had created the *Oldsmobile Rocket Circle* magazine. But he needed someone to write and produce the magazine's center-page spread.

I had planned to call on the companies that had responded to my resume. One such appointment was with Robert S. McNamara, a manager at the Ford Motor Company in Detroit—the same McNamara who later became secretary of defense in the Kennedy and Johnson administrations. When Edwards and Deutsch heard that I was to interview for a job at Ford, they called my wife and said, "We want to hire him. Get hold of him right now."

Though I hemmed and hawed a bit, I returned to Chicago, where Edwards and Deutsch offered me $8,500, plus an unlimited expense account ($60,000 in today's dollars). I wondered whether I could handle a job that big, but Lil said, "There's no question about it." I certainly was knowledgeable enough about lithography to take on the job. I was intrigued with the process and had read up on it, plus, when I was with Studebaker, I had taken a comprehensive course in it.

Lithography is a printing process invented in Germany. The name comes from the Greek words *litho* (stone) and *graphien* (to write). The process is based on the premise that oil and water don't mix. Back then, a slab of limestone or metal was ground smooth and the design was put on the stone with lithocrayon or lithographic drawing ink. Then the stone was etched so the area to be printed would absorb grease and the blank areas would absorb water and thus repel grease. The printing ink was applied, the stone was placed in the press, and the paper was printed. Different stones were sometimes used for each color, but the same stone could be used for multiple colors.

I jumped into my new job with both feet. Things started happening fast, starting with a late-night call from Oldsmobile. The executives liked the magazine and wanted to send it not only to Olds owners, but to all the competition's car owners as well. That meant we had to produce six million copies instead of the 1.6 million copies we were originally planning to run.

We had designed the magazine for the two Harris presses that Edwards and Deutsch had. We could get the print run started on them, but it would take us forever to print six million copies. The only other presses we could get were the faster Meihle presses, but their printing plates were about an inch different in size. To make it work, we had to refit the Harris plates for the Meihle presses, which took a lot of time.

Then there was the problem of binding six million copies. I had to find a bindery to do the job. I still felt as if I were brand new in Chicago, a Minnesota yokel. I found the Bee Bindery in a ramshackle building on Lake Street, right by the Chicago "L." I went up a flight of steps and told the girl at the desk that I wanted to see the owner about a bindery job. She ushered me into Art Blitztien's office. When I told him I had an order in my back pocket to have six million magazines bound, he almost fell right smack off his chair.

"Can you handle this?" I asked.

"We can, but we have to go out and buy more Double K's," he replied.

"What the hell is a Double K?" I asked, and he explained that it is a machine that saddle stitches (staples) and binds magazines.

After he came through on the *Oldsmobile Rocket Circle* job, I gave Art all of our magazines to bind. As a result, I made him and his staff very rich, and he became a life-long friend.

I established myself with Edwards and Deutsch by how I handled that production problem. After that, the company had absolute confidence in me and I became part of a three-man team that developed half a dozen different publications. We created and sold magazines for Holiday Inn, Hudson Motorcars, and the American Gas Industry. We also produced United Airlines' *Mainliner* magazine, the first in-flight magazine, and *Scenicruiser* for Greyhound. Our team got all of those publications up and running beautifully.

CATALOG PUBLISHER

I happened to go back to St. Paul on a trip in 1957 and found that my brother Jim had started this little mail-order company called the Sibley Company, which dealt in general merchandise—stuff like sporting equipment, jewelry, toys, and dishes. It

was a concept that had been developed on the West Coast for discount-catalog owners. They tried to make it look like the customer was buying wholesale when he was really buying at a discount price.

I watched Jim putting together his catalog—cutting pictures out of other catalogs, pasting them into layouts, and writing his own copy. I asked him, "Doesn't it take a lot of time to do that?"

"About six months," he said.

"Well, there are other guys out there doing the same thing you're doing," I told him. "Why don't I go see if we can find them and form a group together? You all would be far enough away from each other so that you wouldn't fear competition."

Jim thought it was a heck of an idea, so I went to work. I called my boss, Sheldon Widmer, on the way back to Chicago from St. Paul and asked him to meet me at this joint on Dempster Street in Evanston, Illinois, my neighborhood at that time. I laid out the idea of putting a bunch of catalog guys together, bringing them in to meetings, and using their different backgrounds to merchandise one large catalog. Sheldon liked the idea, so the next morning he and I discussed the project with Art Meding, the big boss. When we told Meding we figured it would take $80,000 to $100,000 to get it started, he said, "Go for it." I made sure all of my other projects were running smoothly before making up a prospectus and taking it on the road.

Soon I had organized six companies, my brother and five other guys, into a group I named the United Wholesale Distributors Association. Besides Jim's Sibley Company in St. Paul, there was Robinson Wholesale Company in Des Moines, Iowa; McDade and Company in Chicago; Sha-Vel's Wholesale Jewelers in Indianapolis; Dolgin's Wholesale in Kansas City, Kansas; and United Wholesale Jewelers and Distributors of Shreveport, Louisiana. It was the country's first syndicated general merchandise catalog—and an immediate success.

The following year, I put together thirteen catalog houses; the third year, I got eighteen. By this time we were big stuff. Every sales rep who was selling merchandise anyplace was trying to get to the guy at Edwards and Deutsch who was putting out "the catalog," trying to figure a way to get into the book. Our eighteen catalog houses were covering the United States with gross sales that were probably in the neighborhood of $40 million ($280 million in today's dollars). I became one of the top printing salesmen in Chicago. One time I had fourteen railroad cars filled with paper just to print my catalog at Cuneo Bindery in Chicago. I spent four days supervising the job at the bindery, sleeping on skids.

All of the catalog house owners would be on pins and needles as they waited for the next edition of the big, thick book to come out. We always sent them an advance copy. One day I was in the pressroom when they were binding the catalog and saw a bunch of girlie magazines laying around. I interspersed the girlie stuff with pages of the catalog and sent it to the members as if it were their advance copy, with their name and everything on the front cover. This guy down in Shreveport got his mail while the minister's wife was at his counter. Before he had a chance to look at the mail, the guy said to the lady, "Here, why don't you take a look at my new catalog?" If you think *that* didn't raise hell! The next day he got the correct catalog.

My brother Jim was building his inventory so fast that his cash flow wasn't sufficient to cover it. He sold out in 1960 for $12,000 ($84,000 in today's money), which was nothing. The St. Paul businessman who bought him out, Hillard Marvin, is the one who reaped the advantage of the Sibley Company.

For Edwards and Deutsch, the success of the catalog ended with the advent of web presses. Instead of printing on single sheets of paper, the web press printed on a continuous roll that is eleven to fifty-six inches wide and at a speed of nine hundred to three thousand feet of paper per minute. Although the web press had been available for some time, Edwards and Deutsch chose not to use it because it produced lower-quality color than sheet-fed

Ol' Man RIVER

The four partners of United Scientific, a plastics-injection molding company, circa 1960, were (from left) Bazil Banks, Curt Cargill, brother Jim, and me.

I decided it was time for me to move on as well. My expense allowance was $25,000 a year (about $166,000 in today's dollars, which was big money for those days), mostly because I paid the hotel and restaurant bills for all of the catalog members. I had been with Edwards and Deutsch about five years and was living a pretty fast life. I met with clients every night, had two-martini lunches, and, along with most of my associates, was drinking too much. The Chicago lifestyle was getting to me and my family. Lillian and I now had a third child, Elizabeth, born in 1960, so we decided to make a change and returned to St. Paul.

UNITED SCIENTIFIC

After leaving Edwards and Deutsch in 1960, I bought a house in Stillwater, east of St. Paul on the St. Croix River, and invested with my brother Jim and two other men in a little company called Miller Manufacturing and United Screw Products, located at Seven Corners in St. Paul. When I bought in, I owned less than a full quarter share and Jim owned a sixth. I had a verbal agreement with Jim that I was to buy, at some future date, the remaining piece of stock, which would make me a one-quarter owner. I also renamed the company United Scientific.

Between 1960 and 1969 we took that company from $175,000 in sales to $1.75 million. I studied and became an expert on injection molding of plastics. We had a

presses. Then someone tried using color separations on the web press and found that it could turn out color pictures in the catalogs that were almost as good as those from the sheet-fed presses. By using the web press, suppliers of color inserts for the catalog could give the printer just the separations instead of the inserts themselves. It saved them a lot of money.

It wasn't just a matter of quality. Back then, a web press cost $750,000. Meding said, "I can't do it." Edwards and Deutsch resigned the account and the group moved to a printing company with a web press. I don't believe anybody in that whole catalog organization ever called me and thanked me. I had made every one of them a millionaire.

machine shop that had about fifteen screw machines, ten bridge ports, and a few regular lathes. I spent my time doing administrative work, developing new products, and improving the company's image.

One day I was sitting in the Stillwater County Club with a friend who was vice president of Dairy Queen, which is headquartered in Minneapolis. He told me he was shipping powdered milk in cans all over the world. As a premium, Dairy Queen put a glass, the old thumbprint kind, inside each can. I mentally calculated the cost of freight for a heavy glass like that and asked, "Why don't you let me design you a little plastic glass that you can put in there? It will be very attractive and won't weigh anything."

I got a professional piece of artwork done to decorate the glass, which is how we did things in Chicago, and ended up getting an order from Dairy Queen for 4.5 million plastic glasses. My brother Jim was really impressed with what I had done. Following my example, he contacted Northwest Airlines, also based in the Twin Cities, to see if the company could use a personalized glass for serving in-flight beverages. Northwest wanted its own distinctive glass instead of one from Plastics, Incorporated, in St. Paul, which at the time had the market sewed up. I came up with the idea of a plastic glass that was ground to look frosted, similar to Steuben glassware. I believe I was the first person to make a mold with

sandblasted cavities and to work out the draw problems that are innate to a mold like that. I had the Northwest Airlines acronym frosted on the side of a sample glass. After we presented the sample, we got an order for nine million glasses.

Then I designed a new, cow-proof float for the Trough-o-Matic, one of our top money-making products. The Trough-o-Matic hooked onto the side of a large stock tank and automatically turned off the water when the tank was filled. The water was supplied by a hose connected to the device. But the original design caused problems because the cows licked under the float to eat the Styrofoam inside. Our company had gotten into blow molding to make plastic bottles for Hilex bleach and Glenwood Water, so I came up with the idea of using the same technology to redesign the Trough-o-Matic float. My design took out about five parts from the original design and reduced it to a blow-molded float with its own built-in hinge. All we had to add

was a rivet, a rubber washer, and a stainless-steel cotter pin at the hinge. The company still sells more than 150,000 Trough-o-Matics a year. To this day I can't figure out why I did not patent the float. The company has sold about $30 million worth of them in the past forty years.

The Hilex and Glenwood Water bottles were a real pain. They were not only unprofitable, but they also could cause spectacular failures. A heavy cardboard carton supported the bottles for shipping, but if the bottles leaked, the cardboard softened and all of a sudden you had a whole carload in a mess on the floor.

One day, while relaxing in my bathtub, I looked through a legal-size tablet with page after page of reminders of things I wanted to do to improve our business. I had just read a note that said we had to find a proprietary product to replace the blow-mold-

ed bottle business. I stretched my leg and accidentally knocked my daughter Beth's rubber duck into the water. It was floating there in the tub when I grabbed it and shouted, "I've found it! Blow-molded duck decoys!" The next day I went to Gokey's, a sporting goods store in St. Paul, to buy one of its expensive wood duck decoys and made a cast of it in plaster. We put the contrivance in the blow-molding machine and proved that it could be done. Then we made a metal mold and started turning out plastic duck decoys. We packaged twelve to a gunnysack. We had been making one and a half cents on the Hilex and Glenwood bottles. When we started selling the blow-molded ducks all over the United States, we made twenty-five cents per decoy.

A few years later United Scientific had the opportunity to get a big government loan at a low rate of interest to build a new building. Constructing the 13,500-square-foot building became my personal project, and it was a huge undertaking. I contracted with Harry Lovering Construction to do the job. The one-story building, located on Marie Street in West St. Paul, was completed in 1965 and became an important asset to the company.

About the same time I was building my first building, I also began building my first boat. Not only would building *Ugh the Tug* draw me back to the Mississippi River, the project would also become the springboard to a new and prosperous career.

7
BUILDING MY FIRST BOAT

AROUND THE TIME Bill Bowell returned to the Mississippi, the last of the thirteen locks and dams in the St. Paul District of the U.S. Army Corps of Engineers had just been completed. The Upper St. Anthony Lock and Dam in downtown Minneapolis was built in 1963 just one-tenth of a mile upstream of the Lower St. Anthony Lock and Dam, which was finished in 1956. Bookending their construction were three floods: one in 1952, when the Mississippi crested at a record 22.02; a second in 1965, when the river again overflowed its banks, at 26.01 feet; and a third in 1969, when flood levels reached 24.52 feet. Flood stage is fourteen feet.

RETURNING to the RIVER

Though it had been fifteen years since I had owned the *Toka*, boats were imprinted in my DNA. While living in Chicago, I had read every book I could find on boats, studying them like some people study the Bible. I loved the conformation of Maine lobster boats and vaguely hoped to find a hull I could build one on. I resumed hanging around boatyards, and one day in 1965

I spotted an old boat decaying in the yard of the St. Paul Yacht Club. The boat was the *Thomas F.* Built in Duluth, Minnesota, it had once been used as a U.S. Coast Guard harbor boat on Madeline Island in Lake Superior. Although the boat had been heavily built with cypress planking, it was in miserable condition. It also did not look much like a lobster boat, but I was drawn to its hull, which had the lines I was looking for. I bought the *Thomas F.* from Gordy Miller, the dockmaster at the St. Paul Yacht Club, for $300.

Now deceased, Gordy Miller was a legend, the most popular river rat on the St. Paul waterfront. Though he grew up on a farm near Faribault, Minnesota, he was drawn to the river, becoming a pilot for the Central Barge Line in 1937. In 1946 he took over the venerable Dingle Boat Works, which he and his wife, Muriel, operated as a boat repair, dockage, and storage company near Holman Field airport in downtown St. Paul. Gordy operated his Twin City Barge and Towing Company from the same site until the floods of 1951 and 1952 washed away the business. Then the Millers sold Dingle Boat Works and opened a marina and boatyard under the Wabasha Street Bridge, where Gordy sold houseboats and hulls until the big flood of 1965. From there he moved upriver to the St. Paul Yacht Club, where Muriel operated a waterfront restaurant and Gordy bought and sold boats. He was the only one in the area who could operate the huge crane that lifted boats in and out of the water. Gordy belonged to the yacht club longer than any other member, and the Millers' houseboat served as the club office. After the houseboat was damaged by fire in 1970, they restored it and moved the restaurant into it. Later, Jan Halter and Penny Miller (no relation to Gordy) leased it from Gordy and Muriel and changed its name to the No Wake Café.

Gordy Miller—St. Paul Yacht Club dockmaster and Mississippi River icon—sold me Ugh the Tug.

I'm sure Gordy thought I was a nut for buying the *Thomas F.*, but I was drawn to that wreck. I towed the boat to Stillwater and parked it in my back yard. My neighbors laughed when they saw it, and I had to admit it was ugly. Though its hull had the lines of a lobster boat, I had a better idea for its next life. This was river country. Midwest rivers did not have lobster boats on them; they had tugboats and towboats. What I had in my back yard was the beginning of a tugboat I named *Ugh the Tug.*

UGH the TUG

Borge Thompson, one of my employees at United Scientific in St. Paul, was a craftsman and fix-it man. Thompson lived on the outskirts of Stillwater and agreed to let me put the boat in his barn and help me restore it. On an eighteen-by-twelve-inch piece of plywood, I sketched out what the finished *Ugh the Tug* should look like and hung it on the wall of the barn to inspire us.

It occurred to me that if I were going to put a lot of money into restoring a boat, I should do it as a business. So I started a company called Stillwater Tug and Salvage. It sounded good, but we never did get any towing jobs.

Closer inspection of *Ugh the Tug* revealed that while most of its cypress planks were sound (we had to take out a few), two major parts of the hull needed replacing: the horn timber and the knee. The seven-foot-long horn timber—a key part of the skeleton of the hull—was attached to the keel with four eighteen-inch bolts. The knee, which sits on the horn timber, is the major structure of the transom. The huge knee of the *Thomas F.* had been cut from a piece of white oak that was three feet by four inches. Both rotted parts had to be removed and used as patterns for the new parts I was going to have custom-made.

Borge and I labored long and hard to draw those eighteen-inch bolts out of the horn. Even using a hydraulic jack we could pull them out only an eighth of an inch at a time. When the bolts were finally free, I waited for a clear day and then loaded the rotted parts into my El Dorado Cadillac convertible. With the top down, I headed for Neshkoro, Wisconsin, where a remarkable acquaintance by the name of Ferdinand Nimphius had his home and shop.

Ferdinand Nimphius had been a boat builder in Milwaukee, where he constructed several sailboats that won the Chicago-Mackinac race in the 1960s. When the dust settled after his divorce, he had just enough money left to build a small boat in which he intended to sail solo around the world. That plan changed when he and his new girlfriend were driving around rural Wisconsin and spotted a "For Sale" sign on a little farm. They both thought it would be a great place to move to and start over. The farm was in the middle of nowhere; there was not a lake for miles. That was OK with

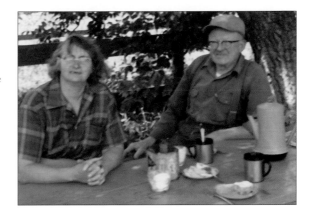

Boat builder Ferdinand Nimphius, sitting with his wife, Betty, at their Wisconsin home. Ferd worked on Ugh the Tug, *the first boat I built, in 1965.*

Ferdinand. All he wanted was a barn in which he could store boats. He sold his sailboat and moved to Neshkoro.

Finding Neshkoro is not easy. It is thirty-five miles west of Oshkosh on Highway 73 and is barely a wide place in the road. When I first drove up to Ferdinand's house, I saw a row of dilapidated buildings encircling the barnyard. The bows of boats stuck out of every doorway. A passel of kids, all seeming to be under ten, flowed out to greet me. Then Ferdinand walked up. We had talked on the phone but had never met. He was a large man with a cherry red face and hair the same color. He wore bib overalls and a red plaid shirt, had a big smile on his face, and was gentle and kind with the children who tumbled about us.

A tour of the boatyard revealed the man's genius. His knowledge of mathematics went far beyond what is required for boat design. The boats under construction in his barns and sheds were for some of the most accomplished sailors on the Great Lakes. One of his major projects at the time was a three-quarter model replica of Columbus's ship, the *Santa Maria*, for a Chicago boat collector.

Ferd agreed to help me with *Ugh the Tug*. He sawed out the new horn timber and knee from the finest dry Wisconsin white oak and built the sitka spruce mast. (Two of Ferdinand's three sons eventually took over his business. Ferdinand died in 1999 at the age of ninety. His wife, Betty, still lives nearby in a little house Ferd built.)

After I hauled the new parts back to Stillwater, Borge and I worked on the boat every spare moment. One of my jobs was to clean out the old caulking between the planks. That caulk had been dry for so many years that it was as hard as concrete. Borge watched me working at it night after night, chipping away with a hammer and chisel. One evening he gave me a circular saw blade he had fashioned out of a larger metal washer. It was just two inches in diameter—the exact thickness of the space between the planks—and wedge-shaped to fit the bevel between the planks. I attached the blade to an electric dill and cleaned out the rest of that hard, dried-up caulk in record time. I still have that hand-wrought blade hanging in my workshop as a reminder of Borge and our friendship.

Not all of the design for *Ugh the Tug* came from my plywood drawing hanging on the barn wall. Carl Lane, an author of nautical books who lived near my winter home in Tavernier, Florida, gave me several ideas, including the placement of a visor around the cabin. Every night during the construction I studied marine catalogs, looking for the trim pieces to put on the boat. The Perko catalog was my favorite because it had the old-style brass lanterns and lights that fit the ambience I was trying to create. I wanted to make the boat look old, not new. Fellow boat builders will understand my emotional commitment to *Ugh the Tug* and why I believed that only the finest fittings should be used on it. I insisted on bronze screws and we used about two thousand of them.

Some existing fittings were fine. The bronze Dorade ventilators on the forward deck were functional, providing fresh air below deck but also trapping rainwater or spray when reversed in heavy weather. The chain plates, two amidships on either side of the boat to stabilize the mast, were hand-drilled and shaped from heavy brass. Also supporting the mast were turnbuckles made of bronze and guy wires made of stainless-steel cable. I made many other parts myself, including the railings, in my basement workshop and hand-carved the six-inch-square Sampson posts that went through the deck to the bottom of the hull. Occasionally my wife would come down to the shop and ask if there was anything she

From this, the Thomas F., . . .

. . . I made this, Ugh the Tug.

could do. My stock answer was, "Put another coat of varnish on the rail." But when I asked Lil to put on another coat for the eighth time, she refused. Her limit was seven, and that's how many coats of varnish the rail got. We painted the hull black, which made the varnish and polished metal work stand out beautifully.

Don Janke, a local carpenter, built *Ugh the Tug*'s cabin. I wanted a little kitchen in the cabin as I liked the idea of brewing coffee and frying eggs while traveling on the river. The only place to put the sink and alcohol stove was under the fold-down bench seat in the cabin. I also arranged for a little hammock to be slung in the cabin, but I can't remember ever using it.

It took a lot of planning, time, and money to turn the $300 *Thomas F.* into *Ugh the Tug*. By the time it was finished in 1968, I had about $12,000 into it—and it was worth every penny. The boat had been a joy to rebuild. The lessons learned and experience gained in refurbishing her served me well. Boats require a lot of upkeep, and in owning several over the years I did a lot of my own brazing and welding in the shop. (I can also take clocks and watches apart and get them to work again, at least most of the time.)

BOS'N'S RIDE on the RIVER

One spring day in the early 1970s, after the ice had gone out, I took my dog,

Bos'n, for a ride on *Ugh the Tug* to Lake Pepin, about forty miles downriver from St. Paul. I had named him after Boatswain, the Newfoundland dog owned by the poet George Gordon, Lord Byron. I had read Byron's poetry while in the service and had visited his home in Mansfield, England, many times. Bos'n (a Doberman) and I were heading back from our adventure when I ran out of gas. I had been trying to get to Wabasha, near the foot of Lake Pepin, where my friends Sharon and Jim Elliot owned the marina and where I could buy my gas from them. Now I was dead in the water and floating back downstream. A big towboat coming downriver, the *Prairie State*, loomed in front of me. I raised it on my radio.

"I'm this little boat right in front of you," I said. "I've run out of gas."

The towboat radioed back, "We'll try to miss you."

"You goddamn well better miss me!" I shouted into the mike.

The captain of the *Prairie State* could tell by my tone that he was dealing with someone of authority like himself. He came back with the suggestion that, when they passed by, a crewman would throw me a line. After I caught it, the towboat pulled me over and gave me five gallons of gas. When I shoved off, however, the polypropylene line got tangled in my propeller.

The next thing I knew, the line had forced the propeller right out of the engine.

I let the boat drift into the Minnesota shore near Minneiska, above Lock and Dam 5. I lifted the engine box and saw that the set screw that holds the shaft in the transmission had come loose. I could fix that, but first I had to cut the line away from the propeller. I took Bos'n ashore, tied him to a tree along the riverbank, stripped to my shorts, and waded in. The water was so cold that I couldn't stand to be in it long enough to clear the propeller. I climbed out and was putting on my clothes when a train roared by. Poor Bos'n! Unthinkingly I had tied him right next to the tracks. But he was a smart dog and he just let the monstrous train go by.

I had a gallon jug of sherry on *Ugh the Tug,* so I took a few sips to warm up before walking to a nearby gas station for help. I told the two fellows at the station that I would pay them $50 if they could get my prop free. One of the men came back with me. He took off his clothes and went in the water, but he couldn't stand the cold either. Back he went to the station to get the other fellow, who was heavyset and could stand the cold water, especially because I kept giving him glass after glass of sherry. He finally cut the line loose and shoved the prop and shaft back into the engine. After I tightened the set screw I told him that if he would go get my dog and put

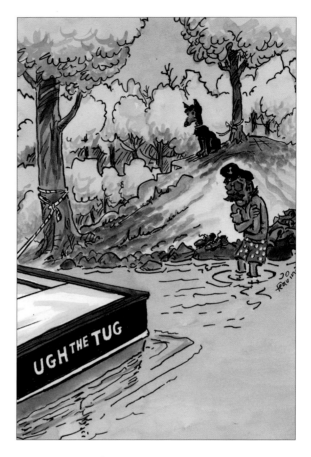

him on board for me, I would pay him $100 instead of $50. In a few minutes Bos'n and I were heading happily back upstream to St. Paul.

A DATE with DESTINY

By 1969, United Scientific was doing pretty well, but my brother Jim and I did not see eye to eye on running the business. I had had all the sophisticated sales training in Chicago and wanted us to develop a product line so that we could have representatives selling our products throughout the country. Jim wanted to do everything himself. That wasn't going to work as far as I was concerned, so I told the other partners they should buy either Jim or me out. They figured that since he had the knowledge in the proprietary sales department, they would be in trouble without him, so they bought me out. I ended up getting cash and an experimental chicken farm in Eleva, Wisconsin, that the company owned. We used to test our plastic chicken feeding and water equipment there. But shortly after I left the company, the other partners split up too. Jim took the product line and the other partners took the machine shop. All of us did well and were satisfied.

For a time after I left the company, I ran the experimental chicken farm. I maintained my residence in Stillwater, but I logged a lot of miles commuting to and from the farm. It needed a lot of work. I redesigned the entire heating system to be more stable than the one invented by United Scientific. To tell you the truth, I soon got tired of hauling chicken shit and began to look for something else to do. I'm an eternal optimist, but I'm also a calculating optimist. I like to plan my future. Each person, as far as I am concerned, must determine his own destiny. It's that simple.

I remembered back to my college days and the *Toka*, the twenty-six-foot Steelcraft I had turned into a sixteen-passenger excursion boat. I thought about the fun I had building *Ugh the Tug*. I knew I wanted to work only six months out of the year. So

the excursion boat idea floated back to me. No one was doing excursion trips around St. Paul. Here we had this great river and no one, except for commercial shippers, was doing anything with it. I did some market studies and everything that I came up with pointed to the fact that I could not lose. Everyone thought I was nuts when I announced my new project, but the time had finally come for me to return to the Mississippi.

8

LAUNCHING the PADELFORD

HARRIET ISLAND was an uninviting place in 1969, particularly for a new excursion boat business. Only one poorly maintained road led onto the island. It dipped under the Wabasha Street Bridge, ran past a wooden walkway to Raspberry Island (then called Navy Island) and a graveyard of abandoned boats, and ended in a parking lot that was a rutted expanse of gravel. This once popular site that had hosted thousands of revelers on Sunday afternoons now stood choked with weeds, its principal visitors the members of the St. Paul Yacht Club, who moored their boats at the upriver end of the island. The Mississippi was heavily polluted, the natural habitat almost destroyed. Highways, junkyards, and industrial buildings had effectively sealed off St. Paul's central business district from the water. Cracked sidewalks, empty lots, and vacant storefronts disfigured the downtown. Few people even thought to look at the river. Those who did saw only massive barges, pushed by towboats, laboring up and down the river.

Few besides those involved in the grain business understood the magnitude of

river shipping. During World War II, the Upper Mississippi had carried some five million tons of cargo annually. By 1969, when Bill Bowell contemplated going into the excursion boat business, shipping on the river had increased to seventy million tons in a season that stretched from March to late November. Neither deterred by hulking barges nor discouraged by the blight on shore, Bowell drove his Airstream trailer to Harriet Island, parked it by the crumbling concrete steps that led to the dock, and launched his fledgling business.

TAKING a RISK

No excursion boats had operated in the Twin Cities area for years. The *Capitol* was gone as was the *Donna May*, which had docked in St. Paul for a short time after World War II. The *Avalon*, which offered excursions out of St. Paul around 1949, eventually succumbed to the changing habits of recreation that ended the romantic era of steamboating. On August 3, 1961, after a round-trip to St. Paul, the *Avalon* left Dubuque at

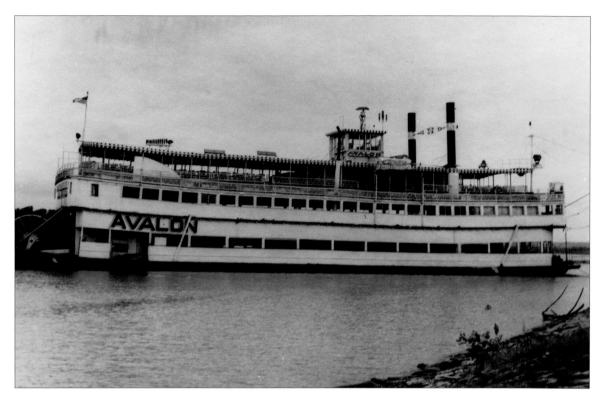

Having plied the St. Paul riverfront from the late 1940s until the early 1960s, the Avalon *is now based in Kentucky, where it offers excursions on the Ohio River as the* Belle of Louisville.

midnight for engagements downriver and never returned. In February 1962 the steamer filed for bankruptcy. It now operates as the *Belle of Louisville* in Louisville, Kentucky.

In 1969 the only excursion outfits on the Upper Mississippi were farther downstream, at La Crosse, Wisconsin; Dubuque, Iowa; and the Quad Cities of Bettendorf and Davenport, Iowa, and Rock Island and Moline, Illinois. The La Crosse and Dubuque excursion businesses were small, each running only one small boat on the river. One operator was a gas station owner

who used a cigar box for a cash register. I figured with my managerial and promotional experience, I could do a lot better. The more I investigated, the more I knew I really had something. My marketing studies weren't scientific or anything. I just saw a need and had the guts to do it. And it did take guts.

My net worth at the time was about $119,000. When I went to the Cosmopolitan Bank in Stillwater for a loan, the board members kind of looked down at me. They ended up lending me the money, but one of the board members made me mad as hell. His wife invited me to a party a couple of months later and damned if she didn't start telling me what a wonderful idea I had to run cruise boats on the river. Her husband had let her read the confidential information I had given him and the bank.

Convinced that the market was there, I planned from the beginning for my company, initially called River Excursions, to grow. As the only excursion boat business in the Twin Cities, I would have no competition. I would base my operations on Harriet Island in St. Paul, which was almost deserted. Gordy Miller, the dockmaster at the St. Paul Yacht Club, had a little restaurant about halfway down on the dock with his wife, Muriel, and the St. Paul Yacht Club had a few boats at the upper harbor under the High Bridge, but that was it. Though the road to Harriet Island was awful, and the entrance to the island looked like a boat junkyard, I had faith that something good would happen there. There was not a doubt in my mind that the business would be successful. It was just such a natural thing.

FINDING a BOAT BUILDER

To go into the boat business, of course, I had to have a boat. So I looked around for a builder who could build a big excursion boat and settled on Dubuque Boat and Boiler Works at Dubuque, Iowa. Known in the nineteenth century

as the Iowa Iron Works, the company had been around since 1870, when it launched the side-wheeler *Clyde*, the first iron-hulled vessel on the Mississippi River. In the 1960s the boat works built more than a dozen excursion boats. The *Julia Belle Swain*, which was under construction at the same time as my boat, was the last excursion boat to be completed in the Dubuque boatyard.

For the design, I decided to combine the best characteristics of two other paddle-wheel boats built by Dubuque Boat and Boiler Works: the *Copy Cat*, for John Fabrick of the Fabrick Caterpillar Tractor Company, and the *Border Star*, for two fellows in Kansas City. As it turned out, my boat ended up being the best of the three. From the *Border Star* I adopted a basic hydraulic system to move the paddle wheel. Dennis Trone, a former naval architect, designed the system, but there were some elements of it that I did not like. Dennis used solid pipe for the slides that the cross bearings ran on. On steam engines, designers usually had the slides in a slide rail, so I modified the system to put my hydraulic rams into what I thought was a more stable slide. I added an accumulator—a vertical air chamber— that cushioned the shock of the stroke. If you don't have a cushion in a hydraulic system, it can knock. Both the *Border Star* and *Copy Cat* had eight-foot-tall second decks that I thought were too high, so I lowered my boat's second deck to seven feet and it made a big difference in the boat's overall conformation.

After finding a builder, I had to come up with a name for the boat. I knew I couldn't name it the *Captain Bowell* as everyone would call it the *Captain Bowel* because of the way my name is spelled. Since my tenth great-grandfather's name was Jonathan Padelford (he is the one who came to this country in 1628), I thought that *Padelford*—"paddle ford"—would be a fitting name for a boat. As it turned out, it was.

GETTING a PILOT'S LICENSE

One problem I had was that I didn't have a pilot's license for boats of a higher tonnage. To qualify for it, I had to put in many hours running a large boat. The *Border Star* was just being completed in the Dubuque boatyard, so I made friends with the captain who had been hired to deliver the boat to its owners in Kansas City. While the *Padelford* was being completed, I persuaded the *Border Star*'s captain to let me sign on as crew and get the additional hours I needed credited.

We were cruising down the Mississippi and heading for the Missouri River and Kansas City on the *Border Star* when the first problem hit us. At two o'clock in the morning, near Princeton, Illinois, the boat lost its hydraulic power. The spotlight was not working (some set screws

had come loose), so the captain ordered me to go on top of the pilothouse to manually move the spotlight and look for a spot where we could land. The boat had a reserve hydraulic system, just enough to get us to shore. We got to the riverbank and standing there watching us, remarkably enough, was a guy dressed in a suit. He extended a ladder so we could get off and tie up the boat. In diagnosing our problem, we found that we needed 250 gallons of hydraulic oil, two seals, and an eight-ton jack. The guy standing on the riverbank just happened to be a hydraulics engineer, and he calmly told us he had all of the stuff we needed. With his help we put everything back together and continued downriver.

For our trip up the Missouri we took on Ray Pritchard, a well-known riverboat captain. (Captains are licensed for different parts of the river.) Pritchard was at the helm when we came to Alton, Illinois, and Lock and Dam 26, the last lock we would traverse on the Mississippi, and there ahead of us was a whole fleet of towboats waiting to go through the lock. The rule is that passenger boats have priority over commercial tows and can precede them through the locks. (Pleasure craft come dead last in line.) The *Border Star* was a passenger boat, but we did not have any passengers aboard, only four crew members.

Pritchard decided on a little deception. He had the crew parade up and down the deck wearing different clothes. One fellow would walk around in one outfit and then dash below, put on a different shirt and hat, and come back out on deck. It fooled the lockmaster, and the towboat operators fumed as they watched the famed Captain Pritchard move our boat to the head of the line. But they had their revenge. There was a strong wind blowing and damned if Pritchard didn't go into the lock skewed and the boat turned around in the lock. The only solution was to back out past all of his snickering colleagues, turn around in the river, and make another run for the lock. This time he came in so close to the lock wall that the rubber tires hanging over the side as bumpers were smoking.

As we approached Mile 14.5 on the Missouri River, which is near St. Charles, all of a sudden there was a hell of a *bang, crash, BOOM!* Immediately I checked the paddle wheel and saw that we had burned out a bearing attached to the pitman arm. I ran to the pilothouse and informed Captain Pritchard. He said to me, "Son"— I was fifty years old—"I'll run in close to the bank. See if you can get a line around something." He ran the boat backward— you can steer a paddle-wheel boat with monkey rudders pretty well backward— until he was a couple of feet from shore. I jumped off and turned to catch the line, but the guy on the boat had nothing but a handful of snarls. The boat passed me and kept going. It went about a mile

downriver before they were able to throw out the anchor, which had only a one-inch-thick line on it. That line twanged like a banjo string, but it held.

I stood there on the riverbank thinking, "My God, I'm building the *Padelford* back at the Dubuque boat works, the same outfit that built this boat. If anything like this ever happened with a load of passengers, it could be tragic." When I got back on the *Border Star,* we made a lot of calls on the radio until we finally hailed a towboat on its way to Kansas City, which agreed to put us on its hip (side) and take us along. I couldn't stop thinking, "I've got to get off this boat, get back to Dubuque, and change the design of my boat." I asked the towboat captain to drop me off at a little riverfront town in Missouri. I walked up to the center of town and discovered that there was no way to get out of there since there were no buses or taxis. So I hitchhiked to the next town, but there was no way to get out of there either. So there I stood, in the middle of the night, thumbing a ride along a highway in Missouri to get to Quincy, Illinois, where I could rent a car.

Finally, I was picked up by a guy who let me ride in the passenger seat of the car he was towing. When we reached Quincy, he let me sleep in a bed on his porch. In the morning I went into town, rented a car, and headed for Dubuque. I skidded into the boatyard, told them what had happened with the *Border Star,* and insisted on

Ol' Man RIVER

having a meeting with the engineers right away. "I want you to put a reserve engine with a screw propeller in the stern of my boat," I told them.

"You can't," they replied. "It's a paddlewheel boat."

"Put the son of a bitch in there!" I insisted.

Because I still had to put in more hours on a large boat to qualify for my hundred-

ton master's license, I flew back to Kansas City to operate the *Border Star*. By then its owners had realized that the boat was underpowered for the Missouri River, and they sold it to Jack Trotter in Little Rock, Arkansas. Trotter hired me to bring the boat to him. The route would take us back down the Missouri, down the Mississippi well past Memphis, Tennessee, and then up the Arkansas River to Little Rock. Trotter hired an old captain to accompany me because I did not yet have a legal

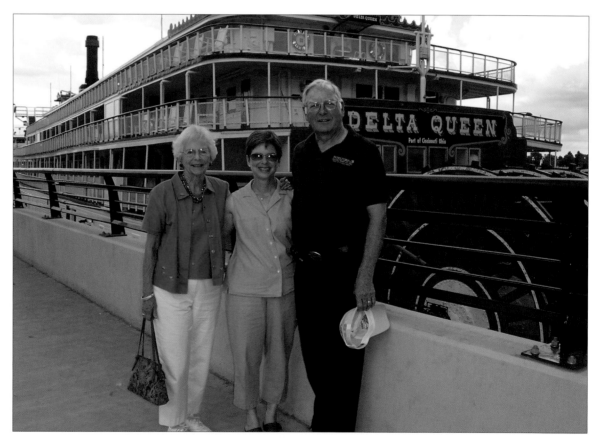

My wife Lillian, our daughter Shelley, and her husband, Jim Kosmo, pose with the pride of the Mississippi River, the Delta Queen. *Lillian, Shelley, and Jim all have played major roles in the success of the Padelford Packet Boat Company from the beginning.*

124

license to run the boat on my own. I can't remember his name, but he had to have been at least ninety years old. Every time we got in trouble and he was at the wheel, he would ask me to take over so he could use the bathroom. Because of the swift current, the under-powered *Border Star* could barely make progress up the river. It took us half an hour to pass under one particular bridge because of the current.

While captaining the boat to Little Rock, I brought along Loren "Whitey" Burnett, an engineer with Dubuque Boat and Boiler Works, who was refining the hydraulic system for the *Padelford*. All the time we were under way, Whitey and I worked on the plans for how I wanted the *Padelford*'s hydraulic system to be.

When we reached Memphis, we pulled the *Border Star* right in behind the majestic *Delta Queen*. The *Delta Queen* was listed on the National Register of Historic Places in 1970 and designated a National Landmark in 1989. Built in 1926, she is the only authentic, fully restored overnight steamboat in the world. The *Delta Queen* is 285 feet long, carries 174 passengers, and operates with a crew of seventy-five. The *Delta Queen* and her sister boats, the *Mississippi Queen* and the *American Queen*—the largest river steamers ever built—give their passengers unforgettable experiences on the Mississippi and Ohio Rivers.

Whitey and I went aboard the *Delta Queen* to look at her steam system and found that the system we had designed was identical, except that ours ran on hydraulics instead of steam pressure. Federal law prohibits using a full head of steam anymore, just enough steam for the immediate purpose. You can't have a full boiler that could explode. The engineer from the *Delta Queen* looked at our plans and gave them his approval.

We were progressing nicely up the Arkansas River toward Little Rock when we came to a bridge that was too low for our smokestacks to go under. My friend Dick Lynn, who was on board, told us to pull into shore. After we beached the boat, Dick jumped off and headed toward an abandoned barn nearby with big, old doors. He took the hinges off the doors, brought them on board, and had our welder weld the hinges onto the backsides of both smokestacks. When the job was finished, the welder cut the smokestacks all around the base at the center of the hinges. We lowered the stacks and easily passed under the bridge.

It was late at night when we reached the Little Rock harbor, where everyone went a bit ape over the big *Border Star*. Then our team scattered. Now that I had qualified for a hundred-ton license, I flew home. Whitey Burnett went back to Dubuque to supervise the installation of the engines on the *Padelford*.

The engineers put a 100-horsepower Caterpillar diesel engine with a screw propeller on the *Padelford*'s stern compartment. It was one of the smartest things I ever did in all my horsing around with boats. The U.S. Coast Guard even picked up the idea and recommended it to other builders. Many copied us because it was so successful. We could use two types of power: propeller and paddle wheel. The *Padelford* is one of the few boats on the Mississippi that is actually propelled by the paddle wheel in the stern. One time we broke a hydraulic shaft on the paddle-wheel hydraulic system and were able to operate for four days on the reserve engine while waiting for a new part to arrive. We never lost a nickel.

One of the final touches I added while building the *Padelford* was its whistle. Made of solid bronze, the whistle cost $4,000 in 1972. It's the finest on the Mississippi and was made by Kahlenberg of Twin Rivers, Wisconsin. Practically every towboat on the river has a Kahlenberg whistle. I had wanted a whistle like that ever since I was a kid growing up on the Mississippi. River people can tell the difference in sound between a spun brass whistle and a cast bronze whistle, which is more expensive.

EARLY SUCCESS

We began running excursions on the *Jonathan Padelford*, a 250-passenger boat with a sixty-five-foot hull, from Harriet Island in St. Paul during the summer of 1970. While I had been supervising construction of the *Padelford* in Dubuque, my wife, Lillian, sent a massive mailing to all potential customers for charters who were listed in the yellow pages. By the time the *Padelford* arrived in St. Paul, we had a backlog of charters. From the first day of operation, we provided facilities for private parties, conventions, proms, graduation parties, and corporate functions. I had been operating the *Padelford* for only a few months when one of my nieces asked to hold her wedding reception on the boat. It was our first of many weddings.

I got permission from the city of St. Paul to operate the *Padelford* from the public dock, and most people were happy to see me come in. At first some of the folks at the St. Paul Yacht Club resented me. One guy in particular gave me a real problem. One day in my first or second year, I came in with a load of passengers and this guy had parked his big yacht right in my space on the dock. And he refused to move. It was a real standoff. Finally, he moved his boat, I unloaded my passengers, and he and I had words. I was furious. Then this guy went into his boat, smeared something red—probably mercurochrome—on his bare chest, and came out screaming, "Look what he did to me!" I had not laid a finger on him, but he brought assault charges against me. Even though I had a witness—a journalism professor from the

University of Minnesota—the judge decided against me and I ended up paying a fine. So I had my ups and downs with the yacht club, depending on who was the commodore. Ninety percent of the time we got along very well. That was important as we were practically living in each other's back yards.

My relations with the city of St. Paul were always good, especially when Harriet Island came under the jurisdiction of Bob Pirham of the St. Paul Parks Department. Bob and I got on well. We had our fights, but we really liked each other. I had the same good relationship with Minneapolis park officials Dave Fisher and Harvey Feldman when I took our boats to Boom Island in that city. Taxpayers in both cities are fortunate to have such outstanding public servants.

From the beginning, the company did well. Our charter service quickly became a mainstay of the summer business, and before long we were running charters almost every night. No one went hungry on our trips. On our daily excursions we offered popcorn, hot dogs, potato chips, and soft drinks. On the charter trips everyone had the same meal, whether it was chicken or steak. As the business grew, the menu became more sophisticated and our offerings ran to five pages. We sold seven kinds of box lunches (among them roast beef with caramelized onions and grilled portobello mushroom sandwiches); six breakfast menus, including a Captain's Choice buffet with eleven categories of items; two pages of lunch and hors d'oeuvres menus; and three categories of dinner menus with seventeen entrees. We installed bars on every deck. If they wished, charter guests could receive five-by-seven color prints of their cruise experience in a souvenir folder when they left the boat.

It was my idea to offer narrated cruises. I knew that tourists come to places where there's history, and St. Paul's history is very colorful. One of the city's first settlers, for example, was a Frenchman with one squinty, piglike eye who sold illegal liquor to the Native Americans and the soldiers at Fort Snelling. "Pig's Eye" Parrant, as the old bootlegger was nicknamed, set up his headquarters at a place called Fountain Cave in the river bluffs. That was the beginning of the city of St. Paul. The town might have been named Pig's Eye if a young Jesuit priest, Father Lucien Galtier, had not come along in 1841. Galtier built a small log chapel on top of the river bluffs and named it for Saint Paul. The saint's name seemed considerably more suitable than Pig's Eye for the growing village.

My favorite story about the river is the one about the railroad swing bridge just above Harriet Island. When it was built in 1915, the bridge was perfectly symmetrical; the section on the left was the

Pierre "Pig's Eye" Parrant is one of my favorite characters on the river. I coached artist Ken Fox as to what the French settler might have looked like and worn. I figured he received the leggings and moccasins in trade for some of his bootleg liquor.

Father Lucien Galtier's chapel in St. Paul.

same size as the section on the right. It was a balanced swing bridge. While the bridge was being built, an old character dressed in bib overalls and smoking a corncob pipe would come to the site every day with a folding chair, a Thermos of coffee, and a can of Sir Walter Raleigh tobacco. He patiently sat and watched the progress on the bridge. When the day arrived for the grand opening, all of the important railroad officials were on hand. After several speeches were made, a ribbon was cut and the signal given to open the bridge. At that point the old man stepped up and shouted, "Don't open that bridge!" While the railroad officials listened in astonishment, the man explained that the opened bridge would swing over his property and he had not given permission for that.

When a surveyor confirmed that the bridge would indeed swing over the old man's land, the railroad tried to buy him off. But he would have nothing to do with it. As he explained, "I'm an old steamboat man who was put out of a job when the railroad came. I wouldn't sell my land to you for any price." He meant it. Since he would not budge, the railroad was forced to cut off a massive piece of the bridge and balance it with a huge block of concrete to shorten the swing. That bridge is still there on the shore of the river.

By offering stories like these on our cruises, I figured we would be selling a lot more than just a boat ride. I tried to make our narration on the boat somewhat cryptic, informative but not wordy, and designed to teach the passengers about the history of the river. The narration I wrote in 1971 is still used for the company's excursions.

BIGGER BOAT, BIGGER FLEET

After one year in business I realized that the *Jonathan Padelford* was too small and decided to enlarge it. I couldn't take the boat back to the Dubuque boatyard because its president, Henry Miller, had

died and the company was bankrupt. So I had a twenty-foot addition put onto the *Padelford* by the Lemont Shipbuilding Company, near Chicago. To get to the boatyard, I had to go down the Mississippi to St. Louis and then up the Illinois River.

The shipbuilder had a synchro sift, which was a highly versatile dry dock. Workers put railroad trucks on the rails of the dry dock and lowered the dock into the water. They then placed the boat on the trucks and raised the dry dock to the level of the yard. Once the boat was on land, workers

The Jonathan Padelford *was in dry dock near Chicago in 1971, when I had twenty feet added to the midsection to accommodate the growing number of passengers.*

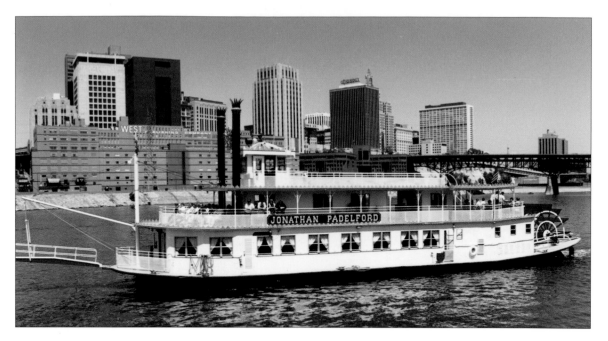

The newly lengthened Jonathan Padelford *cruises past the downtown St. Paul skyline.*

cut it in half and moved the sections apart on the rail trucks. The new twenty-foot section, which had already been fabricated, was then inserted into the opening and joined by welding the three parts together. The additional twenty feet cost only $40,000 and increased the boat's passenger capacity from 250 to 313. Measured from the tip of the boarding swing bridge to the paddle wheel, the boat now measured 125 feet.

In the early 1970s I ran every trip on the *Jonathan Padelford*. To survive the long hours I would steer the boat and do the narration on the upbound leg of the trip. When we turned around at Fort Snelling to head back downstream, I turned on the music on the boat's sound system and asked the passengers to enjoy the tranquility of the river.

Then I handed over the wheel to Tim Jambeck and took a quick nap, getting up just before we made our landing.

I used to love to land the *Padelford* by coming to a dead stop in the middle of the river, where you could draw a straight line to our dock a hundred yards away. By matching throttle to the current, the boat would hold its position. Then, with its rudder pointing toward the shore, the *Padelford* would slide to the dock in a straight line. Invariably the passengers were enthralled and asked how I had done the maneuver. Some would inquire if the boat had a bow thruster to help it land, like towboats and larger steamboats such as the *Mississippi Queen*. No, I would say, it was skill on our part.

The business quickly fell into a pattern. We ran regular excursions four times daily from Memorial Day through Labor Day. Evening dinner cruises ran on weekends from May through October, and we booked charters every day from May through September. Sales climbed every year. We worked seven days a week, sixteen hours a day, all summer. As we added more boats like the *Zebulon Pike*, the business became even more complicated.

THE *ZEBULON PIKE*

In 1972 I heard about a small cruiser operating out of Milwaukee on Lake Michigan that was for sale. It was the sixty-five-foot-long, 120-passenger *Hannah Kildahl*. The owner, whose wife was suffering from cancer, agreed to sell the boat to me for $50,000. To get my new boat home, I had to pilot her through the Chicago ship channel, down the Illinois River, and then up the Mississippi.

When I got the *Hannah Kildahl* to St. Paul I completely remodeled her, adding seats and putting in a spiral staircase going up to the second deck. I renamed her the *Zebulon Pike*, after the young explorer I admired who had come up the Mississippi River in 1805 and signed a pact with

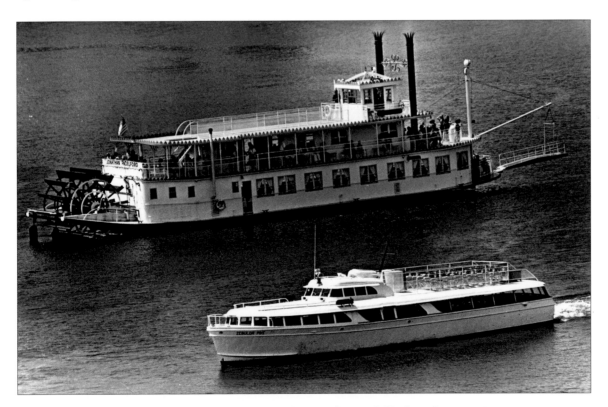

The Zebulon Pike, which I bought in 1972, passes the Jonathan Padelford on the Mississippi.

Dakota Indians for the land on which Fort Snelling would be built. Unfortunately, the *Pike* had been built by someone who was not particularly experienced in boat building. If you don't know how to build a boat in iron, the plating can get warped and it looks bad. The *Zebulon Pike* served its purpose for a few years before I sold it in 1978 to some people in Omaha. I saw an opportunity to buy a much larger boat, the three-hundred-passenger *Maark Twain*, and I needed the money to buy it.

The sale of the *Pike* taught me a big lesson: never sell a boat and promise to deliver it. To get the *Pike* to the buyer in Omaha, I had to take it down the Mississippi and then up the Missouri. Going down the Mississippi was fine, but the Missouri is a bastard of a river. It runs fast, seven miles an hour, and it's a straight shoot.

No sooner had I gotten the *Pike* to Omaha than the new owner decided to move it to Table Rock Lake in Arkansas. He loaded the boat on a big trailer and started moving it down the highway from Nebraska to Arkansas. The problem was he had not bothered to get a permit. He was the kind of a guy who buffaloes his way through things without giving any thought to the rules. He was about to go to jail in Arkansas, or at least face a heavy fine, when he persuaded the governor of Nebraska to intervene on his behalf by calling the governor of Arkansas. Arkansas officials finally let him move the

A jazz band plays aboard the Discovery, *which I intended to use as a ferry at Fort Snelling.*

boat to Table Rock Lake, but they told him, "Don't you ever try to get that boat out of here." The boat just sits down there in Table Rock Lake, rotting away. Running it created such a terrible wake that it made everyone else on the lake mad. It hasn't run in years.

THE *DISCOVERY*

In the winter of 1972 I purchased the *Discovery*, a replica of the keelboats used by Lewis and Clark and Zebulon Pike on their trips up the Missouri and Mississippi Rivers. The *Discovery* was built by the Leavenworth Shipbuilding Company in Fort Leavenworth, Kansas, and originally ran on the Missouri River out of Kansas City. She was fifty-five feet long and carried forty-nine passengers. I intended to use her as a ferry from the landing below the bluff at Fort Snelling to Mendota, but the area did not develop as I had thought it might. I kept the *Discovery* until 1975.

THE *JOSIAH SNELLING*

I bought the 120-foot-long, thirty-one-foot wide *Maark Twain* in the spring of 1973 from a friend in Cincinnati, Ohio, where the boat had been built a decade earlier by Tucker Marine Service. My friend's last name was Maark, and in a fit of whimsy he had named his boat the *Maark Twain*. Maark did not want to sell his boat for cash. Instead, he wanted a reliable buyer who would pay off the debt over a period of time. This was a perfect arrangement for me, so I bought the boat for $150,000 and went down to Cincinnati with my son, Bill Jr., and operations manager Wally Snyder, crew chief Mike Gebhart, and my uncle, Jim Padelford, to pick it up and sail it to St. Paul. I went with them on the Ohio River as far as Paducah, Kentucky, and then flew back to St. Paul. Uncle Jim, an old-time mechanic who could weld and do just about anything, followed the boat on land, pulling my Airstream trailer.

The river was running fast when Bill Jr., Wally, and Mike started up the Mississippi at Cairo, Illinois. They had trouble making two miles an hour. When they finally reached St. Louis and encountered the force of the Missouri River emptying into the Mississippi, they had to get help to get above the mouth of the Missouri. A friendly towboat assisted them. Their next difficulty came when they were about a mile above the mouth of the Illinois River. The Allison gears, which are notorious for separating at the propeller shaft, came out of the port engine. The *Maark Twain* had twin screw propellers, which typically allow you to run a boat on one engine. But when they attempted that, the boat ran in circles. Besides propelling itself upriver, the *Maark Twain* was also pushing a small spud barge ahead of it.

Bill Jr. managed to get the boat tied to some trees on an uninhabited island in the river, but in doing so broke some of the windows and the radio antenna on the boat. The loss of the radio antenna meant he and Mike and Wally could not reach Uncle Jim, who was still following the boat by land. Because they were on an island, they could not walk anywhere for help and they were afraid to use the dinghy to reach the main shore because it was so small.

Fortunately, the radio signals did reach a towboat, whose captain was kind enough to call our office in St. Paul. I flew to St. Louis, rented a car, located Uncle Jim, and met the *Maark Twain* on the riverbank in a tiny dinghy. The first thing I did when I got back to shore was to buy a larger dinghy called a John boat. I also had to go to St. Louis to get parts for the engine. A day or two later when I was bringing the new John boat back to the *Maark Twain*, I lost my balance while stepping onto the deck and fell into the river. Ice was floating all around me. I flipped right back into the John boat, feeling damned glad I had bought a larger one, and began hollering. Uncle Jim and Bill Jr. were down in the hold working on the engine, but fortunately they heard me.

When we finally got the *Maark Twain* to St. Paul, I completely renovated it and put windows on the upper deck. I renamed the boat the *Josiah Snelling*, the army officer for whom Fort Snelling is named. The boat became the sister ship to the *Jonathan Padelford* and the workhorse of the company, running the daily excursions and dinner cruises. The *Josiah Snelling* served the company well until it was sold in 1997.

With all the time and money I was investing in my excursion business, I ran a tight ship. There was no margin for error and no tolerance for laziness. Anybody can run a boat up and down the river, but taking care of the little details and seeing that people are treated properly are the things that matter. I may be a Captain Bligh, but I wouldn't want it any other way.

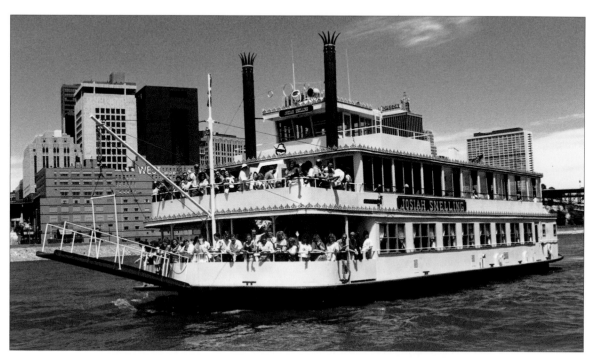

The Josiah Snelling, *pictured at the Port of St. Paul, became the workhorse of our growing fleet.*

9
CAPTAIN BLIGH BOWELL

I WAS A TOUGH ONE when I ran the excursion company. I would not stand for mediocrity, and the minute I saw it I made sure that person no longer worked for me. Mediocrity is when someone walks over a cigarette butt on the deck and doesn't pick it up, or sees a trash can covered with dirt and doesn't clean it up. Mediocrity is when a waiter intentionally serves hot food cold, or leaves a coffee-soaked napkin under the coffeepot instead of replacing it with a fresh napkin. If anybody left an amateurish "Out of Order" sign on the door of a toilet for more than a day without getting the toilet fixed, that was mediocrity as far as I was concerned.

If I'm a son of a bitch, it's because I'm a perfectionist, and sometimes it takes a loud voice to keep things perfect. Someone once asked me when I was piloting the *Padelford* if I considered myself a supreme power. "Definitely," I replied. Any captain who is worth his salt has got to be that way. If he isn't, the job won't get done right. And to get the job done right, it sometimes takes a lot of bluster. I can go through a hundred-mile-per-hour wind

and hardly show a nerve, but a cigarette butt on the deck throws me into a tizzy.

Our business depends on customers telling others what a great time they had. As our mission statement says, "We are a business,

but profits are secondary to providing good, wholesome recreation and entertainment while working in an atmosphere of the enjoyment of life." I've had to motivate some crew members to remember our mission, especially young people. I'm sure there have been some employees who would like to kill me. But the minute they leave and mature a little, they look back and say, "My God, he did me a favor." I've done a lot of kids favors. I remember one crew chief who was the son of a friend of mine. I figured the poor kid was never going to make it, and about the time I had decided to let him go he blossomed and became one of our better crew chiefs for the next couple of years.

I cherish a letter I received from Lisa Haag, one of our crew chiefs, at my retirement. Lisa wrote in part:

> If you hadn't started up the company, my life would not be what it is today. I want to thank you from the bottom of my heart.

> The river is a whole different culture that so few know exists. It is a wonderful place and I am so fortunate for having been a part of it. The six years I worked at the Padelford don't seem long but those years were some of the best. . . . I grew up working hard but working on the boats gave "working hard" a new definition. The most hours I worked in a week were 92. My worst

shift was a 20-hour day with three hours to get ready for the next shift that lasted 12. I wasn't the only one working hours like that, and none of us ever really minded because those boats were as much a part of us as anything else.

> You kept us on our toes, Captain Bowell. I won't say you were easy to work for, but I will say that you made all other work easy. You expected the best and the best is what you got—a concept that seems to be fading in today's world.

> Thank you for having the dream to start the boats. The things I saw, the places I went, the friends I made, the books I catalogued for your library, and knowing you will all be cherished memories for the rest of my life. The Mississippi River will always be a home to me and I have you to thank for that.

KEEPING the PEACE

Some of the parties on the boats got a little wild and I would have to step in. One time some smart aleck was standing on the second deck, heckling me up in the pilothouse all during the trip. This guy kept shouting, "Are you sure you can get us ashore? Are you going to drown us all out here?" He was being really obnoxious. I don't know why. I had never had that happen before or since. As we were about to dock the boat, I could see he was still standing on the deck below me. In front of the pilothouse were the steel cables that run up at an angle toward the king post, the big metal post in the center of the bow. The minute the dock crew had a line on the boat, I jumped over the rail next to the pilothouse, grabbed a cable, and dropped down right in front of the guy. "What did you say to me?" I growled. "Will you repeat that?" Was he flabbergasted! His wife grabbed his arm and they got the hell out of there.

Another time, a crew member came up to the pilothouse to tell me that a bunch of college kids on board were getting out of hand. Two of them were starting a fight. I grabbed the 9-millimeter Browning pistol I kept in the pilothouse, went down to the lower deck where they had squared off, and positioned myself between them. I showed them the butt of my pistol and said, "I'm going to coldcock the first one of you guys who swings." I stood there between them for seven or eight minutes while this little wimp stood off to the side, his eyes as big as saucers. The two guys glared at each other but neither moved. When we got to the dock and booted them off the boat, the little

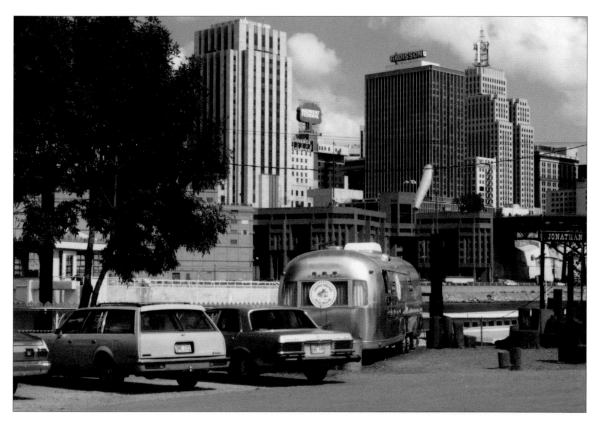

Our early facilities were rather limited. We used my Airstream trailer as a ticket office. Parking was in a dusty adjoining lot. Passengers had to go down steep steps to a rickety old dock to board the boats.

wimp walked up to me and whispered, "Captain, you've got more guts than anybody I've ever seen in my life."

A gun came in handy one time while I was sleeping in the Airstream trailer that doubled as our ticket office on Harriet Island. I was awakened at about two o'clock in the morning by a distinctive click. I recognized it as the latch on the gate on the forward deck of the *Josiah Snelling*. I peeked out the window and saw two men going aboard the boat. I called the police and told them I had a .38-caliber revolver and was going to go after the men—to which

they replied, "Captain, don't make it bloody." Holding the pistol, I crept down the stairs to the dock. Just as I got to the bottom, two young guys came out carrying cases of wieners and buns. I pointed my gun at them and ordered them to sit down. They sat, holding the cartons of wieners on their laps, until the police arrived a few minutes later. "Nice work, Captain," said one of the officers as they took the two youths into custody.

The next day, while I was eating a sundae in a downtown Bridgeman's ice cream shop, damned if one of the would-be robbers

didn't walk into the store. He didn't recognize me, but I knew it was him. He asked the guy behind the counter for a glass of water. The counterman refused him, and when the young man left, I followed him out of the store.

"How did you get out of jail so soon?" I asked him. As he stammered in embarrassment, I handed him a twenty-dollar bill and said, "Why don't you go back in and have a sundae on me?" The kid did not look that bad to me.

DEALING with WEATHER

The weather was always a concern for me if one of our boats got caught in a sudden and severe storm. On the other hand, if I was running the boat, it didn't bother me too much.

You can tell a good riverboat captain by how he reacts in storms. You have to know what to do. A twin-screw propeller boat is easy to handle: You can come back on one throttle and come ahead on the other. This, coupled with steering at the helm, makes the boat highly maneuverable in tough situations. A boat driven by a paddle wheel is entirely different. Because it acts like a sailboat, it's best at backing into the wind. In a tight turn, the captain must be patient because the boat won't respond quickly to steering changes as a car does. The captain must be prepared to add throttle or power; he must know the boat and how it will respond.

We had a rule that if the captain beached the boat in an emergency, the crew had to get a line around a tree or anything else on the shore to secure the boat. One time I was going up the Minnesota River when a tornado hit the Black Dog power plant. We were about three miles below the plant and getting reports of hundred-mile-per-hour winds. A driving rain made visibility difficult. I let the wind take the *Padelford* into the bank broadside. The crew chief, Mike Gebhart, jumped off the boat to tie a line to a tree. With the roar of the wind, he could not hear me tell him that there was not a tree on the bank for half a mile in that area of the river.

When Mike finally realized that, he slid down the riverbank and reboarded the boat, his white uniform covered with mud. As it turned out, we didn't need to be tied to a tree, because the wind was pinning us to the bank. The charter party that night was from the William Mitchell College of Law in St. Paul. A woman from the group was visiting the pilothouse when the storm broke, and she was mesmerized by all the controlled chaos going on there—radio transmissions, weather reports, chatter with other boats in the area. When the storm passed, she left the pilothouse, saying it was the most exciting experience of her life.

During another storm, I decided to beach the *Padelford* across from the St. Paul Pool and Yacht Club near Lilydale. My brother

Ol' Man RIVER

Bob, who has a tendency to get excited, happened to be aboard. As we got close to shore, he took a line and jumped into the water, thinking it was only a couple of feet deep. Instead, it was over his head—and he didn't know how to swim. Bob somehow got to shore with the line and secured the boat. Later we asked him how he did it. He answered that when he hit the bottom of the river, he just walked ashore.

Often when I heard reports about the threat of a storm, I would drive up the hill from downtown St. Paul to Cherokee Park, which overlooks the river and where I could see the western sky. Ninety-nine percent of our weather in the metro area comes from the west, so I could always see what we could expect for the next couple of hours. The storm warnings broadcast on television at that time were not as accurate as they are now. I had the idea of using a Minnesota map on television to show the outlines of the counties affected by a storm. The counties could be colored and arrows used to indicate the directions the storms were traveling. In 1990 I submitted the idea to Stanley Hubbard of KSTP-TV, who turned it over to his station's meteorologists. Within a short time, practically

We had to survive Minnesota winters. The quarter-inch-steel hulls withstood the crushing effect of ice in the harbor. In earlier days, bales of straw were floated around the waterline of boats to cushion their wood hulls.

every local TV station was using the concept. I think it then went national.

RESCUING *UGH the TUG*

The wing dams that would dramatically end the upriver trip of *Ugh the Tug* were authorized by Congress in 1878 to solve the problem of low water on the Upper Mississippi. The dams were designed to project six hundred or more feet from shore and direct the flow of water into a relatively narrow stream, thus increasing its velocity so it could scour a deeper natural channel. The dams were made from willow mattresses, which were sunk to the river bottom and covered with piles of rock. The U.S. Army Corps of Engineers eventually built more than a thousand wing dams in the 143 miles between the Twin Cities and La Crosse, Wisconsin. Many dams lay under less than a foot of water, making them hazardous for small boats. Experienced skippers know to watch the river's surface for the telltale ripples that reveal the presence of a wing dam.

By 1972 I was so busy getting the *Padelford* up and running that I couldn't get away to do anything else. *Ugh the Tug* was just sitting there on the St. Croix River over in Stillwater, so my brother Bob offered to bring it over to Harriet Island in St. Paul. Never mind that he had never run a boat before. Bob loaded his wife, Laurine, and our fifteen-year-old nephew, Mark (brother Jim's son), aboard *Ugh the Tug* and

headed down the St. Croix for Prescott, Wisconsin, where the St. Croix empties into the Mississippi. From there they would come up the Mississippi to St. Paul.

I had had a long and busy day, so instead of going home to Stillwater I slept in the Airstream trailer/ticket office. About two o'clock in the morning my phone rang. Jean, my sister-in law and Mark's mother, was on the line. *Ugh the Tug* had not shown up and she was panic-stricken. I was pretty upset myself and knew that they must have gotten into some kind of trouble.

I looked out the window of my trailer and, fortuitously, there on the dock was fifteen-year-old Scott Madsen, the son of a man I knew. The kid had run away from home. I hollered at him to come help me, then went aboard the *Padelford* and started the engine. The kid threw off the lines for me and together we went down the river, swinging the spotlight back and forth from shore to shore, looking for *Ugh the Tug.*

Soon we passed the downtown St. Paul airport, then the Inver Grove Bridge. I got down the river ten miles, to Mile 827.6, when I caught sight of a bonfire—and my partially submerged boat—on an island. My nephew Mark was frantically waving and calling out, "Uncle Billy! Uncle Billy! We knew you'd come!" Carefully I pulled the *Padelford* into shore between two wing dams, one of which the *Tug* must have hit. The three stranded passengers came aboard the *Padelford*, and while Mark wolfed down all the sandwiches left in the *Padelford*'s snack bar, Bob told his story.

At about six o'clock the previous evening, Bob had been following a towboat up the river to stay in the channel, but must have strayed off course because the boat hit a wing dam. Bob asked Mark to lift the engine cover, and when he saw that the boat was gushing water, Bob knew he had to beach the boat in a hurry. He gunned the engine and headed for shore. Fortunately, the engine sits in the middle of *Ugh the Tug*'s hull, so water never got into it. Bob had done everything right up to that point, getting the boat to shore and protecting the engine. Now all they could do was wait to be rescued. (There was a radio onboard, but Bob did not know how to use it.) I got everyone home safely that night, and we went back the next day to patch the hole and pump out the boat. We started the engine, and everything on *Ugh the Tug* ran fine. But Bob never ran that boat again.

In 1974, I realized I was too busy with boat building to take care of *Ugh the Tug*. I also needed every bit of capital I could find. At lunch with my friend Jim Brooksbanks, I admitted that I was planning, reluctantly, to sell the boat. Jim agreed to buy it and to give me the right of first refusal if he ever decided to sell it.

Jim and his son, Philip, have kept *Ugh the Tug* in pristine condition, exactly as it was

when I sold it to them. They have entered the boat in a number of antique-boat contests, where it has sailed away with the top prizes. Under Jim and Philip's auspices, *Ugh the Tug* won the top award three years straight at the Minnetonka Boat Club's annual gathering at the Treasure Island Casino harbor, near Red Wing. He proudly showed off the big silver cup by placing it on the bow of the boat and filling it with red roses. He has since withdrawn *Ugh the Tug* from competition to give others in the club an opportunity to win.

ROMANCE and TRAGEDY

Around 1977 a petite young woman by the name of Jan got a job with the railroad running the Pig's Eye Bridge just below Holman Field in downtown St. Paul. Jan was later transferred to the Omaha Bridge, about half a mile above Harriet Island. John Halter, one of our captains who ran the *Jonathan Padelford* up and down the river four or five times a day, could not help but notice the attractive woman running the bridge. He began waving to her, which progressed to blowing her kisses, which led to him engaging in all sorts of antics to get her attention, including standing on his head. All appeared to be going well in the courtship until one day, when John saw that another pilot had anchored his boat on the Omaha's sheer fence, the wooden guide that prevents boats from ramming the bridge's main structure. Just as John was wondering what the other pilot was doing there, he saw him climb the sheer fence with a bouquet for Jan.

John began to worry about the competition. He went to a party where Jan was also in attendance, and the two began talking in earnest. On September 12, 1980, John proposed and Jan accepted. Their first child, Sam, was born in 1983. Sam started working on the *Jonathan Padelford* when he was fourteen and was soon joined by his younger brother, Nick.

Another memorable family got its start aboard one of our boats. One year a mallard duck built her nest right on the deck of the *Josiah Snelling.* I had a soft spot in my heart for animals—still do—so I warned everyone to stay away from that mother duck and her nest so she wouldn't be disturbed. Something must have frightened her, however, because one day we realized that the nine eggs were there but the mother duck was gone. It turned chilly that day, and as I was in a restaurant that evening in Minneapolis I began to worry about the eggs being cold. I hurried back to St. Paul and got a big light bulb and reflector to put over the eggs to keep them warm. The next morning I bought an incubator for them. Damned if four of those eggs didn't hatch out baby ducks. We raised those ducklings right there on the boat. By the time we finally released them into the river to live on their own, they still thought of the boat as home and me as their mother. They were so imprinted on me that every time one of

those four ducks saw me, he gave me a long, screeching quack.

Every year we took kids from the same Neighborhood House where I had hung out as a kid on free cruises down the river. The year we had the baby ducks those kids had a great time with them, and the *Pioneer Press* took a picture of the youngsters with me and one of my ducklings.

One year a bunch of kids who hung out in the caves along our route thought it would be great fun to holler obscenities at our passengers. I gave the kids a free pass to

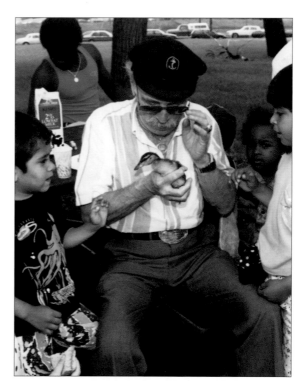

I show off one of my baby ducks to children from St. Paul's Neighborhood House, the same settlement house where I played as a boy.

Barry Thielen, a young crew member who loved the river, died in 1979 after diving off the deck of the pilothouse of the Jonathan Padelford.

take a ride up the river and visit the pilot-house. Most of them seemed to appreciate that I was being nice to them. But when we got to Fort Snelling and began turning around to go back downstream, I looked out of the pilothouse and saw one of the kids standing on the railing. The next thing I knew he dove overboard. Thankfully, he swam safely to shore. Sadly, that would not be the case for one of our crew members.

On a hot midsummer day in 1979 some of the crew of the *Jonathan Padelford* were scrubbing the boat while others were cooling off with a dip in the river. One of the crew was Barry Thielen, a young man who loved old cars and would modify them with some strange configurations. On his days off, Barry would get someone to drive him to Fort Snelling, about five miles upstream from our Harriet Island dock, where he would unload an inflated truck inner tube. Using a hockey stick as a rudder, Barry would leisurely float on the tube back down the river to our dock.

On this particular day, I went to lunch while the crew cleaned the *Padelford*. When I came back at two, the head of the Coast Guard met me with the news that one of my crew had had a tragic accident. Barry had gone up to the pilothouse deck to make a daring dive into the river. He had to have known that the guard on the lower deck projects from the side of the boat. He probably gave himself an extra push to clear the guard, but his feet must have slipped. Instead of clearing the side of the boat, he dove straight down and hit his head on the steel walkway. From there he fell unconscious into the river, and despite the rescue efforts of the other crew, he drowned.

I wanted to dive into the water and find him, but the officer told me it was too late. All of us were grief-stricken, and Barry's parents were beside themselves. His funeral was held on the *Jonathan Padelford*, and I poured his ashes on the churning paddle wheel as we retraced the route he so often took on his inner tube. Later, I wrote a tribute to Barry for a memorial plaque that I placed on the *Padelford*.

10
FLOATING RESTAURANTS

BARGES DO NOT TRAVEL under their own steam. They require tugboats or towboats to move them. The main difference between these two kinds of workboats is the hull. Tugboats have a deep, V-shaped hull and are used near ocean harbors and seaports or on large lakes for maneuvering oceangoing ships into docks or berths. Towboats have a flat-bottomed hull and are used on the more shallow waters of rivers. The hull is heavily reinforced to withstand the constant abuse of grinding into the bottom or going aground. Towboats push (and occasionally pull) barges—and, as in the case of Bill Bowell's *Governor Ramsey*, towboats push disabled excursion boats too.

THE *GOVERNOR RAMSEY*

In the mid-1970s I got the idea to build a big floating restaurant on the river. It was a natural outgrowth of our catering business. Besides, I like to cook. The sauce that we serve on our Cornish game hens on the boats is my recipe. It has cranberries, orange juice, brown sugar, and marmalade in it, and it tastes terrific.

To house my floating restaurant, I bought a two-hundred-foot paddle-wheel boat named the *Missouri Queen*. The forty-foot-wide hull was built in 1940 in Pennsylvania; the boat was finished in West Memphis, Arkansas. Christened the *Arkansas II*, it was the last paddle-wheel boat built for the U.S. Army Corps of Engineers and had been a workhorse on the Lower Mississippi.

When I learned about the boat, it was docked at Sioux City, Iowa, and already renamed the *Missouri Queen*. I bought it from the Iowa Power Company in 1974 and spent two years trying to find someone to bring it upriver to St. Paul for me. When I couldn't find anyone willing to make the trip, I decided to put a crew together and go pick up the *Missouri Queen* myself. When I learned that insurance on the boat while I moved it would cost me $15,000, I took a chance and decided to move it without a dime's worth of coverage.

I left Sioux City on November 16, 1976, on the first leg of our long journey to the *Missouri Queen*'s new home in St. Paul. Since Lake Pepin is the first part of the

Mississippi to freeze, usually around mid-December, I figured we still had a good month to make the trip upriver through the lake and into St. Paul. My brother Dick came down from Fairbanks, Alaska, to help me, and we were joined by pilots Dick Lynn and Keith Keller and crewman Jack Cox, all from Kansas City. The *Queen* would not make the trip under her own power; she had steam engines but no boiler. Instead I planned to push her down the Missouri and up the Mississippi with the *Rosie Bee,* a little diesel towboat.

My friend Rosie Schumacher, a towboat owner from Savage, Minnesota, leased the *Rosie Bee* to me. We got her to Sioux City through a series of roundabout connections. Jim Dye of Dakota Barge Services put the *Rosie Bee* on a tow that he was sending to Joliet, Illinois. Jim dropped her off at Grafton, Illinois, near the mouth of the Missouri. From there, the little towboat cruised up the Missouri for her job with me on the *Missouri Queen.* It was hard going. Sometimes she made only two and a half miles an hour against that strong Missouri River current. The *Rosie Bee* even hitched a ride alongside a larger towboat, the *R. H. Huffman,* between St. Joseph, Missouri, and Omaha, Nebraska.

St. Paul needed a good riverfront restaurant. This architectural rendering depicts the one I hoped to build out of the Missouri Queen. *As it turned out, my idea was ahead of its time in the mid-1970s.*

We found the *Missouri Queen* high and dry in the sand and mud. Using the *Rosie Bee*, it took us two days to flush out the sand from underneath the *Queen* and get her afloat. With the help of Whitey Burnett—the hydraulics expert from Dubuque Boat and Boiler Works, who by then had retired in Panama City, Florida—I devised a unique steering setup using electro-solenoids connected to the hydraulic system of the *Rosie Bee*. That way I could do all of the steering with a solenoid from the bridge of the *Missouri Queen*. The steering handle of the solenoid was only two and a half inches long. To control the throttles, I shouted my orders through a $9.95 Radio Shack intercom to the helmsman of the *Rosie Bee*, who then worked the throttles manually. The wires for the intercom were about 240 feet long and took so much amperage that we had to replace the batteries on the hour.

The *Missouri Queen*, pushed along by the *Rosie Bee*, departed Sioux City and moved down the Missouri at nine miles an hour. The tall superstructure of the *Queen* proved to be a big problem in the high winds of November. The boat swung from side to side in the channel while we struggled to keep her on course. We slid under bridges sideways and, at one point, scraped the riverbank. At Boonville in central Missouri, the *Rosie Bee* sheared two pins in her steering rudders in a blinding snowstorm. When that happened we were heading right for two bridges. Amazingly,

we missed the pillars and passed safely under the bridges.

It took us ten days to make the trip from Sioux City to the Mississippi at St. Louis, Missouri—a distance of 732 miles. When I got to the mouth of the Missouri, a guy called me on the radio. "*Rosie Bee*, are you that boat pushing that big old paddle-wheel boat? Where did you come from, St. Charles?" St. Charles was only fourteen miles upstream.

"No," I replied. "I came from Sioux City." There was a long silence.

"I'll be damned," the guy said. "If any of those Missouri River pilots ever tell me again about how tough that river is, I'm going to tell them what I just seen."

The Missouri River *is* a terrible river to run, because of its seven-mile-per-hour current. Boats built for the Missouri and the Lower Mississippi need three times the horsepower of boats that run in the pool waters above St. Louis—10,000 horsepower compared to 2,500 to 3,000 horsepower. It was smooth sailing at 5.3 miles per hour when we started up the Mississippi. We soon said good-bye to the Missouri River crew and hello to two new crew members: Wally Snyder, our company's operations manager, and Jim Frisbee. Then, at the mouth of the Illinois River, while we were trying to make a landing for the night, a fire broke out in the engine room of the *Rosie Bee*. A hydraulic line had broken, which spewed oil on the hot exhaust, which burst into flames. The crew put out the fire, replaced the hydraulic line, and resupplied the oil, and we were under way in the morning.

Near Louisiana, Missouri—about twenty miles south of Hannibal—we came upon a railroad swing bridge. I signaled the tender to open it and let us pass under but he ignored me. I signaled again. I could hardly control the *Missouri Queen* while pushing her, but he didn't give a damn. He was more concerned with the workmen who were on his bridge than with me and what I was facing while I pushed the massive boat with the little tow in that rapid current. At the last minute he opened the bridge and we safely passed under it. About a mile later we developed a mechanical problem, so I pulled into shore. Still steaming, I marched toward the town along the railroad tracks, and when I came to the bridge I strode into the tender's office and said to him, "You son of a bitch, I should knock the *shit* out of you!" The guy was petrified, just petrified. He was a lot bigger than I was, but I never took that into consideration. Believe me, when I was in the paratroopers, we would walk down the street and defy anyone to even *try* to touch us. That training in how to fight never left me.

Because winter was closing in on us, I decided to run around the clock. We went through Lock 19 at Keokuk, Iowa, on

December 1. Then, all night long, we battled ice around the Nauvoo Bend. By dawn our tow was stranded in the ice with one engine down. We had made only ten miles in thirty-six hours. I called for help and the towboat *Mr. Aldo* of Alter River Towing Company responded. They got the *Missouri Queen* and the *Rosie Bee* free and back downstream on the bank at the Nauvoo Upper Light, Mile 377.3.

We could not leave the boats there, but no matter what we did, we could not get the starboard engine of the *Rosie Bee* restarted. She probably had a frozen fuel line. Both boats became iced in again. I checked on weather reports on the river above Lock 19 and they were discouraging. Winter had arrived. All I could do was to try to get the boats back downriver to Keokuk and leave them there until spring.

With the help of a towboat called the *Yetta Alter*, which broke the ice around the two boats, we got them off the bank and back into the main channel of the river. Then the *Yetta Alter* headed downstream to trade tows with the *Beverly Ann* above Lock 19. My plan was to follow the *Yetta* as she broke the ice in the river, and I spent hours in the dead of night searching for her trail back to Lock 19, a distance of only twelve miles. The trails of three other tows that had passed us that day had frozen solid. You cannot tell the difference between a fresh trail and an old one, as they all look alike. But we found our way, and on just one engine, the *Rosie Bee* cleared the Keokuk lock and landed at Tom Edwards' Iowa Marine Repair basin just below the Coast Guard station. I left both there for the winter.

When spring came we returned to Keokuk to launch our boats for the remainder of their journey up to St. Paul. When we got there, we found that the *Rosie Bee* had sunk at the dock. The packing on the boat's outboard drives had dried up. The guy at the marina pumped her out and got her floating again, and we found that there was not too much damage. The *Rosie Bee* had three engines, so we plundered her middle engine for parts. One of the two remaining engines blew near Clinton, Iowa.

It's typical of the river that you can expect trouble, mechanical or otherwise. You just have to be geared for it. We pulled into a dock where a mechanic removed the blown engine and repaired it for $1,500, a reasonable price. The mechanic's son admired the barrel stove on the *Missouri Queen*. Since I had two of those stoves on board, I gave him one.

Several friends had asked to join us on the trip up the river that spring. One of them arranged to be picked up at Guttenberg, Iowa, at a spot that was owned by a restaurant-owner friend of his. I did not understand the relationship or that docking at this particular place was something of a

The **Missouri Queen** *and the towboat* **Rosie Bee** *in 1976. The* **Missouri Queen** *was stuck in the mud at Sioux City, Iowa, on the Missouri River. It took a couple of days to dig it out with the* **Rosie Bee.**

privilege. We were coming in to pick up my friend when the guy who owned the restaurant got on the radio and began telling me how to do it. "You run your restaurant," I spat at him, "and I'll run this boat!"

"But this is *my* property," he protested.

"I don't give a damn if it is!" I shouted. And I didn't. Getting my boat up to St. Paul was making me testy.

The other passenger-helper we had on board was a minister who had a fifth of vodka with him. On board he found the bestseller *Fear of Flying* by Erica Jong. One night he was reading the graphic descriptions of her sexual conquests and every few minutes he would say, "Oh my God, I can't believe it," and take a sip of vodka. The next thing I knew he went to refuel our gasoline generator. He had a Coleman lantern in one hand and an open gasoline can in the other and everything blew. The minister landed flat on his back, his clothes on fire. When he fell his hand happened to land on a fire extinguisher. He picked it up, doused his clothes, and put out the fire on the deck. About twenty minutes later he appeared in the pilothouse. "We had a little problem," he said. I looked at his face and both of his eyebrows were burned off.

The minister had turned off the generator before attempting to refuel it, leaving me without a spotlight in the middle of the night. I had to cut the engine and let the boat just sit there until daylight. When we got into La Crosse, Wisconsin, we really chewed him out.

The last problem we faced getting the *Missouri Queen* up to St. Paul happened because I was bored sitting in the pilot-house and thought I would play a trick on the crew member steering the *Rosie Bee.* We were going upriver when I saw this red buoy outside of the channel on our left instead of where it was supposed to be on our right. I got on the radio to the *Rosie Bee.* "It looks to me like there is a nice red oil can floating down the river," I told the crew member. "I'll steer close to it and you see if you can't reach out and grab it."

I thought he would radio back that it wasn't a gas can, but instead he panicked and thought we were on the wrong side of the channel. He throttled back hard, and the *Missouri Queen* caught a little wind and swung around toward shore. We found ourselves behind a wing dam. I maneuvered the boat into a tight U-turn and was about to get back into the channel when the *Rosie Bee,* which had a deeper draft than the *Missouri Queen,* caught on the end of the wing dam. We could hear the keel rattling against the gravel. Our boats were now almost crosswise to the river. I tried and tried to get us out, but without success. I finally asked Dick Lynn, a river pilot who was on board, to see what he could do. I had gotten the *Missouri Queen* this close to home without damage, and I sure as hell didn't want to damage her or the *Rosie Bee*. Lynn put a few nicks in our propellers, but he finally got us out of there.

When at last we reached St. Paul, I renamed the *Missouri Queen* the *Governor Ramsey*, after Alexander Ramsey, the first territorial governor of Minnesota. The trip was one of the greatest achievements of my life, because so many people said it couldn't be done, and one of the greatest adventures. The story was written up in *Waterways Journal* and became a legend on the river. As it turned out, however, my

plan to build a fancy restaurant in it was ahead of its time. Restaurant owners whom I approached for a joint project would not grab hold of it.

This was at a time when river gambling was coming back into vogue, and people were looking for big boats. I sold the *Governor Ramsey*, with all of its beautiful chairs and rolls of fine carpet, in 1983 to a guy in Memphis named Bill "Bo" Williamson for just about what I had in it, which was $250,000. I was in St. Francisville, Louisiana, when Williamson died,

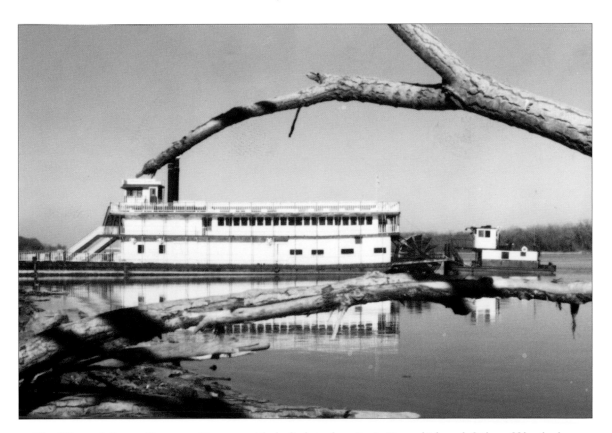

The Missouri Queen/Governor Ramsey *with the little towboat* Rosie Bee, *which pushed the paddle wheeler on her hair-raising trip down the Missouri River and her 650-mile trek up the Mississippi to St. Paul.*

Ol' Man RIVER

The newly named **Governor Ramsey** *as it looked when it arrived in St. Paul in the spring of 1977.*

still owing me $125,000. I got a call from his attorney, who said if I could be in Little Rock the next morning he would give me a check for the money. What it boiled down to is that he did not want anyone to know he was giving me the check. I flew to Shreveport, Louisiana, and then drove to Little Rock. I did not even meet the attorney in his office. We met in the parking lot of his firm. That was the end of the *Governor Ramsey.* I think it wound up as a piece of junk in Little Rock.

THE SHANTYBOAT

I continued to have restaurants on my mind. In 1983, I bought a barge from a

friend in Little Rock and decided to have the hull replated on the spot. We turned it over in the river, floated it upside down, and plated the entire hull with quarter-inch steel plates. When we got it to St. Paul, we built a whole double-deck superstructure on the 128-foot hull, modeling it after a replica of a two-level U.S. Army Corps of Engineers quarterboat. (A quarterboat served as the living quarters for the Corps' engineers while they worked on the rivers at remote locations during the 1900s.) I decorated the interior with splendid brass lamps, white oak wainscoting and ceilings, and many oil portraits of historic river people that I commissioned by Ken Fox. It became the restaurant and catering kitchen that we called the *Shantyboat*. It served wonderful catfish dinners.

In October 1992, a towboat named the *Tiger* pushed the *Shantyboat* restaurant barge, lashed together with our four riverboats—the *Jonathon Padelford*, the *Josiah Snelling*, the *Anson Northrup*, and the *Betsey Northrup*—840 miles down the Mississippi River and 470 miles up the Ohio River to Cincinnati to participate in the Tall Stacks Festival. The five-day celebration drew more than one million people, and the *Shantyboat*—along with a similar catering facility—prepared seventy-seven thousand meals that were served on participating excursion boats. The trip took twelve days to get to Cincinnati and fourteen days to get back to St. Paul. We arrived home in an early November blizzard.

THE *AMERICA*

I was visiting my friend Johnny Nichols in Greenville, Mississippi, in 1988 when he showed me the 184-foot-long towboat *America*. The *America* and the *United States* were the largest towboats built up to that

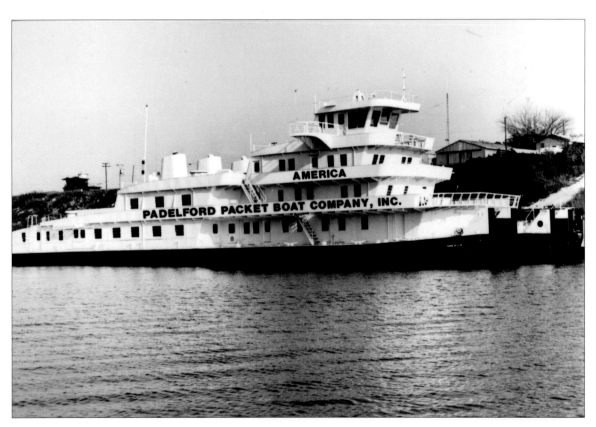

The America *was one of the first 10,000-horsepower towboats to be built. I hoped to turn the* America *into a floating restaurant on the Harriet Island riverfront, but never got her up to St. Paul.*

time and the first 10,000-horsepower boats, each with four engines. Instead of being powerful, however, the boats were really inefficient. The engines couldn't be placed far enough apart and they were cavitating—creating a vacuum in the water. Because of the cavitation, the boats just did not have the push required for a towboat, and they had not been in use for several years.

Thinking the *America* would make a great floating restaurant, I bought it from Johnny and told him he could have the four engines if he would take them out. He did, and he still has those engines twenty-five years later. As it turned out, I owned the *America* for a couple of years, but never did get her up to St. Paul. I sold her in 1990.

Dining aboard the Padelford Company vessels is a traditional mainstay of the business. Whether meals are served on daily excursions or catered for weddings and other special events, the passengers enjoy terrific food on the boats.

I hired the Tiger *of Dubuque, Iowa, to push the four Padelford Company boats 1,300 miles to the 1992 Cincinnati Tall Stacks Festival and back to save wear and tear on the boats. My Airstream motor home, the* Captain's Gig, *and the* Captain's Super Boat *ride along on the barge. We needed the smaller boats for mobility in Cincinnati.*

11
SOLO VOYAGE to NEW ORLEANS

SINCE MAY 20, 1927, when Charles A. Lindbergh climbed aboard the *Spirit of St. Louis* and flew the first nonstop solo flight across the Atlantic, other Minnesotans have dreamed and dared to do the impossible. Just eight months before Gerry Spiess began his solo voyage across the Atlantic in 1979, fellow Minnesotan Bill Bowell boarded the *Charles A.* in St. Paul and headed alone down the Mississippi for New Orleans. His aluminum rowboat was just one foot, eight inches longer than Spiess's ten-foot-long *Yankee Girl.* Lindbergh was twenty-five years old at the time of his historic voyage, traveling 3,600 miles in thirty-three and a half hours. Spiess was thirty-nine, crossing 3,800 miles in fifty-four days. Bill was fifty-seven when he motored 2,350 miles downriver in a record eleven days.

PLANNING the TRIP

Invariably in the fall, when the pressure of the summer excursion season would begin to ease, I felt the urge to get away. I would look out the window at the river flowing past my office and think how great it would be to go out alone in a row-boat and, like a leaf or a log, drift down to New Orleans. Late in 1978 I was thinking my getaway thoughts in my office and must have said something out loud because suddenly, from her office, my secretary, Carole Bernin, called out, "Well, why don't you do it?"

Carole's remark got me thinking. Why *didn't* I do it instead of just dreaming about it? I could make the trip in my eleven-foot, eight-inch, 1951 Alumacraft rowboat. I wasn't crazy about rowing all the way—besides, rowing would take forever—but I could install a 20-horsepower Mercury outboard motor in the boat. With an eighteen-gallon tank to hold extra gas, I would make it between towns. I could take along a six-gallon gas can in case I had to walk someplace to find fuel. And so I began to plan my trip.

I was flabbergasted at how complicated everything got. The first step was to take my boat to Hallberg Marine in Wyoming, Minnesota, to install the motor. When they heard I was planning to go to New Orleans, they wanted to put an aluminum cap on the bow that would keep the water out. But the bow was where I planned to put the gas tank, and with the cap on, it would be hard to get it in and out. I decided to go with a canvas cover.

With the motor installed, I towed the boat to J & J canvas makers in St. Paul to have a cover made for it to keep out rain (or snow) and limit the amount of water that might come on board from the wakes of passing tows. I designed the cover and the top man at J & J made it for me. It was something of a convertible top for the boat, with curtains that could be removed individually. The top, which was just wide

enough to cover the console, folded down for fair weather. There were zippers in strategic places to make it easy to reach the gas tank and other gear.

When the cover was finished I took the boat home to Stillwater, where I kept a running list of all the things I needed to buy for the trip. Every day I would think of something else. I knew I would need earmuffs, a Stearns jacket (which looks like a regular jacket but has a built-in life preserver), a couple of Thermos bottles (one for coffee and one for drinking water), waterproof bags, a portable spotlight, required Coast Guard gear, marine

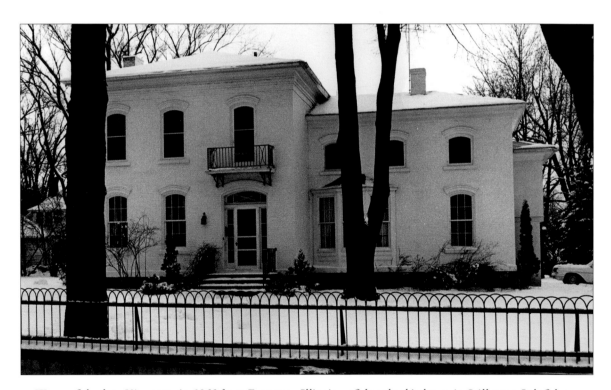

We moved back to Minnesota in 1960 from Evanston, Illinois, and bought this house in Stillwater. It had been built by lumber baron David Tozer in the 1870s. We built a tennis court in the back yard.

radio and antenna, tape recorder, a chain and lock to button up the boat at night, the manual for the motor, bailing jug, first aid kit, camera equipment, a knife, tools, battery gauge, sleeping bag, tent, food, and a list of the names and phone numbers of people I knew on the river. The day before my departure I loaded the boat on the trailer in the driveway at home and it looked pretty full. Then Lillian went out and bought more food.

On the morning of October 17, I still had some errands left to run. By the time we got to Gordy Miller's Harriet Island ramp, it was eleven o'clock. Then I had to run to the bank for some cash. When I got back it was time to launch the boat, named the

Charles A. in recognition of Lindbergh's solo flight across the Atlantic. Wally Snyder, my operations manager, and Carole and Lillian watched as I backed the trailer into the water. The loaded boat settled in the river and kept going down until water lapped at the gunwales. I thought the damned thing might sink.

With a sheepish smile, I announced the obvious—that the boat was overloaded. If I were going to go to New Orleans in a row-boat, I would have to travel light. I began throwing things out of the boat and up onto the dock. Out went the sleeping bag, the tent, loads of food, the ice cooler. I put my toothbrush in one hip pocket and a flashlight in the other. I still had a few luxuries with me—my pipe and tobacco and a pocket full of credit cards.

"I'll rough it," I said, and shoved off.

FROM ST. PAUL to WABASHA

The first mile and a half taught me a painful lesson about the river: A wind from the south makes the going miserable in a small boat. Blowing against the current, the wind produces a chop that is bone-jolting. I seriously wondered if my fifty-seven-year-old back and kidneys could survive the pounding. I banged down the river, going under the Inver Grove Bridge, past Pine Bend and Grey Cloud Island, and into the graveyard of tree stumps above Lock 2 at Hastings.

I called the lock on my radio. "WZD4614, the *Charles A.*, to Lock 2."

"Lock 2, back to the *Charles A.* Where are you? Upbound or downbound?"

"I am just above you, in a rather small boat."

"Lock 2 back to the *Charles A.* I can't see you, but I think I see the tip of your antenna above the gate. Stand by—the water's up. We'll open the gate."

The *Charles A.* entered the lock to the stares of the personnel standing on the wall. They were wondering what a VHF radio was doing aboard such a little craft. I held onto the lock drop line with one hand and stuck a foot out of the boat against the wall to steady myself as the water level dropped. When the gates opened, I putt-putted out of the lock and into the river below Hastings. Fortunately, bluffs close to the shoreline reduced the force of the wind, making for a smoother ride. My speed was about twenty-five miles an hour.

At Lock 3 at Red Wing, I was held up for an hour while I waited for a tow ahead of me. Then I buzzed on through Lake Pepin, a twenty-five-mile stretch of the river where I was tormented again with backbreaking chop. About halfway through the lake, I seriously wondered whether the big gas tank at the bow might pound itself right down through the boat. Slackening my speed I followed the lee shore, which was on the Minnesota side, reluctantly jouncing past Lake City and the promise of a warm motel room. My goal was to reach Wabasha at the foot of Lake Pepin, where friends Sharon and Jim Elliot owned the Wabasha Marina. They had no idea I was making this crazy trip. Sharon answered my radio call. I tried to disguise my voice, but she said, "Hi, Bill. What are you driving on the river this time?"

Sharon's question took me back to an earlier stop I had made at their marina, when I took the *Tiger Lily*, my River Queen houseboat, on a trip downriver with my brother Jack's son, Stephen. (*Tiger* was for me and *Lily* was for Lillian.) The River Queens were some of the finest houseboats on the Mississippi at that time. At fifty-two feet mine was the largest built. With its twin inboard-outboard engines it was a gas hog, but it was a nice boat to live aboard or take a vacation on.

Stephen and I stopped at Wabasha Marina to get gas from Sharon and Jim. I pulled into their dock, and while Stephen jumped out to tie up the lines, I went into the bathroom to wash my hands. I was wearing a two-carat diamond ring that I took off to wash my hands. The ring slipped out of my hands, rolled around the sink, and disappeared down the drain. I looked under the sink and found that the drain went straight down to the river. Horrified, I hollered to Stephen to mark the boat's position on the dock.

The ring was practically a family heirloom. I had gotten it back in my days at Edwards and Deutsch, from one of the catalogs we published. Sol Abrahamson, one of the catalog members from Shreveport, Louisiana, sold me the ring for a minimal amount of money. It was set with three square-cut stones and two smaller stones on the side. The larger stones were examples of perfect color—along with cut, clarity, and carat, one of the 4 C's of diamond grading—and I used them when demonstrating that grading during lectures I gave on gems to the catalog group. (I had read quite a bit on gemstones, and even thought of going to Los Angeles for a course in gemology, but I never did.)

I had to mark where the ring was on the bottom of the river. I found a half-inch box wrench, tied a piece of string to it, and dropped it down the sink until it hit bottom, about nine feet. I stripped to my shorts and dove overboard, but I could not stand the pressure on my ears as I tried to get to the wrench. I made several attempts, even dropping an anchor line over the side so I could use it to pull myself down, but I couldn't get deeper than five or six feet.

I remembered my friend Robbie Murray, a legend in Stillwater. He flew airplanes, went skydiving, and did underwater diving. The guy was fearless, so I called him and in no time he was in Wabasha to help me. I explained to Robbie that he should find the ring under the wrench that was tied to the string I had dropped from the sink. He dove overboard, and in less than thirty seconds was back up with a triumphant grin on his face and the diamond ring in his teeth. I tried to pay him for a job well done, but he refused. A few years later I had the diamonds reset in rings for Shelley and Beth, my daughters, and Sandra, my daughter-in-law.

Anyway, I don't know what the Elliots were expecting when I called them on my radio on this voyage, but Jim's eyes, which

o'clock, I got through most of the next few locks without a wait. Thinking I could improve my time, I decided to cut across some of the wing dams to shorten the distance. I sailed right over the first ones, and just when I was feeling confident about taking the shortcuts, I hit a wing dam with a big bang. I got the boat into shore immediately and found that I had wrecked the prop. I had also knocked a chunk off the skeg of the motor (a piece of the casting) and started worrying that I might have bent the shaft. Fortunately, I had a new prop with me and was able to replace the damaged one without too much difficulty.

Instead of gaining time, of course, I had lost several hours, and it was growing dark by the time I arrived at Lock 9 at Lynxville, Wisconsin. To my dismay a big double tow was laboriously going through the lock, so I had to wait for an hour before I could enter. When the lower gate finally released me, I opened the throttle and roared toward McGregor, Iowa, fourteen miles downriver. I wanted to reach the town before dark because the boat had no running lights. (I hadn't planned to run at night, so I didn't equip the boat with them.) But the buoys became increasingly more difficult to spot, and when pitch darkness fell upon me, I had to run the river as they did in Mark Twain's day—by hit or miss.

As I strained to see, I felt something wet around my ankles. Reaching down, my

are big anyway, grew wider than usual when he saw my rowboat. Neither he nor Sharon could believe I was serious about going all the way to New Orleans in it. I had a big steak dinner and a delightful evening with these two long-time river people. I had logged eighty miles that first day. Only 1,623 more to go.

FROM WABASHA to KEOKUK

The weather the next day was fair, and after getting under way at about ten hand plunged into water. No wonder the boat was feeling sluggish; it was filling with water. I was sure I had holed the boat on the wing dam or some of the rivets had popped loose. Afraid the boat was going to sink, I headed to shore near Island 63 just below Harper's Slough and grabbed a low-hanging branch, holding on while bailing water like mad with my two-pound coffee can. Then I sat quietly on my seat and waited. The boat wasn't taking on water. I figured that, in the dark, I must have picked up a mass of weeds that had wrapped itself around the engine's lower unit above the prop and acted as a scoop, bringing water over the transom. I had not realized what was happening as I was concentrating on the blackness ahead of the boat.

I continued to gingerly steer my way in the darkness. I knew that, once around Old Town Bend and below Harper's Slough, the channel follows the Iowa shore all the way to the dimly lit river town of McGregor, a distance of eight miles. In McGregor were my friends John and Ruth Bickel, who lived in a hotel—a former brothel for rivermen—that they had restored. Cold, wet, and weary, I trudged to their door and rang the bell. Inside, John and Ruth were having cocktails with their friends J. O. and Mildred Ward and Harold Ward and his wife, Minnie. I joined them for drinks and dinner and later slept in one of the rooms of the old hotel, drifting off to sleep amid the ghostly bed squeaks of long ago.

I filled my gas tanks at Myers Marina and was back on the river by eight the next morning. At Lock 10 in Guttenberg, Iowa, I met the *Colonel George Lambert* going upriver—a beautiful towboat built at Twin City Barge and Towing by Jack Lambert, who claimed to be a descendant of George Lambert, for whom Lambert's Landing in St. Paul is named. I stopped for lunch in Dubuque with old riverboat captain friends Eldon Newdt, Art Bull, and Bob Kehl.

At Lock 12 along the Iowa shore near Bellevue, an upbound tow was about to lock through, so I tied up alongside the wall to wait. While I sat there my radio crackled into life. The towboat *Cooperative Venture*, owned by Alter Towing Company, was calling me. They too were waiting to go through the lock, said the captain, but they had a problem. Their radioman was standing on the wall of the lock, waiting to come back aboard the towboat with equipment he had taken in to town to be repaired. Would I be willing to pick up the fellow and run him out to the *Cooperative Venture*?

Glad to help, I ran my boat over to where the radioman was standing. When I saw the amount of equipment he had, however, I realized it would swamp my small boat. The solution was to unload my gear into a pile on the wall, take the radioman and his equipment onboard, run him out to the *Cooperative Venture*, and return for my gear.

Ol' Man RIVER

The crew of the big towboat rewarded me with a tour. By the time I got my own gear loaded back up, it was time for me to go through the lock.

When I came into the Clinton Pool at Lock 13, there was that damned south wind again, making the waves hit the bottom of the *Charles A.* and boom like a Chinese gong. To go full speed I practically had to put my elbows on my knees and hold my butt off the seat. Otherwise I got a whack that jarred my whole body. By the time I reached Clinton, Iowa, every bone in my body ached. I parked the boat in a slip in the marina, filled up with gas, and got a ride with some fellows to the Travelodge. The next morning I asked the woman at the motel desk to call me a cab to take me back to the marina. "We don't have a cab in Clinton anymore," she replied. "The one we used to have was lousy, and now they won't even answer the phone. As far as we know, there aren't any cabs."

I couldn't believe it. I had planned to get an early start. Instead, I had to hitchhike down the road, lugging my marine radio, camera, and heavy gear. Fortunately, a guy picked me up and took me all the way to the marina.

I wasn't going very far very fast. Going through the locks chewed up great chunks of time as I often had to wait in line more than an hour. My speed on the river seldom topped twenty-five miles an hour. I took the curtains off the boat in hopes that the southwest breeze would blow through and increase my speed, but it did not seem to help. My rough ride through the Nauvoo Bend near Keokuk, Iowa, reminded me of when I had stalled in the ice with the *Rosie Bee* and the *Governor Ramsey.*

Holding my knees so long in one position made them painfully stiff. I tried to stretch one knee at a time, particularly my right knee, which has always been weak. Every muscle hurt as I climbed in and out of the boat throughout the voyage. At some locks I climbed onto the wall to watch towboats locking through. By the time this trip is over, I told myself, either I will be in good physical condition or a complete wreck.

As the sun went down, I motored across the pool at Keokuk and came up on the city just as its lights were blinking on. To get down to the marina I had to go through the Keokuk lock, the largest lock on the Mississippi, which turned out to be fairly easy. All I had to do was wrap a line around the bollard and hang on as the bollard floated down the wall of the lock. By the time I got out of the lock, it was pitch dark. I felt my way along the shore about a quarter of a mile and pulled into a small marina. Happily, someone was there to help me in. I closed up the boat, got my gear together, and, this time, remembered to bring my Thermos bottle. (I had forgotten it the day before and had to go all day without coffee—a fairly serious predicament for me.) I walked about eight blocks to the Holiday Inn, where I checked in. It was after seven o'clock and I had been going since seven-thirty that morning. I had traveled from Mile 510 to 364, about 155 miles, putting me 220 miles from St. Louis. It was my best day yet, but I was absolutely beat.

FROM KEOKUK to MEMPHIS

The weather the next day was beautiful, as was the scenery. The fall colors were absolutely gorgeous. I had a south wind at first, but then it veered off, the chop died down, and I made great time down to Lock 21 at Quincy, Illinois. When I saw that there was one double tow in the lock and another double tow approaching, I drove like mad to get down to the lock ahead of him. The lockmaster did not see me and I could not raise him on the radio, so I landed the boat and walked up onto the bank to talk with him. He agreed to lock me between the two double tows, which saved me a lot of time. My little boat attracted a lot of attention from people watching bigger boats pass through the locks and from folks aboard cruisers on the river. People seemed to be interested in my trip, and everyone, almost without exception, said they wished they were making the trip themselves.

One morning as I was making breakfast on the boat, I discovered that an animal had eaten a hole through the lid of the coffee can where I kept my cereal. When I checked the rest of my supplies, I found that some of my apples had also been eaten. The tooth marks were not those of a little mouse. I worried for a time that I might put my hand into one of the food bags and get nipped by the rat, or whatever rodent was onboard, before it abandoned ship.

Sailing past St. Louis, I took a picture of the Eads Bridge and the Eero Saarinan Arch, and pulled in for lunch at the *Robert E. Lee* docked along the levee. I had gone about only fifteen miles farther downriver when I came to little Kimswick, Missouri. I had heard from friends on the *River Queen* about a little place called Hoppy's Landing that was a good place to stop. Although it was only 2:30 in the afternoon, I was feeling exhausted. "To heck with it," I said to myself. "I'm not going any farther today."

I ended up staying there two hours, watching owners pull their boats out of the water. The *River Queen* pulled up and I joined my friends for the cocktail hour. Then the wife of the owner of Hoppy's told me I could get a motel room about three miles away and that they would be happy to take me there. So I had them pull my boat out of the water. When I looked it over I saw that I had some water in the gear casing. This was not a good sign. I refilled the casings with grease and made a mental note to check it again in a couple of days to see if I was losing grease. If I was, it would mean that, when the prop hit the wing dam after I left Wabasha, the shaft might have been bent. That would have damaged the seals, causing them to leak.

As we rode to the motel, I felt exhausted. Perhaps I had pushed too hard. Yet I had made very few miles, experiencing my worst mileage day. I was now about 160 miles above Cairo, Illinois. From now on, I would have to check frequently for sources of gasoline. Marinas are far apart downriver, and the Mississippi is lined with big levees, where a person might walk for miles trying to find fuel. I wanted to avoid that problem.

The next day I made better time despite meeting a lot of towboats. The only problem with them was that I had to slow down to let their wakes pass me. There were so many towboats that I made a list of them. At one point I went on Channel 13 and said, "WZD4614, the *Charles A.* twelve-foot skiff, has just survived the wakes of the *Ray A. Eckstein* and the *Dixie Power* and is proceeding on downriver toward New Orleans." One of the captains came on the radio and was laughing about my trials, as was I. I reached the mouth of the Ohio River around four o'clock and kept going until I got to Mile 922 on the Lower Mississippi at Hickman, Kentucky. Keep in mind that the Upper Mississippi *begins* at the mouth of the Ohio River and the Lower Mississippi *ends* there. The upper

river begins at Mile 0 and travels north to Mile 857.6 at Minneapolis. The lower river begins at Mile 0 at Pilot Town, Louisiana, ninety-five miles south of New Orleans, and travels north to Mile 953.8 just below Cairo, Illinois.

The following day I made it all the way to Memphis, Tennessee, getting in about 5:30. My friend Tom Meanly was there, working on the *Memphis Queen*, his new excursion boat, and he was amazed to see me motor up in my little skiff. When I pulled it in and tied it between the old *Memphis Queen* and the new *Memphis Queen*, I greeted Tom and accepted his invitation to stay the night on his cruiser. The next morning I checked the lubricant in my boat's lower unit and it was all right; there wasn't any water coming out of it. I thought about putting new spark plugs in but that was complicated, so I figured to hell with it. Instead, I went over to the boat store and bought three cans of pipe tobacco and a case of outboard motor oil and took off.

FROM MEMPHIS to NEW ORLEANS

When I got out on the river, a miserable wind caused a terrific chop, the same kind of pounding waves I had faced when I began my downriver leg. I kept plugging away, following the river as it meandered below Memphis, buffeted by the wind. One minute you've got the breeze one way and the next minute you've got it another.

SOLO VOYAGE to NEW ORLEANS

When the wind would smooth out, I made decent time. At two that afternoon, I arrived at the harbor of Helena, Arkansas. Outside the harbor were the damnedest big rolling waves—something a twelve-foot boat had no business being in.

The marina at Helena had nothing but gas for sale. I had eaten breakfast, but nothing but a piece of cheese and a Bit-O-Honey bar since then. When I ate the candy bar, I reminded myself to be careful or I'd crack a tooth. No sooner did I have the thought than I bit down, a tooth cracked, and I spit out a piece of porcelain. I resolved not to eat any more of those candy bars, but I did, of course.

I had come only seventy-five miles from Memphis and I hated to stop. So I decided to go ahead, chop or no chop. I reached the mouth of the Arkansas River, Mile 582.2, at dusk and began looking for lights. Nothing. I went upriver on the Arkansas and could barely see where I was going. I finally found a spot to tie up to between some pilings. I wanted to fasten the boat securely while I was asleep so that it wouldn't drift down into the wide-open Mississippi with all those towboats. On the other hand, I wanted to be able to release the boat in a hurry if, for some reason, I had to get out of there. I reached down into my food locker and all I could find was a chunk of cheese and a quart of scotch. I ate the cheese, drank the scotch, put up the curtains, and tried to figure out

how I could lie down in the boat to get some sleep. I arranged the paddle to straddle the two seats, then put my head back on my life preserver and my butt on the rear seat. I not only survived the night in the boat, I actually slept for twelve hours straight.

The next morning was so foggy that towboats had pulled over to shore to wait until it lifted, but I kept going. As the day wore on, the weather improved, and I got to Greenville, Mississippi, about 10:30 in the morning. I put in new spark plugs and went on to Vicksburg and Natchez, Mississippi. I kept at it because I wanted to get to New Orleans before one o'clock on Saturday. That would make it eleven days from the time I left St. Paul.

I couldn't believe the harbor at Baton Rouge. It was overwhelming. The ocean-going port was filled with huge ships that made tremendous wakes. At first I couldn't find a place to tie up, but then I got the bright idea of pulling the boat out of the water and right up onto the dock, which I did with the help of some people there.

The last day of my solo voyage down the Mississippi covered a stretch of the river filled with these big ships. Just as I was coming into New Orleans, the Coast Guard stopped me and told me the river was closed to outside traffic for a few miles for a race between the *Mississippi Queen* and the *Natchez*. I had to pull over and wait until the race was finished. I sat there for two hours even though the best part of the race lasted for only a few minutes. There went my hope of getting in before one o'clock! As it was, I tied up in New Orleans alongside the winning boat, the *Natchez*, at about 2:30.

I had made the 1,698-mile trip in eleven days, which I believe is some kind of a record for boats under twelve feet. I flew home, and Lillian and I drove back to New Orleans to pick up the *Charles A.* and tow it back to St. Paul. My urge to "get away" had been more than satisfied.

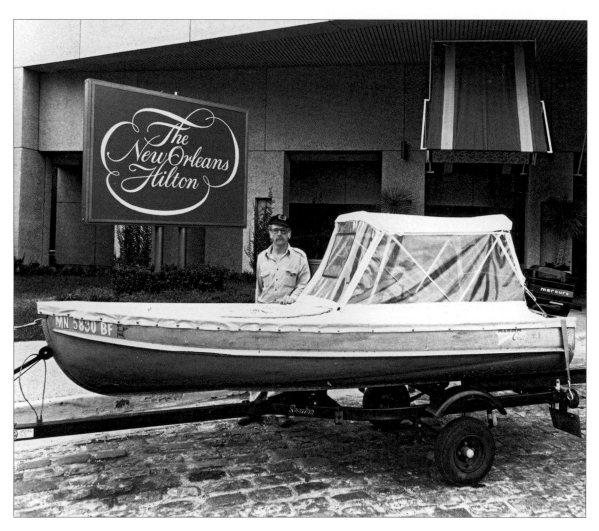

The Charles A. *and her skipper as I prepare to trailer the boat back to St. Paul after my solo trip down the Mississippi River in 1978. I purposely stayed at this posh hotel, carrying my luggage in transparent plastic bags. I wanted to emulate John Steinbeck in* Travels with Charlie, *when he raises eyebrows by pulling up to Chicago's swankiest hotel with his camper in tow.*

12
EXPANDING the FLEET

I CONTINUED TO BUY, sell, build, and renovate boats to keep up with the changing needs of the company. I was always buying barges. I bought the first one back in 1974, if I remember right, for office space. It was for sale on the river at Muscatine, Iowa. I drove down there, took a stroll around the barge—which had an office already built on it—and wrote the guy a check for $12,000 on the spot. It was a hell of a buy. We had it towed up to St. Paul, did a lot of renovation on it, and used it for several years as our office. In the early 1980s I bought another barge for storage space and to house our maintenance operations.

THE *VIKING EXPLORER*

My friend Jack Trotter of Little Rock, Arkansas—the owner of the *Border Star*, which I captained while getting my hundred-ton pilot's license—owned another boat, called the *Arkansas Explorer*. The *Arkansas Explorer* was not a paddleboat but an elegant, 110-foot oceangoing yacht with twenty-four staterooms. In the spring of 1980, when I heard that Jack was selling the *Arkansas Explorer*, I bought it for

$550,000 (even though its condition was a mess) and renamed it the *Viking Explorer*. I took possession of the mini-cruiseliner in New Orleans, and, to bring it home to St. Paul, started sailing it up a section of the Mississippi that was confusing territory for me. Oceangoing ships steaming at twenty miles an hour charged up and down the river between Baton Rogue and New Orleans. I had traveled that stretch in the tiny *Charles A.*, but that experience did not prepare me for navigating those waters in a larger craft.

For crew I had friends Chris Matson and his older brother, Harry, and Wally Snyder, who had worked for me at the Padelford Packet Boat Company. (By this time, we had retired our old business name of River Excursions.) As we moved carefully up the crowded shipping channel, fog rolled in and I wasn't sure where we were. All of a sudden a huge ship came around an unexpected bend in the river. It loomed over us, its stacks poking just above the fog. The big ship was coming at us in such a way that I was going to have to pass him on my starboard side instead of the proper port side.

Ol' Man RIVER

But he shifted at the last minute to pass properly. Wrenching the *Viking Explorer* around, I did a U turn right in front of him, almost under the bow wave of his ship.

The ship's whistles and horns screeched at me through the fog. I hated to think what that captain must have been saying in his pilothouse. But I had no choice. My radar

was going, but it was the old-type radar and no good that close to an obstacle. We narrowly avoided a collision—and I learned a lesson about the big boats. I said to my crew, "Fellows, I've had enough. We're going to pull in." We had no business being out on the river in that fog. We tied the *Viking Explorer* to a barge on the riverbank and waited for the fog to lift. When we gathered on the deck we noticed the familiar odor of a pig farm. The smell was so strong that I asked my guys to investigate inside the barge. Twelve feet below deck were scores of pigs! It was obvious that the barge owner was stealing corn from downriver grain barges from Iowa and Minnesota and feeding it to his pigs. He could easily divert the sweepings from the barge covers to net a vast quantity of corn.

We continued upriver until we reached Memphis, where we spent the night. The Memphis harbor is fronted by an island, and to get into the main channel of the river, boats have to go south until they are past Mud Island and then sail around the island's southern end. Every river captain knows there is a sandbar extending south of Mud Island. I thought I was well past the sandbar when I made my turn around the end of the island, but I wasn't. I hit that damned sandbar going full throttle because I needed the extra power to swing around into the strong current. Every bell and whistle on the *Explorer* went off, bringing the crew racing up on deck, including one guy who was stark naked.

My first order to the crew was to check the bilge to make sure we hadn't poked a hole in the *Explorer*'s keel. Fortunately, we hadn't. The keel was plated with eight-inch-square steel, with two-by-ten-inch-thick plating covering the bottom. That boat was really built. Next, I called my friend Tom Meanly, owner of the *Memphis Queen*, who used one of his excursion boats to try to budge the *Explorer* off the sandbar. He couldn't. The boat was stuck, but good. To complicate matters, the water was receding and the *Explorer* began to list. We tried the harbor service next, which hooked an 800 horsepower towboat to the *Explorer*. As the towboat pilot and I worked to connect the two boats, I glanced back to check his position. I couldn't believe my eyes: there were my three crew members, standing on the other boat's deck in their life jackets. They had abandoned ship! I was the only one on board the *Viking Explorer*. "Why, you chickenshit bastards!" I shouted at them. "What the hell are you doing over there?"

Even the harbor service boat could not move the *Explorer* off the sandbar. I phoned around for a towboat with more horsepower and a barge to provide a little leverage. A boat with 2,000 horsepower answered my call. Within an hour the skipper brought his barge alongside and finally pushed my boat off the sandbar. The *Explorer* was not damaged in the least.

In the midst of all of this, the Coast Guard hailed me on the radio. "I understand you went aground on Mud Island," said the caller.

"Yes, I did."

"How come you didn't report it to us?"

I was flabbergasted. "Listen, you son of a bitch," I growled. "I'm worried about my boat! I'm worried about my crew! Do you think I'm going to worry about a damned report to the Coast Guard? You're out of your damned mind!" I was furious at the guy. I never heard from him again, but the next day I saw that a new buoy had been placed where I had run aground. Locals named the buoy "Bowell's Shoal."

Meanwhile, TV stations sent their camera crews and newspapers sent their reporters to cover the event. The front page of one paper ran a photo of the *Explorer* heeling over with the headline "*Viking Explorer* Goes Aground." I later learned that the local

harbor service had two boats in dry dock that had gone aground in the same place.

By now I was under a lot of pressure to get home because the excursion season was starting and I still had about a month's worth of work on the boat to clean her up. We high-tailed it to St. Paul, where I hired Frank Clark, the talented architect who did the décor for the Lowell Inn in Stillwater, to renovate the *Viking Explorer*'s interior. The locals made bets that we could not complete the job in thirty days, but we did. Those tradesmen did a gorgeous job. The boat had mahogany trim on all the stateroom doors. My cabin on the second deck looked like the captain's stateroom on a plush yacht.

We used the *Viking Explorer* to do river cruises with thirty-four passengers: three-day trips to Prairie du Chien, Wisconsin; five-day trips to Dubuque; and fourteen-day trips to St. Louis. I bought a Greyhound-type bus that met the boat at each town so we could give shore tours. I often drove the bus myself. I felt I was an expert at double-clutching the gears, which I had learned to do years before in the CCC.

I captained the *Viking Explorer* on these cruises, which were very popular. My days began before dawn, when I woke up to the rumble of the diesel engines three decks below my quarters behind the pilothouse. After a quick shower I went to the pilothouse, where a crew member had a mug of hot coffee waiting for me the way I like it, black. My special mug had a boating scene on it. I liked that mug for two reasons: first, though it looked expensive, I had paid only fifty cents for it at a discount house, and second, it had a picture of a sailboat on it. The mug was a reminder of the secret desire I have harbored much of my life: to sail, single-handedly, around the world.

The small pilothouse of the *Viking Explorer* warmed up quickly, thanks to its tiny heater, which dissipated the early morning chill. Since any delay in getting the boat under way meant a loss of miles for that particular day, I had my efficient but sleepy crew cast off the bow and stern lines early. I always left the breast line, the final umbilical cord that ties a boat to the dock, until last, to be released only on my curt command. Soon we would be moving forward on the dead calm river, with only the quickening breeze a telltale of our increasing headway.

I measured time by the hours and minutes traveled on the river. On one morning, I observed a passenger—a woman who was an early riser—standing on deck below the pilothouse and looking upriver at the trees just beginning to show their fall colors. The two of us silently watched as a mallard rose from the water in front of the boat and a great blue heron lifted off from a nearby log. We saw the foliage along the riverbanks become sharper and more vivid

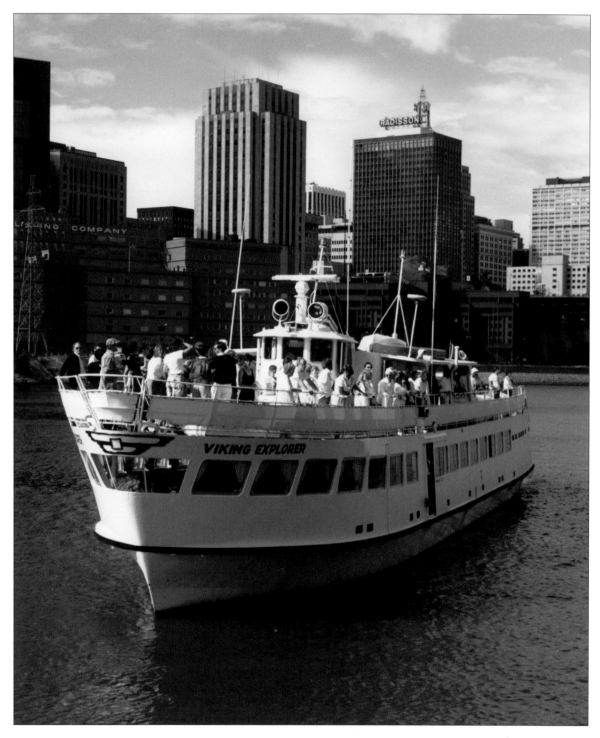

The Viking Explorer *heads out from St. Paul on a weekend excursion to Prairie du Chien, Wisconsin.*

with the sunrise. As the gray haze of the river gradually cleared, other passengers came out on deck, greeted each other, and went back inside for their morning coffee. The quiet contemplation of dawn on the river that the passenger and I shared was over. It had been but a moment, but I was certain that she too loved the river and had been moved, as I always have been, by something as simple as the beginning of a new day on the Mississippi.

The *Viking Explorer* was designed to run year-round. Late in the fall I sailed the boat back to New Orleans and across the Gulf of Mexico to Fort Myers, Florida, where we ran tours around the coast to Fort Lauderdale, giving us income year-round. Summer crew members that we wanted to keep for the following year worked the winter months on the *Viking Explorer*, which was helpful both to them and to me.

The *Viking Explorer* had one flaw that gave me problems. The railing extended farther over the side of the boat than did the bumpers that protect the hull when the boat comes up against a wall or dock. The railing in that position made the boat look good, but it was a hazard. Once when I was going through a lock, and we were just about stopped but keeping a little forward motion, I saw a man talking with a fellow passenger. Without thinking, and without even facing the wall of the lock, the man put his hand on the side between

the wall and the boat's rail. I knew I didn't have enough time to holler to him to take his hand off the rail before it hit the lock wall. Grabbing the controls, I backed off the port engine and came ahead on starboard to take pressure off the rail, but the guy's hand was trapped. He reacted by yanking his hand free, taking the skin right off and exposing all the bones and ligaments. It was a gruesome sight. Although my actions at the helm probably saved his hand from being crushed, his injury cost us about six thousand dollars. But he was the nicest person there ever was and so was his wife.

I had other moments requiring quick action aboard the *Viking Explorer*. Once, when we were on the Lower Mississippi, a terrible thunderstorm caught up to us. The river was running at seven miles an hour as sheets of rain made visibility horrible. I was looking for a place to pull in when I spotted a granary in the middle of the river. I talked with somebody on the radio about the advisability of tying up on the pilings around the granary, and he said, "Boy, if you go in there, be careful. There's a real bad current." Well, I chose to go in anyway, even though I could see that the water was rushing mad. I brought the boat close to the dock and ordered a crew member who wasn't all that experienced out on the forward deck to throw a line. When, on the first try, he did not make it, I hollered at him, "Get the hell out of there!" He jumped back, the current jerked the boat, and the pilings took a big chunk out of the *Viking Explorer*'s rail. We finally tied up someplace farther upstream.

The worst episode was in Florida. We were in Pensacola, headed for Boca Grande. I got a morning weather report saying the present four-foot seas were decreasing, which was the condition I was hoping for. But by two o'clock the following morning, I was looking at eight- to twelve-foot waves. I had been at the helm for nearly twenty-four hours and was exhausted. I had another captain take the wheel so I could go to my cabin to rest. I had no sooner stretched out on my bunk when a crewman burst in and shouted, "The bow window's busted and we're taking on water!"

I rushed to the pilothouse and told the captain, "Back on the throttle and just hold your headway into the waves." Then I ran below to face my crew, an inexperienced group of four young people. They just stood there looking at me, petrified, and I knew I had a panic on my hands. Just then I saw that our boat's fish bowl had tipped over, spilling water and gravel on the carpet. The marble table in the forward lounge had also tipped over and broken in half. "Where's Shakey?" I asked. Shakey was our pet fish, one of those little guys you have to keep in a bowl by himself or he'll eat all the other fish.

"Shakey is all right," someone said. "He's over there." Propped up in the corner of the room was a Styrofoam cup with Shakey inside, swimming around. Well, that broke the panic for the crew. They figured if I was worried only about the fish, things couldn't be *that* bad.

We plugged the hole with a mattress that we threw across the bow window, which had a five-inch gap and was about to collapse. I had one of the guys search for a prop or brace. He came back with a couple of two-by-fours, which I told him to cut into several pieces. The poor guy was seasick, but began sawing with the rustiest old saw I ever saw. He would make a few sawing motions and then throw up in a bucket, but he kept at it. He would saw, throw up, and then saw some more. We nailed the chunks of two-by-fours to a piece of plywood backing the mattress and put a brace from the cleat up to the ceiling. It was a crazy-looking affair, but it held the mattress and bow window in place. We rode out the storm, and the next day the seas quieted and we continued the voyage. When we crossed the Gulf, we never took passengers.

CHARTING NEW WATERS

The Tennessee-Tombigbee Waterway is the largest water resource project built in the United States. The waterway contains ten locks and dams, a 175-foot-deep canal connecting the Tennessee River with the Tombigbee River, and 234 miles of navigation channels. Building the Tenn-Tom required the excavation of nearly 310 million cubic yards of soil, making it the largest earth-moving project in history. (The Panama Canal involved the excavation of 210 million cubic yards of earth.) The project took twelve years to build and was completed on December 12, 1984, at a cost of $1.9 billion. Near the midpoint of the waterway is the place where Hernando DeSoto and his army of one thousand men crossed in 1541 on their trek from Florida to the Mississippi River.

Winter cruises on the *Viking Explorer* soon fell into a pattern, with three-night cruises along the Caloosahatchee River and across Lake Okeechobee to West Palm Beach, Florida. In the spring I brought the boat back to St. Paul via the Gulf, crossing to New Orleans and cruising up the Mississippi. After five years or so I wanted to try something different. To avoid the

river's strong current and heavy barge traffic, I decided to take a shorter route. In the process the *Viking Explorer* became the first overnight vessel to travel along the new Tenn-Tom Waterway.

The adventure began when the *Viking Explorer* arrived at Mobile, Alabama, a few days ahead of schedule after an easy crossing of the Gulf from Boca Grande to Pensacola. We had made 337 nautical miles in thirty-three hours. On May 4, 1985, we boarded our passengers and cruised north along the Mobile River at eight miles an hour against a current of two to three miles per hour. Compared to the big Mississippi, the Mobile River is narrow, the water heavy with a red sediment. The first day, we made ninety miles, the last two covered in the dark, running on radar and trying to miss the debris floating downriver.

The Viking Explorer *and the touring bus we would use to take passengers on day trips. I bought the mini luxury yacht in 1980 and ran it year-round on the Mississippi and Caloosahatchee Rivers.*

Ol' Man RIVER

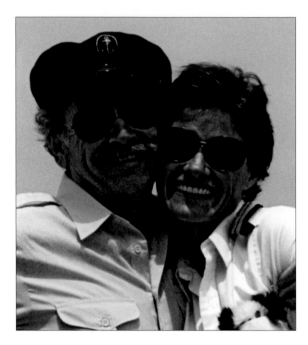

Joey Claeys, captain of the Viking Explorer, *gets a hug from her boss.*

The second day was similar to the first, with birds singing from the wooded riverbanks. We passed through the Coffeeville Lock, and, because there are few public places to tie up along this stretch, we put the bow in the bank and threw a rope around a tree. The following day we ran on radar until midmorning because of fog. At many towns we were met by the mayor, the media, and citizens. At Mile 248 we passed Epes, Alabama, a small town perched high above the river on limestone bluffs.

We soon came upon a blue heron rookery, with thousands of nests. I had never seen such a large rookery, so I turned the boat around and paused at the spot so everyone could absorb the scene. A little farther on

I saw a huge flock of wild turkeys on the riverbank, so again I turned the boat around. When I pulled the bow right into the shore to give the passengers the best view, those turkeys never moved.

The town of Columbus, Mississippi, gave us a royal welcome. Passengers viewed historic homes from the bus that had been following our boat up the river. Crowds of spectators, drawn by our radio and television coverage, watched the 110-foot *Viking Explorer* go through the Tenn-Tom locks—eight of them in one day. The passengers were mesmerized by the constantly changing panorama of beautiful hillsides, craggy bluffs, clear water, and abundant wildlife. We followed the Tenn-Tom to the Tennessee River, which passes through Tennessee and Kentucky before it joins the Ohio River. We picked up the Mississippi at Cairo, Illinois. Traveling the Tenn-Tom Waterway saves about three hundred miles compared to following the Mississippi through New Orleans, and has the added benefit of avoiding the fuel-consuming current of the Lower Mississippi. The route also offered a viable alternative to the crowded Lower Mississippi when I took the *Explorer* for the return trip to Florida for the winter.

I captained the *Viking Explorer* much of the time it was in Florida. The boat really made money, even when I was not there. But I ran into problems when I went back to St. Paul on business and left the crew to run the boat. When I wasn't on board, they would get into marijuana and cocaine. When the federal government passed a law allowing the Coast Guard to confiscate any boat that had drugs aboard, I knew I could not operate the *Explorer* in Florida anymore. I sold the boat in 1992 to a friend in Seattle. Now called the *Wilderness Explorer,* the boat runs trips on Glacier Bay in Alaska. It carries five- and six-person kayaks, which passengers use to get close to the shoreline without disturbing the wildlife.

THE *ANSON NORTHRUP* and *BETSEY NORTHRUP*

Steamboats did not run on just the Mississippi and Missouri Rivers. The Red River, which originates in Minnesota and flows north into Lake Winnipeg in Manitoba, also had steamboats. The driving force behind steamboating on the Red River was Sir George Simpson, governor of Canada's Hudson Bay Company, who wanted to reduce shipping costs for goods transported from Winnipeg (then called Fort Garry) to St. Paul. The St. Paul chamber of commerce strongly agreed with Simpson, and in the fall of 1858 offered one thousand dollars to the first person who could put a steamboat on the Red River. Minnesota lumberman Anson Northup, who had built the first hotels in St. Paul and St. Anthony in 1848 and 1849, got them to raise the ante to two thousand dollars.

Northup bought the *North Star,* a steamboat docked above the Falls of St. Anthony.

Taking advantage of the high water in the spring of 1859, he ran the *North Star* up the Mississippi past Fort Ripley north of Little Falls and on to Pokegama and Sandy Lakes. He was looking for a way west to Red Lake, which empties into the Red River near Grand Forks, North Dakota. He was unsuccessful and brought the boat back downriver to Crow Wing. There he dismantled the *North Star* and hauled the pieces 150 miles through the snow, arriving on the Red River April 1, 1859, about ten miles north of present-day Moorhead, Minnesota. It took about six weeks to reassemble the boat, including its twenty-two-thousand-pound boiler.

Northup launched the boat, now rechristened the *Anson Northup,* on May 19, 1859. He sailed upriver to Fort Abercrombie in Dakota Territory, about forty-five miles south, before turning north to Fort Garry, reaching his destination on June 10, 1859.

Northup hoped to negotiate lucrative freight contracts with the Hudson Bay Company. When he could not come to terms with the company, he sold his steamboat to the Burbank brothers for eight thousand dollars. The Burbank brothers had made a secret agreement with the Hudson Bay Company to give the company a 50 percent discount on freight charges in return for its underwriting of the boat's purchase. The Burbanks renamed the *Northup* the *Pioneer* and hired experienced Mississippi riverboat captain

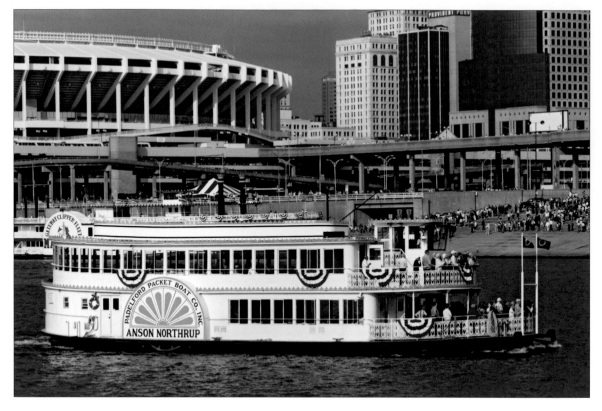

*The **Anson Northrup** draws a crowd in Cincinnati in 1992 for the Tall Stacks Festival.*

Edwin Bell to sail it. Bell made one more trip to Fort Garry in 1859 before the river froze. The Hudson Bay Company bought out the Burbank brothers in 1861 and took over the boat. The *Pioneer* sank during the winter of 1861–1862 at Cook's Creek, near Selkirk, north of Fort Garry.

I began construction on the 350-passenger side-wheeler *Anson Northrup* in late January 1988 at the Leevac Shipyard in Jennings, Louisiana. I named the ninety-two-foot boat for the Minnesota pioneer who captained the first steamboat on the Red River. His last name was really spelled

Northup, but I thought that was too hard to pronounce, so I took some liberties with it and added an R to the spelling of his name, much to the dismay of at least one person at the Minnesota Historical Society. (Even some of the waybills of the original *Anson Northup* spelled the name with the extra R.) The *Anson Northrup* was specially designed to operate under the low Burlington Northern Santa Fe Railway bridge on the Mississippi, between the Upper and Lower St. Anthony Locks, to the Camden Avenue Bridge in Minneapolis. The boat arrived at Boom Island Park in Minneapolis in mid-June, just in time to begin daily public excursions and Sunday evening dinner cruises.

In 1989 I bought the *Brandon Paul*, a car-truck ferry in Tiptonville, Kentucky, and renamed her the *Betsey Northrup*, after the wife of Anson Northup. We moved the *Betsey Northrup* to Mississippi Marine in Greenville, Mississippi, in the fall of 1989, where they transformed her into a two-deck, 360-passenger party barge. The main deck was enclosed and the second deck was left open, but with a canopy. The two *Northrup* vessels combined have a capacity of 710 passengers.

Minnesota gubernatorial candidate Wheelock Whitney and state Supreme Court judge Kathleen Blatz join me on the Anson Northrup *in May 1988.*

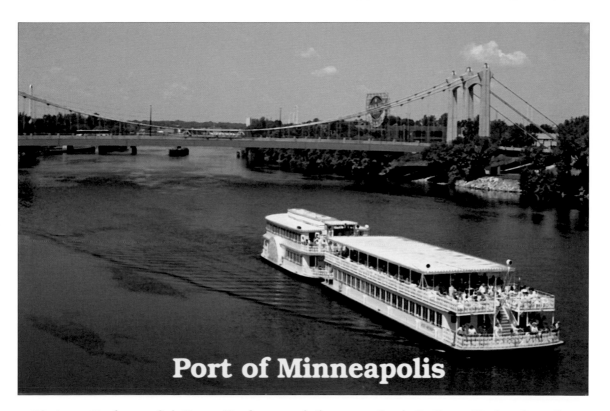

Port of Minneapolis

The Anson Northrup *and the* Betsey Northrup *were built to pass under the Burlington Northern Santa Fe Railway Bridge in Minneapolis. Here, the boats approach the Hennepin Avenue Bridge.*

The Little Charlie, *which was commissioned to move the* Betsey Northrup, *has a telescoping pilothouse.*

Because we needed a towboat to move the *Betsey Northrup*, we bought a full-size tow in 1991. At first we called it *Ugh the Tug III*, but that got to be confusing, so we changed the name to *Little Charlie*. Charles was the name of Betsey and Anson Northrup's son.

UGH the TUG II

I had *Ugh the Tug II* built for me in 1992 in Pensacola, Florida, by my friend Frank Patti. I designed *Ugh the Tug II* as a prototype vessel that would move small barges and docks, hoping I could get someone interested in building them for marinas around the country. I was always dreaming, looking for another project. *Ugh the Tug II* is built exactly like a big towboat, including tow knees on the front, heavy Sampson posts, winches, a mast, cabin, and two diesel engines. With the winch on the front of the vessel you can lift a dock. You can push a small barge, push debris— it is so maneuverable you can do just about anything with it. It has all the steering that a big towboat has, including a backing rudder, which helps you steer backward. The boat is twenty-five feet long and has a draft of about four feet. The guys who work at the Padelford Packet Boat Company really love that little boat.

Ugh the Tug II did give us a scare once. When Frank Patti was building the boat, he put two Chinese engines in it, which were pretty cheap. I didn't complain, because he charged me only $27,000 for the boat and he probably had $35,000 of his own money in it. One morning in 1996, our crew came to work to discover that *Ugh the Tug II* was gone—it had vanished from its mooring at the dock. They called me and said someone must have stolen the boat during the night. I told them to go look in the water with a pike pole. Sure enough, there was our boat, sitting on the bottom of the river under at least ten feet of water. It turned out someone had left a pump on to get some bilge water out. When they pulled the electrical plug, the engine reversed its cycles and acted like a siphon, filling the boat with water all night long.

We got a diver to put a line on the boat, then pulled it up and had it floating again by noon. The insurance company bought us two new engines and this time I made sure we got Yanmar engines, the kind I had wanted in the first place. *Ugh the Tug II* was painted up and is still in operation. It is a classic boat.

The raising of Ugh the Tug II *after the workboat sank in 1996 at the dock on Harriet Island.*

The antique popcorn wagon and calliope I sold in 1990 when I thought I might be going broke.

KEEPING the COMPANY AFLOAT

By 1990 I began to worry that I might be going broke. I had the refurbishing of the *America* project going and cash was in short supply, so I decided that, to be safe, I had better unload some of my possessions. Fortunately for me, the emerging casino boat operators were looking for big boats to buy, so I was able to get back the $225,000 I had invested in the *America*.

I also had a popcorn wagon mounted on the chassis of a 1925 Model T Ford and a matching calliope. I got $25,000 apiece for

each of those. Then I sold the *Governor Ramsey* and lucked out on that one too. I raised half a million dollars in a hurry. My cash flow problems were solved. Then, all of a sudden, business conditions turned around and the Padelford Packet Boat Company was making money again.

THE *HARRIET BISHOP*

In 1995 my son-in-law Jim Kosmo, Shelley's husband, and my nephew Stephen Bowell—both executives in the Padelford Packet Boat Company—attended a U.S. Coast Guard meeting with me in St. Louis. On our way home to St. Paul, as we crossed the Missouri River at St. Charles, Jim pointed out an excursion boat sitting in the river under the bridge. It was the *Spirit of St. Charles*, which had been built by Dave Flavin, a friend who had operated the 475-foot-long excursion boat in connection with the motel he owned. When gambling boats became popular, Dave sold the *Spirit of St. Charles* to a big gaming outfit in Las Vegas called Palace Station. The company soon realized that it would be wasting its time running an excursion boat and put it up for sale.

Before driving any farther, we decided to take a look at the *Spirit of St. Charles*. We were impressed by how well it had been maintained, and all the way home we talked about what we could do with the boat if we bought it. Adding another boat would take the pressure off the *Josiah Snelling*, which had become the principal boat in our fleet. When we reached St. Paul, I called the lady in charge of Palace Station's St. Charles operation. She led me to believe that I could buy the *Spirit of St. Charles* for $650,000 and I made the offer. Palace Station had no idea what the boat was worth. But a couple of days later, she called to say she was getting higher offers for the boat from someone else in the Twin Cities. When I tried to reach her the next day, I was told she had gone to Las Vegas for a management meeting. I packed my suitcase and flew there immediately.

At the corporate office of Palace Station, I announced to the receptionist that I was

St. Paul mayor Norm Coleman (second from left) and Governor Arne Carlson declared May 20, 1995, Captain William Bowell Day in Minnesota. Joining in the celebration was U.S. Congressman Bruce Vento (right).

from St. Paul, Minnesota, and was interested in buying the boat the company had for sale in St. Charles. The receptionist called an executive, who took me to a conference room. There I laid my checkbook on the table and said I was ready to pay cash for the boat. The executive went into another room to talk with his boss and returned a few minutes later. "You've bought yourself a boat," he said.

Palace Station paid for my lodging in Las Vegas while our lawyers worked out the details. A few days later I flew back to St. Paul, knowing I had increased my net worth by at least $750,000. The boat I had purchased for $650,000 was practically new and worth at least $1.4 million. We renamed the *Spirit of St. Charles* the *Harriet Bishop,* and it quickly replaced the *Josiah Snelling* as the flagship of the Padelford fleet. She features a forty-eight-tone calliope on her top deck.

My fortunes at the time were further boosted by St. Paul's Riverfront Development Corporation, whose enthusiastic mission was to renew citizens' interest in a great resource right in their own back yard: the Mississippi River.

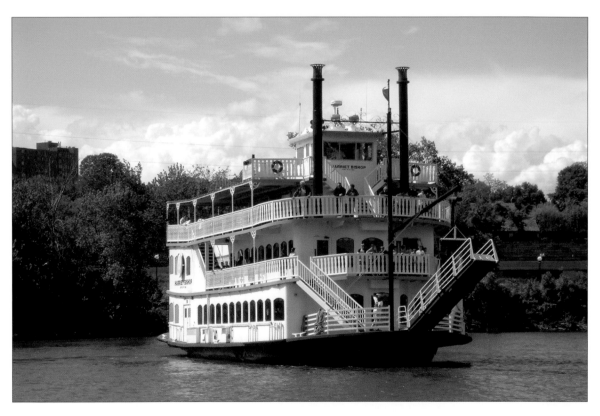

The Harriet Bishop *was a lucky find. It replaced the* Josiah Snelling *as the workhorse of the fleet.*

13
RIVER CRUSADER

THROUGH THE YEARS I have made it my mission to protect the Mississippi, and have become involved with various professional and civic organizations that have the river's best interests at heart. The first such organization happened to be my brainchild and that of Henry Miller, then president of Dubuque Boat and Boiler Works and builder of the *Jonathan Padelford*. Hank and I became close friends as we spent hours talking about the future of the passenger boat industry.

I told Hank about my success with catalogs, and with founding the National Association of Discount Catalog Houses and developing it into a major organization. From that experience I had learned the importance of group togetherness. Why, we asked ourselves, can't we do the same thing for excursion boat operators? Hank put together a list of about thirty-five excursion boat operations in the country and we began contacting the owners. We scheduled our first meeting for March 15, 1971, at the Bel-Air East Hotel in St. Louis and invited the other operators to attend. Sadly, Hank never made it. He

died after suffering a heart attack in September 1970 while on his private stern-wheeler, the *Rufus B.*, near St. Louis.

NATIONAL ASSOCIATION of PASSENGER VESSEL OWNERS

In March 1971, seven other excursion boat operators and I did meet, and we organized the National Association of Passenger Vessel Owners. I was elected president of NAPVO, Dennis Trone became vice president, and Jack Trotter was elected secretary-treasurer. Trone was the engineer-designer who succeeded Hank as president of Dubuque Boat and Boiler Works. Trotter operated the *Border Star*. The biggest expenditure the members had was insurance, so the association began working on that right away.

One year we held NAPVO's annual meeting in Little Rock, Arkansas, where the members stayed at a downtown motel. About thirty-five of us went to a dinner party, had a nightcap in one of the rooms, then went off to bed for the night. Our daughter Beth was in bed and Lillian and I were just getting undressed when there was a knock on our door. Thinking we had probably left something in a friend's room and he was returning it, I opened the door without looking through the peephole. There stood a guy with a sawed-off shotgun in his hands.

"Give me all of your money," he said as he quickly pushed his way past me into the room. Lillian stared in disbelief and said, "You've got to be kidding." "No, ma'am, I am not kidding," he replied. "We've got the motel surrounded. The switchboard is cut off and no one can do anything." Lil looked over at Beth and the guy said, "Don't worry. Nothing is going to happen if you do what I tell you." I started to walk toward the guy, but he raised his gun and said, "That's close enough! Just put your money on the bed." I had three hundred bucks in my pocket and Lil had thirty. We placed the money on the bed. "Now turn off your lights and go back to bed," he ordered. "Forget anything happened." And he left.

I locked the door, got Lil and Beth into the bathroom, and told them to lock the door behind them. Then I put my ear to the door connecting our room to the next room down the hall. I heard men going through the same hold-up. I wondered if the robber was telling us the truth about the phone being cut off. I picked up the receiver and the desk clerk answered in the gruff, unprofessional voice of one of the burglars.

"Can I help you?" he asked.

Oh, shit! I thought. "Yeah," I replied. "We're being robbed up here."

"Do you want to speak to the management?" the clerk asked.

"No, why don't *you* tell them!" I retorted and hung up. I looked around the room, trying to think of some way I could outsmart the robbers. I picked up the phone again and dialed 8 to bypass the switchboard and get a long-distance operator. "Connect me with the Little Rock police immediately," I told the operator. When the police came on the line, I said, "We're over here in the motel and have just been robbed. The guys say they've got the whole hotel tied up. I can hear the thief in the next room robbing somebody else."

"We'll be right over, but stay on the phone," the dispatcher told me. In a short time the police showed up quietly, without lights or sirens. From my window I saw a cop in the courtyard below. I stepped out on my balcony just as one of the robbers ran across the courtyard. I hollered to the officer, "There goes one right there! Get him!" I shouted to Lil that I was going down to my car to get my .38 revolver and help the police. I ran to the bottom of the steps, where a cop had collared the guy who robbed me. "Hang onto that son of a bitch," I said. "He's got all my money." The cop handcuffed the guy to a balustrade and asked me to help him catch the others. "We think they're in the room over there," he said, pointing down the hall. "You open the door and I'll cover." I turned the knob and pushed the door open. Fifteen terrified people were sitting on the floor of the room, all having been robbed. "I'm going to go out to my car for my .38," I told the cop. "These guys are all over the place."

When I got my gun, I went back to the room. "I just saw one go through the courtyard," Lil said. Soon we heard *boom, boom, BOOM!* There were three guys in the yard and the police got two of them. By then, the media had gotten wind of what was going on and showed up with cameras. I ended up on television the next day, with my .38 sticking out of my back pocket as I directed the police. As I was talking with the police chief the day after the robbery, he said, "When we were talking to you on the phone, we really didn't believe you—that anybody could be that calm so close to the action." I told him I was a former paratrooper and had been in much worse situations.

That may have been the most exciting meeting the National Association of Passenger Vessel Owners ever had. I served the rest of my presidency until 1979 without incident. The organization, now known as the Passenger Vessel Association, has about six hundred voting members and an office in Washington, D.C., staffed with an executive secretary, lobbyists, and safety engineers.

KEEPING the RIVER CLEAN

When I started my company in 1969, the Mississippi River was so polluted that used condoms floated by the Harriet Island dock, where passengers boarded our boats. It was a big embarrassment. I did not want my customers to get a bad impression of my river. The other problem was that when logs and debris floated downriver in the spring (or whenever the water was high), they had a tendency to lodge right between our barges and boats and the shore. I developed an absolute fetish about keeping my part of the river clean. So I decided to do something about it and soon became an expert at cleaning debris.

Around 1983, I built a special little boat I named the *Captain's Super Boat*. It was nineteen feet long and had two outboard jet engines that pulled water in and shot it out, giving each engine a torque (pushing power) that far exceeded the 35 horsepower they are rated for. I put a deck on

The Super Boat's job was to get rid of trees like this.

the boat, a tow pole, and a pair of tow knees on the bow that could go up and down. I came up with the idea of adjustable tow knees, and I wish I had bothered to patent them. I could lower the knees if I were pushing a log that lay low in the water. Then, when I wanted to go fast, I could raise the knees so they wouldn't spray water all over me.

I did work with the *Captain's Super Boat* that you wouldn't believe. When we had to move a particularly awkward log, I would take a pair of old-fashioned ice tongs, fasten a line to them, and grab the log with just the right amount of tension. By attaching the line to the tow pole, we could lift and drag the log away from the shore and our boats. We would tow all this debris out to the channel and send it on its way

The jet-engine outboard motors on the Captain's Super Boat *have tremendous pushing power, which came in handy during the 2001 floods in St. Paul.*

downriver. I think Gordy Miller came up with the idea of the ice tongs, and they worked beautifully.

SAINT PAUL RIVERFRONT CORPORATION

The revival of the Padelford Packet Boat Company in the early 1990s was due, in part, to changes taking place in St. Paul. The city was rediscovering its river. When Norm Coleman became mayor in 1994, he placed the rebirth of the Mississippi at the heart of his administration. With funds from Twin Cities foundations and corporations, the Saint Paul Riverfront Corporation set about restoring Harriet Island, building a public dock, developing housing on the river, and promoting a vision for the redevelopment of downtown St. Paul. Hundreds of volunteers soon were planting thousands of trees and shrubs along the shores to sustain birds in their annual migration up the Mississippi River Valley. Through the creation of the new Harriet Island Regional Park, city dwellers regained their sense of place, realizing that they lived not just anywhere, but in a historic town at the head of navigation of one of the great rivers of the world.

To keep citizens informed of its progress, the Saint Paul Riverfront Corporation began a series of annual events called—almost as a joke—the Millard Fillmore Dinner, after one of the nation's least distinguished presidents. The first dinner, held in 1994, attracted 125 attendees. The 2004 dinner packed in sixteen hundred—the absolute capacity of the convention center's dining room. At the time of the first Fillmore dinner, river historian Mark Vander Schaaf pointed out to SPRC members that the former president had actually visited St. Paul as part of the Grand Excursion of 1854, a promotion of the Illinois Central Railroad to celebrate the arrival of the first train from the East Coast to the Mississippi River. Twelve hundred leading easterners, including newspaper editors, university professors, and Fillmore, rode the train to Rock Island, Illinois, where they boarded steamboats bound for St. Paul. The event was the largest of its kind in the history of the young nation. Newspapers in the East printed enthusiastic stories about the bountiful "West," resulting in such a flood of immigration that, within four years, Minnesota met the population requirement of five thousand and qualified for statehood.

All of which led to the suggestion: Why not re-create the Grand Excursion in 2004 on the 150th anniversary of the original trip? The event could showcase how every community in five states along the route had staged its own return to the Mississippi. Under the leadership of the Saint Paul Riverfront Corporation, the idea took hold in river towns from the Twin Cities to the Quad Cities. For eight years planners worked together to bring the largest flotilla of river steamboats in a century to the Upper Mississippi. Led by Bill Bowell's *Jonathan Padelford*, the boats steamed into St. Paul on July 3, 2004. Cannons boomed, choirs sang, governors and mayors made speeches, and the world's largest balloon arch swayed a welcome not only to the boats, but to the thousands of people cheering on the bridges and banks.

Norm Coleman came to see me down on the river when he was running for mayor of St. Paul in 1993. I still remember his visit. My son-in-law Jim Kosmo was with me, and we were among the early people who backed the candidate. When Coleman became mayor, one of the first things he did was reorganize the Saint Paul Riverfront Corporation and put Patrick Seeb in charge. Coleman really meant it when he said he was going to reconnect the city to the river.

I always wondered why they didn't put me on the SPRC board. Then again, it might have been a good idea *not* to have me on it. I was already much too busy. When I had the *Viking Explorer,* I was flying back and forth to Florida and other river towns almost every week, piloting trips on the

In rare time off, I used to go fishing in the late 1990s with Mayor Norm Coleman of St. Paul and his son, Jacob, up by Lock and Dam 1 and around Pig's Eye Lake north of Newport.

RIVER CRUSADER

Explorer and piloting trips in the Twin Cities as well. I was on the go seven days a week. I didn't get much sleep.

At first Patrick and I did not get along. He and the Saint Paul Riverfront Corporation had their own ideas for the river. One day I told him, "You're going to find out that I own this river down here. You are in my territory and are doing things with my river without asking me." I can't remember what Patrick was doing; he was just doing things without consulting with me. I felt I was the king of the hill. I think Coleman recognized that immediately, and Patrick, after our initial blowup, backed off. He must have admitted, "By God, that guy *does* own the river." We got along terrifically after that. He has done a remarkable job and is respected by everyone. I am one of his greatest fans. In fact, when the SPRC hosted one of its Millard Fillmore dinners, Patrick had a little fun at my expense with a pretty good bit he had going with news anchor Don Shelby of WCCO-TV about being chewed out by Captain Bowell.

One of Patrick's biggest accomplishments was the Grand Excursion reenactment. When I rode in the pilothouse of the *Jonathan Padelford* as it led the procession of Grand Excursion boats into St. Paul on July 3, 2004, I was inspired and thrilled. Ed Stringer, who was my attorney at Briggs and Morgan when I first started the business, was in the pilothouse with

me, along with his wife, Virginia, as well as Nina Archabal, executive director of the Minnesota Historical Society, her husband, John Archabal, and Charles Zelle of the Saint Paul Riverfront Corporation. Watching us lead the flotilla were 150,000 cheering people who had gathered to welcome us. It was a remarkable sight. When I went down to the Mississippi in 1970, I was almost alone. Now tens of thousands were celebrating the river.

THE UNIVERSITY of MINNESOTA CENTENNIAL SHOWBOAT

The story of the *Minnesota Centennial Showboat* goes back to the mid-1950s, when Frank M. Whiting, director of the University of Minnesota's theater department, decided to revive an old river tradition and stage student performances on a theater floating in the Mississippi. "Doc" Whiting began talking about his idea with Twin Cities activist Tom Swain, who had been charged by Governor Orville Freeman to come up with projects to celebrate Minnesota's centennial. With $25,000 from Whiting's department and $25,000 from the Minnesota Centennial Commission, the two men went shopping for a boat they could convert into an old-fashioned showboat.

They found the *General John Newton*, a boat built in 1899 by Dubuque Boat and Boiler Works and docked just north of

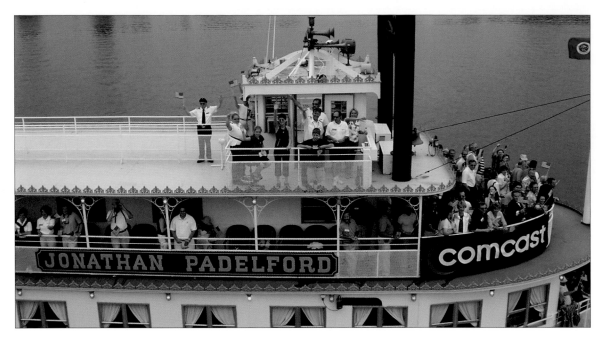

The Jonathan Padelford *leads the Grand Excursion parade of boats into the St. Paul harbor with several dignitaries on board. I can be seen on the left giving the river man's salute.*

New Orleans. For a time the boat had been used as a floating courtroom and freight boat for the U.S. Army Corps of Engineers. The University of Minnesota bought the decommissioned *General John Newton* for one dollar, and after its engines were removed, the boat made its permanent home in an area on the Minneapolis campus known as the river flats, just below the student union. The *General John Newton* was turned into a floating theater that staged its first show, *Under the Gaslight*, in 1958. More than twenty thousand people from forty states and twelve countries came to see the show's 103 performances. In its second season, forty thousand people from forty countries came to see *Billy the Kid*. The *Minnesota*

Centennial Showboat had proved itself and had even turned a profit for the University of Minnesota.

Though successful, the boat began to fall into disrepair, with little money from the university for maintenance. By 1992 a College of Liberal Arts committee began researching how much community money could be raised to save the *Showboat* and where it might come from. Wherever the boat ended up, it would have to meet code requirements: that is, be moored at a dock with a ticket booth and adequate restrooms. Dock facilities alone would cost about $750,000. By the time Norm Coleman became mayor and reactivated the Saint Paul Riverfront Corporation, the College of Liberal Arts committee reported that St. Paul's reawakened civic pride made it the likely place to raise funds for the *Showboat*, but only if it were docked at Harriet Island. Coleman committed the city to building the dock and restrooms at the soon-to-be-renovated Harriet Island Regional Park. Paul Verret, president of the Saint Paul Foundation, helped to inspire other significant donors. After years of looking for a new home, the *Showboat* was finally towed from its four-decades-old berth at the university to the Upper River Services boatyard in St. Paul for renovation. But in late January 2000, a spark from a welder's torch smoldered and ignited, consuming the *Showboat*.

When I left work the evening of January 27, 2000, I saw smoke coming up from the South St. Paul section of the river, but until the next morning, I had no idea it was the *Showboat* that was burning. Up until then, I had not given much thought to the kind of boat the University of Minnesota was going to put on Harriet Island. Now that it was lost, I didn't like the idea that there wouldn't be a *Showboat* at that expensive new public dock on the island. I also was concerned that if the *Showboat* didn't go in there, perhaps another excursion boat would. The contract the Padelford Packet Boat Company had with the city of St. Paul excluded that possibility, but you never know what can happen in a political situation.

I sat down with folks from the U of M and the city of St. Paul to see what we could do. From the university we had Tom Trow, director of community and cultural affairs for the College of Liberal Arts; chair Lance Brockman and program director Sherry Wagner of the Department of Theatre Arts and Dance; and Vic Wittgenstein and Mike Hahm, director and special services manager, respectively, of the St. Paul Parks Department. The insurance money had not been collected yet, but the university had quotes of around $4 million to build a new *Showboat*. That kind of money was out of the question.

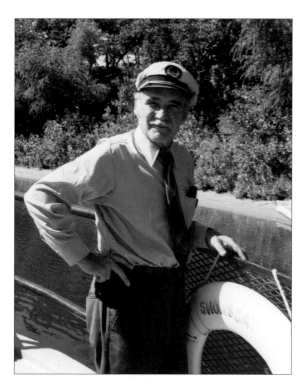

My friend Frank "Doc" Whiting, the chair of the University of Minnesota's theater department, gave birth to the original Centennial Showboat *in 1958.*

When we heard of a boat for sale on the Illinois River at Morris, Illinois, a group of us went down to see it. It was a monster of a casino boat and a bargain at $1 million, but the interior was a mess and the boat was the wrong size for Harriet Island and the St. Paul dock. It would have been a mistake to try to make that boat into the new *Showboat*.

So I called a meeting of the key people at the Padelford Packet Boat Company and told them, "I am going to build the new *Showboat* for the University of Minnesota." I ran into a lot of negative reaction from the assembled executives, so I ended the meeting. Twenty minutes later I called Stephen Bowell, my nephew and the president of the Padelford Packet Boat Company, into my office. He had not been negative in the meeting, so I said to him, "You and I are going to build the new *Centennial Showboat* for the university." I knew it would be my last major project for the company.

During my years on the river, I had made friends with many people in the boat-building business. Because of my contacts and experience, I knew I could build a boat for much less than the university could because the university had to abide by its own maze of internal rules and regulations. Stephen and I hashed out the deal with folks from the U of M. Stephen worked for untold hours with Tom Trow on all the contractual details.

I promised to build the boat for the University of Minnesota for $2 million. If the cost ran over that amount, I would pay it out of my own pocket. The university would own the boat and the Padelford Packet Boat Company would have a maintenance contract to run it—the ticket office, food service, everything. We would also pay for any repairs up to $1,000 in any given year. The university would stage its plays for eighty-five days of the year and the Padelford Packet Boat Company would get use of the boat as well.

For my concept of what the *Showboat* should look like, I went to my files and pulled out a drawing of an old river showboat. I took it to Timothy Graul, a naval architect friend in Sturgeon Bay, Wisconsin, and we teamed up to turn my concept into the plans for the *Showboat*. Then I called John Nichols, a prince of a guy who owns Mississippi Marine, a boatyard in Greenville, Mississippi. John built the *Betsey Northrup* for me and had the facilities to build a big boat.

My ace in the hole was my brother Dick. I persuaded him to move to Mississippi from his home in Palmer, Alaska, to be my yard superintendent on the project. Dick and his wife, Roxanne, moved into my Airstream motor home right in the shipyard and stayed for two years. Thanks to Dick, who is a plumber by trade but a bit of a mechanical genius, the *Showboat* has a state-of-the-art heating system, with

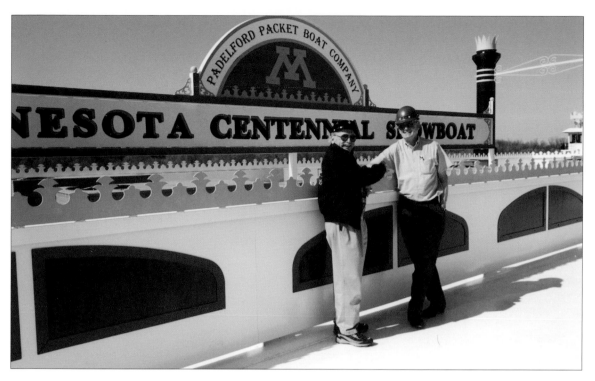

John Nichols, owner of Mississippi Marine, built the new University of Minnesota Centennial Showboat in Greenville, Mississippi. We brought the boat up the Mississippi River to St. Paul in the spring of 2002.

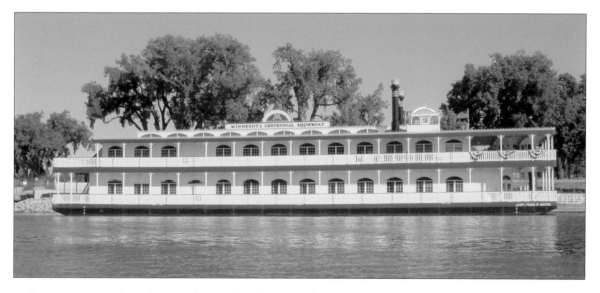

I was near tears when I brought the new Showboat into the St. Paul harbor. I knew it would be my last major project as I was selling the company to my children upon my retirement.

Ol' Man RIVER

plastic heating pipes in the deck as well as many other technical improvements. John Nichols wanted to keep Dick on his payroll when the *Showboat* was finished, offering him a position as vice president. A week after the *Showboat* left Greenville, however, Dick was in Nome, Alaska, working on an addition to a hotel called the Aurora. The thirty-three-room addition measured 175 by fifty feet—almost the exact size of the *Showboat*.

The entire *Showboat* is built of steel. Even the ornate railings that appear to be Victorian gingerbread trim are made of laser-cut steel. When it was time for the first shipment of steel to be delivered to the boatyard, the money from the insurance had still not come in. Tom Trow wrote to the insurance company and explained that because of the great public and student interest in the new boat, he could not promise that the insurance company's slowness in paying would not get into the newspapers. He did not want anyone to be embarrassed. The check was in the mail practically the next day.

To make the finances work, we told the U of M that we would have to be able to sell wine and beer on the boat. For that to be possible, the university's board of regents would have to give permission. For a time this appeared to be a major stumbling block. We pointed out that the license would belong to the Padelford Packet Boat Company, not the university, that I had

sold wine and beer on the river for twenty-five years without generating a single call to the police, and that the city of St. Paul was already selling wine and beer at the renovated Wigington Pavilion on Harriet Island. University of Minnesota vice president Sandra Gardebring explained to the regents that this could be a deal-breaker with the Padelford Packet Boat Company, and that it would take the sale of wine and beer for the *Showboat* to be competitive. The regents approved the contract.

Early in the process I realized that, to get the boat we all wanted, I would have to spend more than the $2 million agreed upon. We asked the university for another $200,000. Pure and simple, they did not have it. I ended up investing another $250,000 of our company's funds.

The partnership that built the *Showboat* was extraordinary. Lance Brockman and I designed every single element. There is hardly a bolt in it we did not see and approve. Lance wanted to keep the intimate charm of the original *Showboat*, so the auditorium has the same number of seats, 219, as the original boat. But the stage is bigger and deeper, the boat is half again as big, and the public areas are enlarged. We knew what was required to run a successful dinner theater, and the University of Minnesota went along with our judgment.

Because I had built several boats before, I knew what to watch for. Altogether I made

about twenty trips to Greenville to oversee the building of the *Showboat*. The whole proposition was like it was made in heaven. Everybody got along so well. Everyone was helpful. It was just one of those unbelievable deals. Tom Trow, Lance Brockman, College of Liberal Arts dean Steven Rosenstone, university president Mark Yudof, the board of regents—all worked together to make this a success.

The day the new *Showboat* arrived in St. Paul—April 27, 2002—was a very big day for me. Lance, nephew Stephen, and I

boarded the boat down around the Pig's Eye Bridge and rode it up to Harriet Island. Two tugs gently nudged the boat into its berth at the new public dock. The media and a crowd of friends were there to witness the turning over of the boat to President Yudof. The weather was beautiful as I stepped out on the upper deck in my captain's uniform and raised my arms in the river captain's salute. I was close to tears. I was eighty-one years old, and this was my last big project. I had taken on the job because I knew I could do it. The deal I had made with Stephen was that I would

With me and Mayor Norm Coleman (second from right) are the University of Minnesota people who made building the new Centennial Showboat *possible. From left: theater department chair Lance Brockman, president Mark Yudof, and College of Liberal Arts dean Steven Rosenstone (far right).*

remain employed by the Padelford Packet Boat Company without a salary until I finished the *Showboat*—a period of four months. And now I had brought her into port. On July 4, 2002, I renamed the *Showboat* the *Captain Frank M. Whiting,* and a new generation of students performed the first show on that stage after nine years of waiting.

Most people do not realize that two arms raised overhead are a special salute from one river man to another. You can stand on the bank of the Mississippi today when a boat passes, and if you raise your arms you are going to see the captain come out of his pilothouse and do the same. As I raised my arms there on the deck of the *Centennial Showboat*—my last boat—I was saluting the legions of river men and women I have known and all of the people who preserve the mystique of America's great and wondrous river.

My arms are raised in the river man's salute moments after I deliver the University of Minnesota Showboat *to St. Paul on April 27, 2002.*

14
REFLECTIONS

IN THE NEW MILLENNIUM, Harriet Island is a far different site than the deserted spot where Bill Bowell had launched his Padelford Packet Boat Company in 1970. The Riverfront Development Corporation projects are much in evidence. A new public dock extends from the shore of the new Harriet Island Regional Park. An ornamental walkway and broad steps lead to the water. A refurbished Clarence Wigington Pavilion, brick ticket office, playgrounds, and broad lawns welcome visitors. Harriet Island hosts a continuing series of festivals, concerts, and fireworks displays. The Taste of Minnesota festival has moved its annual Fourth of July extravaganza from the State Capitol grounds to Harriet Island.

The Minnesota Boat Club's historic 1910 building on nearby Raspberry Island has been restored, and the organization's three hundred members, one-third of whom are active rowers, host such events as the U.S. Masters National Rowing Championships. A pair of hundred-foot-high stairways lead from the Wabasha Street Bridge down onto the island, which also houses the Schubert Club's Kugler Band Shell.

The St. Paul Yacht Club, which in the 1960s felt fortunate to dock eighty boats, now houses more than two hundred in its upper and lower harbors. The lower harbor, where twenty-five "year-rounders" live on floating permanent homes, is one of the few remaining communities of its kind on the Upper Mississippi. The cleanup of pollution in the water and along the shore, the emphasis on a return to the Mississippi by the Riverfront Development Corporation, and the Yacht Club's mission of fostering education and safe, affordable boating on the Mississippi all have fostered the community's growth.

The Mississippi River itself has changed. While pollution still exists, the waters are cleaner than they have been in more than a century. Fish have returned. Shepard Road was moved back from its former site along the river, and the area—now known as Upper Landing Park—boasts a biking trail and green space for the Science Museum of Minnesota at the foot of Chestnut Street. Riverfront housing stands on the former site of the Kaplan Junk Yard. And the capital city of St. Paul has new high-rise office buildings and a new downtown park, called Landmark Plaza, as well as a new vision of itself as a river city at the head of navigation of the Mississippi.

SELLING the COMPANY

Age is a great motivator. We all know we are not going to live forever.

My father died February 13, 1962, in California at the age of sixty-nine because of alcohol. My mother lived to be eighty-five and died July 11, 1981, in Denver, Colorado. My parents separated in California because of Dad's drinking, and later they divorced. Four of my eleven siblings have died as well: Mary, who lived in southern California with her husband, Bob Benson, a plumber; Robert, who settled in Texas and became a manufacturer; Phyllis, who lived in California with her husband, Len Billings, who traveled the world while working for a large corporation; and Jack, who lived in Denver and worked

in automobile sales. Jimmy lives in Texas and is retired; Nancy Jeanne married Danny Kohl and is retired in Sun City, Arizona; Patricia and Donna live in Las Vegas, Nevada; Richard is a plumber in Alaska; and Tommy moved to Colorado and is an automobile wholesaler. Betty Jane lives in California.

I was the executor of my uncle John Walter Bowell's estate, my father's brother, and after going through all of his files, I decided to organize mine so that my heirs would not have such a mess on their hands. In 2001 I sold the Padelford Packet Boat Company to my children and nephew because I wanted to keep the business in the family and have the Bowell name continue to be connected to it.

I sold the company and its four excursion boats—the *Jonathan Padelford,* the *Anson Northrup,* the *Betsey Northrup,* and the *Harriet*

The newly refurbished Harriet Island Regional Park includes Wiginton Pavilion and a new public dock, where passengers can board any of the Padelford boats for cruises along the Mississippi.

A Bowell family gathering in August 1992 on the Jonathan Padelford. *From left, beginning with me: son-in-law Jim Kosmo, granddaughter Sara Brucker, daughter Shelley Kosmo, granddaughter Anne Brucker, daughter Beth Myers, grandson Jonathan, son William Bowell Jr., and wife Lillian Bowell.*

Bishop—to my son, Bill Bowell Jr.; my daughters, Shelley Bowell Kosmo and Elizabeth Bowell Myers; and my nephew, Stephen Bowell, who is my brother Jack's son and like a son to me. Stephen had worked summers at the Padelford Packet Boat Company beginning in 1975, when he was fifteen. He has a business mind and an accounting background, and was making a large salary at a major car dealership in Denver as its finance manager before coming back to St. Paul to lead the company. I named Jim Kosmo, Shelley's husband, the company's executive vice president; he has a master's degree in business. Shelley is the sales manager and does all the bookings; Beth does all the bookkeeping from her home in De Bary, Florida. Bill Jr. served as the showboat manager of the *Captain Frank M.*

Whiting before the rest of the family bought him out. Although I left active management of the company in 2002, I continue to serve as chairman emeritus.

Upon my retirement, my daughter Beth presented to me this story about her experiences with the Padelford Packet Boat Company:

FULL CIRCLE

April 1970—I am a nine-year-old girl standing on the St. Paul Yacht Club dock. I'm wearing a white sailor dress with a red tie and a matching hat. My mother, my twenty-three-year-old sister and her seventeen-month-old daughter are waiting with me. A Channel 4 news

Ol' Man RIVER

cameraman is there, weighted down with heavy equipment. At last, the moment we have been waiting for arrives. Coming up under the Wabasha St. Bridge is the biggest boat my nine-year-old eyes have ever seen. My dad is in the pilothouse waving. The cameraman starts filming. We're all jumping up and down and clapping. I think I am the luckiest kid in the world.

July 1970—I have recently celebrated my tenth birthday. I'm in the galley of the *Jonathan Padelford* working with my cousins Mark, David, and Jeff, my brother Bill, and Max and Mike Gebhart. I am making 25 cents an hour serving Cokes and hotdogs and running the cash register. I think to myself, "I'm making a fortune and I'm surrounded by handsome men. I am the luckiest kid in the world."

REFLECTIONS

July 4, 1976—I'm sixteen years old and cooped up in an Airstream trailer ticket office. There are so many customers wanting to ride on the *Padelford,* I have to turn some of them away. At the end of the day my money is off and my ticket numbers are screwed up. My mom is a little annoyed with me for having made so many mistakes. Meanwhile, all of my friends have spent the day at Square Lake. I'm beginning to feel sorry for myself. Cousin Steve has come from Colorado to work on the boats for the summer. He thinks it's the greatest thing in the world. Well, he can have it! I beg my parents to let me quit and go work at McDonald's or somewhere—anywhere but here. They agree to let me try something else. I think I am the luckiest kid in the world.

Labor Day, 1979—I have finished my first year at college. After school ended for the year, I was summoned by my parents to resume employment with the Padelford Packet Boat Company.

Ol' Man RIVER

I returned reluctantly but quickly realized that this was a fun place to be. I am working with other college students, including my boyfriend. After-hours parking lot parties and visits to Awada's with the crew make for an enjoyable summer. The end-of-the-year crew party on the *Tiger Lily* is a blast. I drive home thinking, "I'm the luckiest kid in the world."

October 1985—I have just finished my fourteenth summer with the *Padelford*. Over the years I have been a ticket seller, crewmember, money counter, charter coordinator, and gift shop manager. I'm tired of the long hours and working several weeks without a day off. I'm twenty-five years old and wonder if there is life outside of the Padelford Packet Boat Company. I decide to expand my horizons and move to Orlando. Once I arrive in Orlando, I'm so happy to be there that I amuse my mom and my friend by shouting for joy in a restaurant parking lot. I'm the luckiest kid in the world!

November 1992—I'm married and I have a two-year-old son named Jonathan. I am working part-time at Holiday Isle Beach Resorts in the Florida Keys. I've been working here for a few years. The owner's executive assistant comes to me and tells me she is leaving Holiday Isle and that the owner requested that I take her place. I am astounded at the compliment. Out of 350 employees I am his first choice. I

think back to when I was sixteen years old and how lousy I was at working. I know that my education at Padelford had served me well. This is the greatest job offer I have ever received, but it means working full-time and overtime. I have a two-year-old and he is my first priority. I tell Mr. Roth thank you so much but I just can't do it. I go out to dinner with my husband and we celebrate the wonderful job offer that I turned down! And I think to myself, "I'm the luckiest 'kid' in the world."

March 1998—I'm living back up in Orlando with my husband and have two children now. I'm knocking myself out, driving in rush hour on the interstate and taking my kids to daycare so that I can earn very little money! My dad has this great idea. With modern technology I can live in Florida and work for Padelford doing the bookkeeping. My husband turns our garage into a beautiful office for me and I'm in business. No more suits and rush-hour traffic! I'm the luckiest "kid" in the world.

February 6, 2002—A day unlike any other. A milestone. [Sister] Shelley, [cousin] Steve, [brother] Bill, and I are buying the Padelford Packet Boat Company. We have been through the mill the last few months, but the day has arrived. The papers are signed and we toast with champagne. We celebrate with the crew, we celebrate with the family.

Everyone is happy. I think to myself, "I'm the luckiest 'kid' in the world."

Summer 2002—I stand at the dock with my children, watching the *Jonathan Padelford* coming in for a landing. My son Jonathan can't wait to get on the boat so that he can go back in the galley and help sell Cokes and hotdogs. I realize that I have come full circle. As the boat lands at the dock, Jonathan's enthusiasm wells up within him and he says, "Mom, I must be the luckiest kid in the world!"

For more than thirty years the Padelford Packet Boat Company has been a successful business, but my wife, Lillian, has been the glue that has kept our family together through all our highs and lows, including our separation.

About thirty years ago I met Dorothy Calabrese, a divorced mother of four-year-old Jason and sixteen-year-old Jaime. Dorothy was thirty-seven and attractive; I was fifty-three. I fell in love with her. A relationship developed seven years later, in 1981. Lillian and I separated, and Dorothy and I began living together in our condo in Minneapolis. I sold the Stillwater house in 1985. Dorothy and I used to live in the Florida Keys in the winter, where I kept my twenty-three-foot diesel boat *Shamrock;* now we winter in Scottsdale, Arizona. With my encouragement, Dorothy has pursued her lifelong interest in buying and selling antiques. I helped her set up a library of books on antiques,

which she loved and studied every night. She quickly became an expert in identifying and pricing antiques. She specializes in glass and sells through two venues, Blake Antiques in Hopkins and Riverwalk Antiques in Minneapolis. She also does estate sales.

I have maintained a friendly relationship with Lillian, who lives in downtown St. Paul in the summer and in De Bary, Florida, in the winter. I have a great deal of respect for her intellect. When we started the Padelford Packet Boat Company, she did the bookkeeping and handled reservations. When we lived in South Bend, Indiana, she helped start a Lutheran church. When we lived in Stillwater, she served on the council of Trinity Lutheran Church. She is active in her church in Florida, plays tennis, and enjoys playing bridge.

PORTRAIT GALLERY

Back when I was getting the boat company started, I hired a young man named Ken Fox to keep the *Padelford* freshly painted. I was surprised to learn that Ken not only could paint the sides of boats, he could paint portraits as well. Before long, I was digging into the Minnesota Historical Society archives to select old photographs and line drawings of famous river people that Ken could use in painting their portraits. To date, he has done two dozen paintings for me of such famous Minnesota characters as explorer Zebulon Pike, Father Lucien Galtier, Governors Henry Sibley and Alexander Ramsey, painter Seth Eastman, and schoolteacher

The Virginia *was the first steamboat to arrive at Fort Snelling, on May 10, 1823. This is the only painting of the* Virginia *and one of the prizes in my collection of historic paintings by artist Ken Fox.*

Harriet Bishop. (See Appendix IV for a complete list.) Over the years I have commissioned more than forty paintings of historic, river-related individuals.

Ken and I collaborated on some of the paintings, such as the one depicting the arrival of the *Virginia* at Fort Snelling in 1823. The *Virginia* was the first steamboat to make it past the rapids at Rock Island, Illinois, and up to the Falls of St. Anthony. There were no existing drawings of the *Virginia*, so I went to Wheeling, West Virginia, where the boat was built in 1819, to research the mechanical detail of riverboats built at that time. Ken used my sketches for his painting, making it the only authentic rendition of the *Virginia*. His work also shows the fright of the Indians at the sound of the steam exhaust. Constantine Beltrami, the Italian explorer who carried a red silk umbrella into the north woods, is depicted standing on the deck of the steamer. The Indian agent Major Lawrence Taliaferro is standing next to him.

Ken's painting of the Jackson Street Landing in 1858 is taken from a daguerreotype owned by the Minnesota Historical Society. He also painted Pierre "Pig's Eye" Parrant, the infamous whiskey seller who was one of St. Paul's first residents, using my suggestions for what Pig's Eye looked like. The Minnesota Brewing Company used Ken's painting as inspiration for one of its beer labels.

As a spoof, I had Ken paint a portrait of what my great-grandfather Bazel Bowell might have looked like, with a strong resemblance to me but wearing period clothing. Ken did a good job on it, and when it was finished, I hung it over the beautiful fireplace in my Stillwater house. When Dr. Tom

This remarkable painting of the Jackson Street Landing in 1858 by artist Ken Fox was based on a daguerreotype from the Minnesota Historical Society's collection.

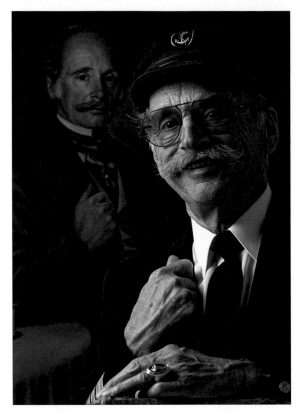

I had Ken Fox paint my great-grandfather's likeness.

I bought this painting for Lil's birthday in 1957. We later learned that it had been painted by Karl Jutz, a famed nineteenth-century German artist.

Murphy, a friend who came over on Wednesday evenings to play chess with me, saw the painting, he remarked, "You are the most egotistical son of a bitch I ever knew." Ken Fox still spends the summer seasons painting the boats in the Padelford Packet Boat Company fleet.

My love of art goes a long way back, probably to the time I spent on Macalester's yearbook and my later work in publishing. I have collected turn-of-the-century bronzes since 1951, when I bought a statue of two girls by French sculptor Ernest Rancoulet. One holds a harp and the other is holding a horn. Another of my favorites was done by Emile Pinedo. It's a nude lady standing in front of a boudoir mirror. The one that tops the list is an Asian bronze of a cow lying down. It is about ten inches long, has great detail—every muscle shows—and has an exceptional patina. It reminds me of visits to Lillian's relatives in the Spring Grove area of southern Minnesota.

I made one of my luckiest art finds when we were living in Chicago, about 1957. Lillian and I visited an antiques show in Evanston, Illinois, where we lived at the time. Hanging on the wall was a beautiful barnyard scene of a mother hen with baby chickens and ducks. We inquired and found out that the price was $350. Lillian was quick to point out that we could not afford to buy it. We went home without it. The next day I went back and bought the painting without telling her. Our friends down the block, Lois and Dean Milburn, agreed to secretly keep the painting in their closet until Lil's birthday, which is November 28. She was delighted when she received the present.

I noticed a little flaking of the paint on the bottom of the piece and took it to an expert in downtown Chicago to have it repaired. When I went to pick it up, he surprised me by offering me $1,000 more than I had paid for it. We refused the offer. He then showed me a book that listed all the paintings by Karl Jutz, a famous nineteenth-century German artist. The barnyard scene, titled *June Bug Hunt,* was among those listed.

The oil painting hung in our dining room in Stillwater for many years. Lillian was in Florida and I was driving down the road somewhere in Minnesota when I began to think about the painting sitting in a cold house and wondered what the cold would do to the flaking problem. In 1985 I decided to send a picture of the painting to Sotheby's in New York. They came back with an offer to show the painting in an upcoming show of German art. They would list the painting at $38,000. Lillian refused the offer. About a year later they came back with another offer of $50,000. She again refused.

NATIONAL MISSISSIPPI RIVER MUSEUM and AQUARIUM

Just as I love art, I love reading. I think that comes from Cecilia Collins, my English teacher at Harding High School. I still remember her talking about Stephen Crane's *Red Badge of Courage.* My love of reading expanded my personal library to twenty-seven hundred books on the river. I have not attempted to collect rare books, although a number of them are in the library. My book collection is a working library. I want it to be a repository for all the major books and journals dealing with the commercial end of the river industry. Over the years I have put together a bibliography of river books, and there are now six thousand on my list. That list has been my source as I continue to buy books through the Internet and expand the library.

A lot of the books in my library have stories behind them. A couple of years ago, when I visited Manassas, Virginia, near Washington, D.C., I asked the owner of the local bookstore if he had any books on the river. At first he said no, but then he remembered he had just gotten one in. Its cover was torn off, but as I looked at it I saw that it was a copy of E. L. Corthell's *History of the Jetties at the Mouth of the Mississippi River.* Corthell was chief engineer to James Buchanan Eads, designer of the first bridge to cross the Mississippi at St. Louis. The book was obviously a presentation copy, as it had been leather-bound and had gold trim on its edges. I asked the bookseller how much he wanted for the book. He asked me if fifteen dollars would be too much. So I bought the book and threw it in the trunk of my car. Two weeks later, as I was cleaning out the trunk, I pulled out the book and thumbed through the pages. The book was inscribed,

Among the portraits of famous Minnesotans painted for me by Ken Fox are (clockwise from left) Zebulon Pike, who selected the site for Fort Snelling; Harriet Bishop, St. Paul's first schoolteacher; Father Lucien Galtier, St. Paul's first Catholic priest; and Abigail Snelling, wife of Josiah Snelling, a commandant at the fort that bears his name.

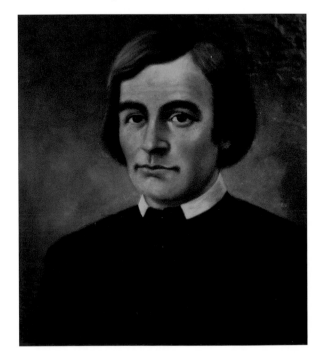

REFLECTIONS

"Presented to the Honorable Montgomery Blair by his sincere friend, James Buchanan Eads, 1882." Blair was postmaster general during Abraham Lincoln's administration, and the famous Blair House in Washington, D.C., is where he lived.

As I was getting up in age, I began wondering what would happen to all of my river books and my gallery of historic portraits. After a while I thought it might be nice to donate them all to the National Mississippi River Museum and Aquarium. The museum was the brainchild of John Bickel of McGregor, Iowa. John and his wife, Ruth, are two of my close river friends and often joined me for trips on the *Viking Explorer*. As early as the 1960s John began talking about his dream of a river museum and hall of fame that would celebrate the lives of the great people of the river. Joining him in championing that idea were Jack and Skippy Bell, two other McGregor residents and friends.

By 1985 John was discussing his idea for a National Rivers Hall of Fame with me and Jerry Enzler, director of the fledgling Dubuque Riverboat Museum. When Bill Woodward of the Dubuque Historical Society joined the discussion, the planning became serious and productive. In 1987 the group formed an "America's River" partnership with the Dubuque County Historical Society, the city of Dubuque, and the Dubuque Area Chamber of Commerce, and set a goal of raising $25 million for a museum and pedestrian walk along the Mississippi.

The Logsdon, *a 1935 towboat now on display at the National Mississippi River Museum and Aquarium.*

That goal was just the beginning. When the state of Iowa chipped in $40 million, the planners enlarged their vision to encompass what eventually became a $188 million investment in the National Mississippi River Museum and Aquarium and its components: the William Woodward Discovery Center, the Fred Woodward Riverboat Museum, the Woodward Wetland, the Boat Yard, and the National Rivers Hall of Fame. Through my friendship with the Bickels, their son Corky, and Jack Bell, I became a believer in the museum and its potential national significance.

As I debated about where to donate my books and paintings, I found another way to help the Dubuque Riverboat Museum. Back in the 1970s a group of us in St. Paul tried to establish a transportation museum in the old Union Depot railroad station in downtown St. Paul. A friend of mine, Jimmy Dye, was selling his towboat business and wanted to donate the *Logsdon*, a 1935 towboat—a real artifact—to our museum as a tax deduction. Since our museum was not able to accept the boat at that point, I took care of it. Unfortunately, we were never able to get the transportation museum idea off the ground, so I made a gift of the *Logsdon* towboat to the Dubuque Riverboat Museum.

While I was mulling over the decision of where to leave my library and paintings, I went down to visit the Padelford Packet Boat Company. Somehow I thought that my office would have been kept pretty much the same as it had been when I occupied it. I had hung all the awards I had won on the walls, including two special honors I received in 1991: the National Rivers Hall of Fame Achievement Award and the John Bickel Award, also from the National Rivers Hall of Fame. My other honors came when Governor Arne Carlson proclaimed May 20, 1995, as Captain William D. Bowell Sr. Day in Minnesota and the Minneapolis and St. Paul mayors did the same thing. I received WCCO's Good Neighbor Award. Anyway, when I got to my old office I found file cabinets up against the walls, covering (among others) the John Bickel Award and the Rivers Hall of Fame Achievement Award. Well, that helped me make my decision, and I started talking to Jerry Enzler, the director of the Dubuque museum, in earnest.

My collection of books, paintings, steamboat whistles, and other artifacts was moved in 2004 to its new home in the $54 million National Mississippi River Museum and Aquarium. The collection constitutes the Captain William Bowell River Library. I gave the museum $1 million to establish the library, which I hope will grow into a national and international center for river studies. The building is on the former site of Dubuque Boat and Boiler Works, which built the *Jonathan Padelford* in 1970. We threw a big Captain's Ball for 350 people at the new convention center on the river the night before the opening and held a ribbon-cutting ceremony for the library on Saturday, June 26.

My goal is to have a painting of each of the fifty-six individuals in the National Rivers Hall of Fame. In the past year or two, Ken Fox has created twenty-six of the paintings, which I commissioned him to do. We have thirty more to do,

RETIREMENT

When I cut the ribbon in June 2004 to mark the opening of my library at the National Mississippi River Museum, I said that I was

Ruth Bickel and Captain Doc Hawley of the Delta Queen *help me celebrate the opening of my library.*

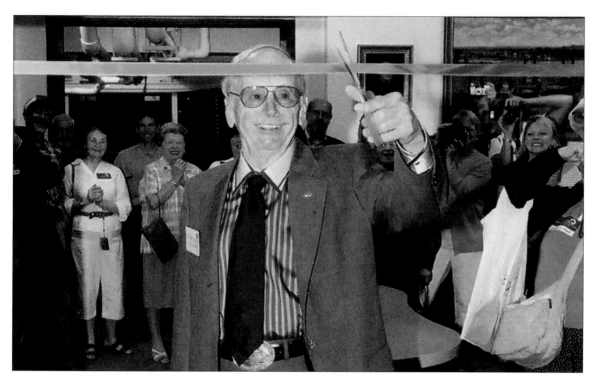

Above: I cut the ribbon to the stacks of my new library in Dubuque. Below: I rest my hand on the glass case that holds a rare edition of Corthell's History of the Jetties at the Mouth of the Mississippi, *which bridge engineer James Eads gave to Montgomery Blair, who was secretary to Abraham Lincoln.*

My family poses at the opening of my river library. Front row, from left: daughter Shelley Bowell Kosmo, me, and Dorothy Calabrese. Back row: nephew Stephen Bowell, son-in-law Jim Kosmo, son William Bowell Jr., and daughter-in-law Lori Bowell.

Five well-known riverboat captains at the opening of the Captain William Bowell River Library. From the left are captains Ruth and Bob Kehl, the first to start riverboat gambling on the Mississippi; me; Captain Doc Hawley, who for many years piloted the Delta Queen; *and Captain Gary Fromelt, former president of the Passenger Vessel Association.*

seeing the dream I envisioned thirty-five years ago come to fruition. What a great way to leave footprints in the sands of time.

Looking back on my life I cannot see anything I would want to change. Being in the excursion boat business and seeing all of the smiling faces of passengers as they came off the boats was a daily inspiration. I felt as if I were accomplishing something every day.

I still have so much to look forward to. I am still creating, still exploring. I have signed up to take a sculpture class and I continue to write about the river and the people before me who ran on it. I also went back to Normandy in 2002 to find that pretty French teenage girl whose family had helped me and my fellow paratroopers cross the Douve River after D-Day. Her name is Paulette Lelievre Laurence, and she told me I was the only one who had come back to thank her and her family for the risks they had taken. I shared a memorable meal with the family, and the local paper wrote a story about us and printed our picture together. My children are planning a trip in October 2005 to visit the monument to the 507th Parachute Regiment, located in Amfreville, France, and I want to be there when they see it.

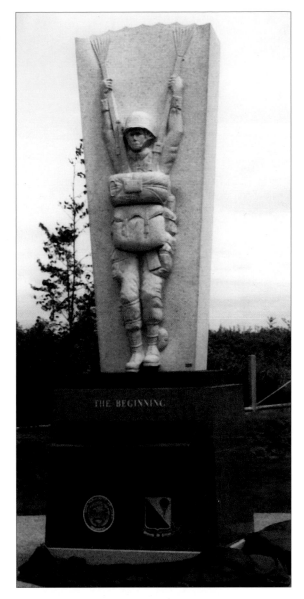

In 2002 I went back to Normandy, France, to visit the D-Day memorial to the 507th Parachute Infantry Regiment near Amfreville.

I find I cannot go into retirement without owning a boat to putter around in. Because *Ugh the Tug II* is now used for the cleanup tasks on the Mississippi River that had been done by the *Captain's Super Boat,* and because the *Super Boat* is seldom used, I bought the *Super Boat* back from the Padelford Packet Boat Company and am redoing the whole thing. I also hope to rent a canal boat and travel along some of the old canals in New

York that served as highways for pioneers traveling west. The state is trying to develop the canals and the old towns along their banks into tourist attractions. Four of the canals—the Erie, the Champlain, the Oswego, and the Cayuga-Seneca—are connected, and the boats you rent are identical to the canal boats available in England. The boats were pulled by mules and horses that were stabled right on board. My great-grandfather Henry James Padelford drove mules on the Erie Canal for years before he migrated to Minnesota in 1856. When I make that canal trip to New York, I plan to research the area in hopes of discovering more details of his life.

When I am on the river, I never really know what is coming up next, whether it will be good or bad. Whatever it is, I relate to it— the tranquil nights on moonlit waters, the frightening moments in rushing floodwaters, the natural beauty of the river's wildlife. Eight decades after beginning my life on the Mississippi, I still cannot cross the stream on a bridge without looking down and saying to myself, "That's *my* river."

Soon I will board the *Captain's Super Boat* on a trip up the Mississippi above St. Anthony Falls, looking for new adventures on these waters. This *is* my river, after all—and it is time I explored more of it.

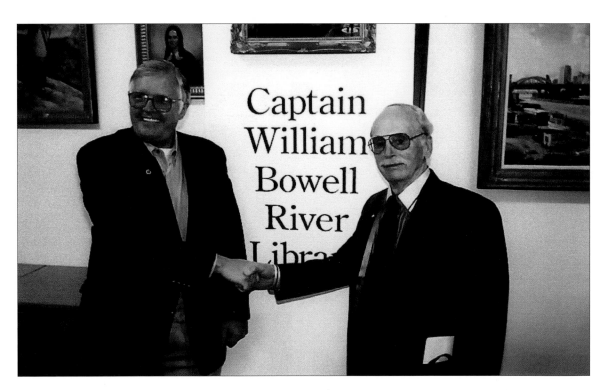

Paul Verret is the nephew of John Verret, chaplain of the 507th Parachute Infantry Regiment. Paul is president emeritus of the Saint Paul Foundation and was involved in such riverfront projects as the Grand Excursion.

APPENDIX I

BOATS OWNED AND OPERATED

I bought my first boat in 1951. Since then I've bought and/or built twenty-one more, and took the helm of three others.

BOUGHT or BUILT	NAME	HISTORY	LENGTH	PASSENGERS	SOLD
1951	*Toka*	Steelcraft cruiser built in 1946. Redesigned and rebuilt as excursion boat (welded by Red Olson, Stillwater, Minn.).	26 feet	16	1952
1951	*Charles A.*	Alumacraft rowboat used in 1978 as pleasure craft and motored from St. Paul, Minn., to New Orleans, La.	11 feet, 8 inches		
1965	*Ugh the Tug*	Formerly the *Thomas F.*, a U.S. Coast Guard boat built in Duluth, Minn. Redesigned and rebuilt as tugboat by Capt. Bowell and Borge Thompson (Stillwater, Minn.) with Ferdinand Nimphius (Neshkoro, Wis.) and Don Janke (Stillwater, Minn.).	26 feet		1974
1969	*Jonathan Padelford*	Designed and built by Dubuque Boat and Boiler Works (Iowa); lengthened 20 feet in 1971 by Lemont Shipbuilding Company (Chicago).	125 feet	313	in service
1972	*Zebulon Pike*	Formerly the *Hannah Kildahl*, a cruiser.	65 feet	120-plus	1978
1972	*Discovery*	Replica of Lewis and Clark keelboat built by Leavenworth Shipbuilding Company (Fort Leavenworth, Kan.).	55 feet	49	1975
1973	*Josiah Snelling*	Formerly the *Maark Twain*, built in 1963 by Tucker Marine Service (Cincinnati, Ohio).	120 feet	300	1997
1974	*Governor Ramsey*	Formerly the *Missouri Queen*, the former *Arkansas II*, last paddle-wheel boat built in Pennsylvania and completed in West Memphis, Tennessee, for U.S. Army Corps of Engineers in 1940. Purchased from Iowa Power Company (Sioux City, Iowa).	200 feet		1983
1978	*Pen Yan*	Wooden runabout used as pleasure craft.	16 feet		
1979	*Shamrock*	Fishing boat used as pleasure craft in Florida.	20 feet		1985
1979	*Tiger Lily*	River Queen houseboat used as pleasure craft.	52 feet		
1979	*Captain's Gig*	Sea Ark cruiser used as pleasure craft.	23 feet		

Ol' Man RIVER

BOUGHT or BUILT	NAME	HISTORY	LENGTH	PASSENGERS	SOLD
1980	*Viking Explorer*	Formerly the *Arkansas Explorer*, a Blount-built mini cruise ship with 24 staterooms. Refurbished by Frank Clark (Stillwater, Minn.). Now sailing as the *Wilderness Explorer* with the Glacier Bay Cruiseline of Alaska.	110 feet	34	1992
1983	*Captain's Super Boat*	Custom-made workboat.	19 feet		in service
1983	*Shantyboat*	Restaurant barge built to look like a U.S. Army Corps of Engineers quarterboat.	128 feet		
1988	*Anson Northrup*	Side wheeler excursion boat built by Leevac Shipyard (Jennings, La.).	92 feet	350	in service
1988	*America*	Towboat intended to be rebuilt into a floating restaurant in St. Paul, Minn.	184 feet		1990
1989	*Betsey Northrup*	Formerly the *Brandon Paul*, a car-truck ferry from Tiptonville, Ky. Rebuilt into party barge at Mississippi Marine (Greenville, Miss.).	108 feet	360	in service
1991	*Little Charlie*	Towboat with telescoping pilothouse used to push the *Betsey Northrup*.			in service
1992	*Ugh the Tug II*	Towboat built by Frank Patti (Pensacola, Fla.). Designed by Capt. Bowell and Whitey Burnett.	25 feet		in service
1995	*Harriet Bishop*	Formerly the *Spirit of St. Charles* of St. Charles, Missouri. Three-deck excursion boat.	140 feet	475	in service
2002	*Captain Frank M. Whiting*	Showboat designed by Timothy Graul (Sturgeon Bay, Wis.). Built by John Nichols of Mississippi Marine (Greenville, Miss.) under supervision of Capt. Bowell. Owned by the University of Minnesota and managed by the Padelford Company.		499	in service

OTHER BOATS OPERATED

BOUGHT or BUILT	NAME	HISTORY	LENGTH	PASSENGERS	SOLD
1970	*Border Star*	Operated in Kansas City, Missouri while upgrading my Coast Guard license.			
1976	*Rosie Bee*	Towboat used to bring *Governor Ramsey* (the former *Arkansas II*) from Sioux City, Iowa, to St. Paul..			
1991	*Dubuque Casino Belle*	First gambling boat on the Mississippi built for Bob Kehl at Patti Shipyard. I was on the maiden voyage from Pensacola, Fla., to Dubuque, Iowa.			

APPENDICES

APPENDIX II

RIVERS WORKED

In fifty years, I've sailed on twenty-one bodies of water.

Arkansas River

Atchafalaya River

Caloosahatchee River

Gulf of Mexico (from Pensacola to Fort Myers, Florida)

Illinois River

Intracoastal Waterway (from Jennings, Louisiana, to Key West, Florida, and from Stuart, Florida, to Miami to Key West)

Lake Michigan

Lake Okeechobee

Lake Ponchartrain

Minnesota River

Mississippi River

Missouri River

Mobile River

Ohio River

St. Croix River

St. Lucie Canal (Okeechobee Waterway)

Tchefuncte River

Tenn-Tom Waterway

Tennessee River

Tombigbee River

White River

APPENDIX III

HONORS AND AWARDS

1972—Governor's Award for Top Tourist Attraction of Minnesota, Governor Wendell Anderson.

1972—Grand Marshall, Minneapolis Aquatennial Boat Parade.

1979—Grand Marshall, St. Paul's East Side Parade.

1991—John P. Bickel Award, given by National Rivers Hall of Fame.

1991—National Achievement Award, given by National Rivers Hall of Fame.

1992—National Association of Passenger Vessel Owners Innovation Award.

1992—National Association of Passenger Vessel Owners Certificate of Appreciation for outstanding service and contributions to NAPVO.

May 20, 1995—Proclamation of William Bowell Day, City of Minneapolis, Mayor Sharon Sayles Belton.

May 20, 1995—Proclamation of William Bowell Day, City of St. Paul, Mayor Norm Coleman.

May 20, 1995—Proclamation of William Bowell Day, State of Minnesota, Governor Arne Carlson.

1995—Good Neighbor Award, given by WCCO Radio, Minneapolis.

June 9, 2002—Proclamation of William Bowell Day, City of Minneapolis, Mayor R. T. Rybak.

June 9, 2002—Proclamation of William Bowell Day, City of St. Paul, Mayor Randy Kelley.

2003—Lifetime Achievement Award, given by St. Paul Convention and Visitors Bureau.

APPENDIX IV

PORTRAIT GALLERY

I commissioned twenty-six paintings of historic river people, boats, and buildings from artist Ken Fox of the Padelford Packet Boat Company. The paintings were given to the Captain William Bowell River Library, which opened in June 2004 at the National Mississippi River Museum and Aquarium in Dubuque, Iowa.

HISTORIC RIVER PEOPLE

Count J. Constantine Beltrami—an Italian count who fancied himself an explorer. Although he lacked the skills of a woodsman, Beltrami sailed to Minnesota and Fort Snelling on the *Virginia* in 1823 and came within a few miles of discovering the headwaters of the Mississippi.

Harriet E. Bishop—a Vermont schoolteacher who traveled to Minnesota in 1847 as part of a program led by reformer Catharine Beecher to educate and civilize frontier children. Bishop started St. Paul's first public school and first Sunday school.

Captain William D. Bowell Sr.—founder of the Padelford Packet Boat Company in St. Paul, Minnesota, in 1969 and recipient of the 1991 National Rivers Hall of Fame's Achievement Award and John Bickel Award.

Jonathan Carver—an English explorer whose *Travels through the Interior Parts of North America*, published in 1778, was the first English account of the Mississippi River region and one of the most widely read travel books of the time.

Seth Eastman—an army officer and commander at Minnesota's Fort Snelling in the 1840s, best remembered as one of the foremost painters of the Dacotah on the Upper Mississippi.

Jean Baptiste Faribault—a Frenchman who traded furs with the Winnebago, Fox, and Sioux in the early 1800s in Prairie du Chien, Wisconsin. In 1819, Faribault moved to Pike Island on the Mississippi, then retired with his family to the southeastern Minnesota town that now bears the name of his son, Alexander Faribault.

Father Lucien Galtier—a French Catholic priest who in 1841 built the first log chapel in the Minnesota frontier village known as Pig's Eye. Galtier renamed the town for Saint Paul, the Apostle of Nations, and in 1858 the city became the state capital.

James Madison Goodhue—the founder of Minnesota's first newspaper, the *Pioneer Press*, in 1848. Goodhue arrived in St. Paul from Wisconsin with a three-hundred-pound printing press in tow.

Father Louis Hennepin—a Belgian Recollect missionary who came to New France (Canada) in 1675. Hennepin was the first European to describe Niagara Falls and to discover, in 1680, the Falls of St. Anthony at the present-day site of Minneapolis.

Colonel Henry Leavenworth—the first commander of Minnesota's Fort Snelling, arriving in 1819. He later established Fort Leavenworth in Kansas and was promoted to general.

Lieutenant Stephen H. Long—an army engineer who led an 1819 expedition to survey the territory between the Mississippi River and the Rocky Mountains. Long was a graduate of Dartmouth College and a professor of mathematics at West Point.

Anson Northup—a St. Paul contractor and fur trader who, for a prize of $2,000, agreed in the fall of 1858 to put the first steamboat on the Red River near Moorhead, Minnesota.

Lieutenant Zebulon Montgomery Pike—an army officer sent by President Thomas Jefferson in 1805 to explore the Upper Mississippi with twenty soldiers. Pike signed the first Indian treaty west of the Mississippi and purchased the land on which the Twin Cities were later built.

Philander Prescott—an early fur trader, married to the daughter of a Dacotah chieftain, who supervised farming for the Dacotah, built a flour mill on Minnehaha Creek in Minneapolis, and perished in the Sioux Uprising of 1862.

Pierre "Pig's Eye" Parrant—the first person of European descent to live within what is now the city of

St. Paul. The former fur trader arrived in St. Paul as a bootlegger with a blind, sinister-looking eye.

Alexander Ramsey—the first governor of the Territory of Minnesota from 1849 to 1853. Ramsey was also the mayor of St. Paul, Minnesota's territorial capital, in 1855, as well as the governor of the state of Minnesota from 1860 to 1863. Ramsey served in the U.S. Senate from 1863 to 1875.

Henry Rowe Schoolcraft—a geologist and ethnologist who discovered the headwaters of the Mississippi at Minnesota's Lake Itasca in 1832. Schoolcraft also served as Superintendent for Indian Affairs for the Territory of Michigan in the 1830s.

Dred Scott—a slave owned by Fort Snelling army surgeon John Emerson in the 1820s. Scott sued for his freedom before the U.S. Supreme Court and lost, but the decision played a major role in the election of Abraham Lincoln as president in 1860.

Henry H. Sibley—a fur trader who became the first governor of the newly formed state of Minnesota in 1858. General Sibley led the army in the suppression of the Sioux Uprising of 1862.

Abigail Snelling—wife of Colonel Josiah Snelling, commander of Minnesota's Fort Snelling.

Josiah Snelling—army colonel who laid the cornerstone for Fort Snelling in 1820 at the confluence of the Minnesota and Mississippi Rivers and who remained its commander until 1827.

Major Lawrence Taliaferro—the Indian Affairs agent for the Minnesota Territory from 1819 to 1839 who wrote detailed descriptions of early life in Minnesota's Fort Snelling area.

HISTORIC BOATS AND BUILDINGS

Anson Northup—the first steamboat sailed on the Red River in 1858–1859 near Moorhead, Minnesota. Built by fur trader and St. Paul contractor Anson Northup at Lafayette, North Dakota, the boat was carried in pieces from Crow Wing, Minnesota, to the Red River.

Father Lucien Galtier's log chapel—the first church built in the city of St. Paul, Minnesota, in 1841.

Jackson Street Landing in 1858—also known as Lambert's Landing, this levee was built at the foot of Jackson Street in St. Paul and was the first landing encountered by boats coming up the Mississippi River to the capital city.

The Steamship *Virginia*—the first steamboat to navigate the treacherous rapids at Rock Island, Illinois, and make her way upstream to Fort Snelling, arriving on May 10, 1823. The boat was 118 feet long and eighteen feet wide.

APPENDIX V

NATIONAL RIVERS HALL OF FAME

I have commissioned paintings of the fifty-six inductees in the National Rivers Hall of Fame from artist Ken Fox of the Padelford Packet Boat Company. Half are completed and on display at the National Mississippi River Museum and Aquarium in Dubuque, Iowa.

THE PATHFINDERS

Jim Bridger explored the Yellowstone, Green, and other rivers of the West beginning in 1822 to become one of the region's most celebrated scouts.

Zadok Cramer published *The Navigator* in 1801, the bible for early flatboat and keelboat pilots on the Allegheny, Monongahela, Ohio, and Mississippi Rivers.

Louis Jolliet and **Jacques Marquette** explored the Mississippi River from the mouth of the Wisconsin to the mouth of the Arkansas in 1673.

Rene-Robert Cavelier La Salle explored the Mississippi Valley to the Gulf of Mexico in 1682, claiming it for France.

Meriwether Lewis and **William Clark** made their epic journey up the Missouri River to the Columbia and the Pacific in 1804–1806.

Major Stephen Long captained the steamboat *Western Engineer* up the Missouri River in 1819.

Ol' Man RIVER

Alexander Mackenzie crossed North America to the Pacific, exploring the northern Rockies and the Mackenzie River in 1792–1793.

Zebulon Pike explored the Upper Mississippi River in 1805 and searched for its source, reaching as far as Leech Lake in the Territory of Minnesota.

John Wesley Powell explored the Grand Canyon in a perilous 1869 boat expedition on the Colorado River.

Sacagawea guided Lewis and Clark to her Shoshone homeland, where they secured horses to cross the Rocky Mountains in 1805.

Henry Rowe Schoolcraft discovered Minnesota's Lake Itasca as the source of the Mississippi in 1832.

THE BUILDERS

De Witt Clinton built New York's Erie Canal, which opened in 1825 to connect the Great Lakes to New York and revolutionized water transportation.

James Buchanan Eads built the first ironclad gunboats in North America and designed the revolutionary steel-arch Eads Bridge, opened in 1874 in St. Louis, Missouri.

Charles Ellet Jr. built America's first wire suspension bridge in 1842, over Philadelphia's Schuylkill River.

John Fitch demonstrated the world's first operational steamboat to delegates at the Constitutional Convention at Philadelphia on the Delaware River in 1786.

Robert Fulton, working with Robert Livingston and Nicholas Roosevelt, created the first commercially successful steamboat, the *North River Steamboat of Clermont,* on the Hudson River in 1807.

William Hopkins revolutionized Mississippi River steamboat building with the metal-hulled raft boat *Clyde,* built by the Iowa Iron Works of Dubuque in 1870.

James Howard established his boatyard in 1834 in Jeffersonville, Indiana, building such vessels as the *John W. Cannon* and the *J. M. White (III).*

James Rees began building engines, machinery, boilers, and steamboats in Pittsburgh in 1854, exporting them around the world.

John Roebling built the longest suspension bridge in the world at the time in 1867, crossing the Ohio River at Cincinnati. His son, **Washington Roebling,** completed the Brooklyn Bridge over New York's East River in 1883, based on his father's design.

James Rumsey unveiled his revolutionary steamboat in 1787, a jet-propelled version, to George Washington on the Potomac.

Henry Miller Shreve built the first steamboat designed to handle the strong currents of the Mississippi and Ohio Rivers in 1812.

William Peter Sprague, "the patriarch among the boat builders of the west," oversaw maintenance for more than one hundred steam towboats in Pittsburgh in 1899.

THE RIVER PEOPLE

Black Hawk, a Sauk chief, crossed the Mississippi in 1832 to reclaim his tribal homeland, which resulted in the Black Hawk War.

Betty Blake led the effort to have Congress exempt the *Delta Queen* from the Safety at Sea Act in 1970, and later built the luxurious *Mississippi Queen.*

John W. Cannon, owner and captain of the *Rob't E. Lee,* escaped death in 1849 when his first steamboat, the *Louisiana,* blew up and killed eighty-six in New Orleans.

Mary Becker Greene began piloting in 1896 and eventually became the matriarch of Cincinnati's Greene Line, owner of the *Delta Queen.*

Daniel Smith Harris captained the *Grey Eagle* in 1858 when it set the record for the earliest spring arrival in St. Paul, Minnesota, a record not broken until 1947.

Orrin Ingram founded the Dole, Ingram, and Kennedy Lumber Company in Eau Claire, Wisconsin, in 1857, which continues today as the Ingram Barge Company.

Joseph LaBarge received his master's license in 1840, eventually becoming the longest running and most famous pilot on the Missouri River.

Thomas P. Leathers built the steamboat *Natchez VI* and set the record in 1870 from New Orleans to St. Louis at three days, twenty-one hours, fifty-eight minutes.

Grant Marsh brought wounded soldiers back from the Plains Indian Wars aboard his *Far West* in 1876, along with news of Custer's defeat at the Battle of Little Big Horn.

Mary Miller of Kentucky was the first woman in America to earn her steamboat master's license, in 1884.

"Diamond Jo" Reynolds built the *Lansing* in 1862, and started the Diamond Jo Steamboat Line in 1868 as the leading grain shipper on the Upper Mississippi.

Nicholas J. Roosevelt piloted the first steamboat voyage on the Ohio and Mississippi Rivers aboard the *New Orleans* in 1811. His wife gave birth on the journey.

Isaiah Sellers set a record of three days, twenty-three hours, nine minutes on the *J. M. White* for the New Orleans to St. Louis route in 1844. Sellers's record stood until 1870, when it was broken by the *Natchez*.

John Streckfus and the Streckfus Steamboat Company of Rock Island, Illinois, purchased boats from the Diamond Jo Steamboat Line in 1911, giving new life to the *St. Paul*, the *J. S.*, the *Capitol*, and the *Washington*.

Ernie Wagner captained the *Delta Queen* from 1962 to 1976 as the sole surviving tourist steamboat in the United States.

THE ARTISTS, WRITERS, AND MUSICIANS

Louis "Satchmo" Armstrong of New Orleans launched his career as a jazz musician by playing the cornet on the Streckfus steamboat line on the Mississippi in 1919.

John James Audubon journeyed up the Missouri River by steamboat in 1843, illustrating the birds and wildlife, collecting specimens, and taking copious notes on flora and fauna for his illustrious *Birds of America*.

George Caleb Bingham painted *Fur Traders Descending the Missouri* in 1845, one of his many works depicting the western rivers.

Richard Bissell published *A Stretch on the River* in 1950, one of his several classics about the Mississippi.

Karl Bodmer, a Swiss artist, traveled up the Missouri aboard the steamboat *Yellowstone* in 1833 to paint Indians and scenes of the West.

Henry Bosse, a German-born draftsman, photographed construction of wing dams and other engineering changes on the Upper Mississippi beginning in 1883.

Ben Lucien Burman wrote *Steamboat 'Round the Bend* in 1933, a well-loved book brought to the silver screen with an Oscar-winning performance by Will Rogers.

George Catlin traveled west in 1830 on the first of many trips to paint the Indians along the western rivers.

J. P. Doremus built a floating photo gallery in 1874 to photograph steamboats, waterfronts, bridges, lumberyards, log rafts, and river towns from the river.

Stephen Collins Foster composed "Old Folks at Home," more popularly known as "Swanee River," in 1851.

E. W. Gould wrote *Fifty Years on the Mississippi* in 1899, a monumental study of early steamboats and people.

Fate Marable, the "wizard of the ivories," played jazz aboard the Streckfus steamboat line in 1907.

Constance Lindsay Skinner began the *Rivers of America* series in 1937 and edited seven of the highly successful books, including *The Kennebec: Cradle of Americans*.

Mark Twain, one of America's foremost authors, made the Mississippi River known throughout the world. He received his pilot's license in 1859.

Captain Fred Way Jr. published *Way's Packet Directory, The Log of the Betsy Ann, The Allegheny, The Inland River Record*, and *The S & D Reflector*.

This book was designed by
Mary Susan Oleson
NASHVILLE, TENNESSEE

FONT USED: COCKTAIL